I0821886

Revealing and Concealing in Antiquity

Aarhus Studies in Mediterranean Antiquity (ASMA)

XIII

ASMA is a series of monographs and anthologies published by the research programme Classical Antiquity in the Department of Culture and Society, Aarhus University, Denmark. The programme includes researchers from a wide range of disciplines studying Graeco-Roman Antiquity, such as Classical Archaeology, Classical Philology, Ancient History, the Study of Religion, and Theology. The aim of the series is to publish significant new research in Classical Studies and to provide an interdisciplinary platform for the study of the ancient world. Thus, the series reflects both individual and collective scholarly engagements with new and innovative research of the highest international standard.

Revealing and Concealing in Antiquity

Textual and Archaeological Approaches to Secrecy

Edited by
Eva Mortensen and
Sine Grove Saxkjær

Aarhus University Press |

Revealing and Concealing in Antiquity

Cover by Jørgen Sparre
Illustration: Locrian *pinax*, Type 5/2 (Courtesy of Soc̀ietà Magna Grecia)
The book is typeset in Adobe Garamond and printed by Narayana Press
Printed in Denmark

ISBN 978 87 7124 389 5
ISSN 1399 2686

Aarhus University Press
Langelandsgade 177
DK-8200 Aarhus N
www.unipress.dk

International distributors:
Gazelle Book Services Ltd.
White Cross Mills
Hightown, Lancaster, LA1 4XS
United Kingdom
www.gazellebookservices.co.uk

IS Distribution
70 Enterprise Drive, Suite 2
Bristol, CT 06010
USA
www.isdistribution.com

The publication of this book was made possible by a grant from Aarhus University Research Foundation

PEER
REVIEWED

/ In accordance with requirements of the Danish Ministry of Higher Education and Science, the certification means that a ph.d.-level peer has made a written assessment which justifies this book's scientific quality.

Contents

Preface

Revealing and Concealing in Antiquity comprises an interdisciplinary exploration of the concept of secrecy in the ancient world, offering a range of new possibilities for interpreting the ancient literary sources and the material record. The volume originates from a seminar on secrecy held in September 2013 at Aarhus University, Denmark, within the research programme *Classical Antiquity: Tradition and Transformation.* The seminar was attended by junior researchers from Classical Philology, Classical Archaeology, Theology and Study of Religion, who all presented aspects of their research within the framework of *secrecy*.

This volume construes secrecy in four different areas: secrecy in narratives, secrecy in text structures, secrecy in the gap between public and private life, and secrecy in connection with rituals, cult and worship. In this way, we examine the concept across disciplines and in relation to different social contexts; in addition, the various contributions range from the 5th century BC to Late Antiquity – one article revolves around the reception of antiquity, thus taking us to the Renaissance – while the case studies are drawn from a broad geographical span, including Magna Graecia, Asia Minor, the Levant, the northern Roman frontier and Denmark. Incorporating such different places, times, contexts and scholarly backgrounds allow us to draw out comparisons that might otherwise be invisible.

Hugh Bowden from King's College London kindly agreed to set the scene for the discussion and elucidation of secrecy in antiquity, at the seminar as well as in this publication. His introductory chapter revolves around revealing and concealing, and the significance of ideas of secrecy in ancient Greek religion – myths, divination, initiation and mysteries – and how this reflects upon the human condition.

The ten other contributions of the volume explore the meaning and implications of different forms of secrecy in the ancient world. The concept of secrecy – that is, the act of concealing and revealing as well as the social functions attached – exists and works in innumerable spheres and domains. In the first section, *Secrecy in Narratives*, three contributions work with a narrative context through very different viewpoints and case studies, exploring how narratives have the ability to reveal and conceal. Erin Jeanne Wright presents the theories of Georg Simmel, pivotal for the study of secrecy, and in relation to the Gospel of Mark, she reviews the narrative as a revealing medium and explores how the author manipulates listeners as well as time and place in order to repeat a cycle of secrecy in a narrative context. In the dramatic narrative in focus in Uffe

Holmsgaard Eriksen's contribution, concealment and secrecy are important factors. The narrative which is explored is about God disguised as a human in order to deceive the Devil, as developed by five 4th-century AD authors and the Byzantine poet Romanus the Melodist. The narrative as a concealing medium is examined further by Eva Mortensen, in the context of the cityscape of early Roman Ephesus. She deconstructs the narratives expressed in the material record, and considers how the patrons behind them intended either to reveal or conceal parts of the city's past in the public urban space.

The second section of the book, *Writing to Reveal or to Conceal?* contains two contributions which explore the ability of texts to hide and unveil knowledge and information at different levels. Trine Arlund Hass examines bucolic poetry from the Renaissance, more precisely an eclogue written by the Danish medical student and author Hans Philipsen Pratensis, in which references to the works of the great authors of antiquity occur as hidden themes that can only be revealed by the learned reader. Whereas the focus here is on 'intertextuality', the following article by Søren Sindberg Jensen reviews concealment and revelation as strategies for dialogues and disputes within early Christian Arabic writings. He considers to what degree Christians in the early Islamic period emphasise the revelation and concealment of God's knowledge in their encounters with Muslims.

In the third section, *Between Public and Private,* three contributions are concerned with the liminal space between the public and the private – the private seen as 'the secret'. Signe Krag explores spatial settings and architecture in relation to the private and the public spheres by examining Roman funerary buildings in Palmyra. The many portraits found in the buildings as well as the funerary rituals taking place here furthermore elucidate how memories and emotions shape a sphere of privacy and secrecy just as the physical walls did. What we consider 'the private' is exposed in an epitaph on a gravestone from Carnuntum on the northern Roman border, and this startling lack of secrecy, as well as other inscriptions bordering on the obscene, is the focus of discussion in Niels Bargfeldt's article. Maria Munkholt Christensen moves the discussion away from the funerary sphere through her examination of the relation between private and public in Christian prayer. She identifies how the 3rd-century AD Christian authors Tertullian, Cyprian and Origen contradict themselves in their instructions regarding prayer to be conducted in private as well as in public, and the implications this had for the individual.

The last two articles of this volume treat topics concerned with *Secrets in the Cultic Sphere.* Wiebke Friese reconstructs the ritual background and the architectural setting of the Glycon Neos Asclepius cult in Roman Paphlagonia, which combined well-known mystery and healing rituals with new rituals – so creating an atmosphere of secrecy. In the contribution by Sine Grove Saxkjær, the 5th-century BC terracotta *pinakes* from Locri Epizephiri, South Italy, are explored in relation to their ambiguous imagery and potential revelation of cult practices which took place in the Mannella sanctuary.

Acknowledgements

First and foremost, we wish to thank all the contributors to this volume as well as all participants in the seminar. We would especially like to express our gratitude to Hugh Bowden, who kindly accepted our invitation to participate in the seminar as well as contributing to this volume. The seminar was funded by the Aarhus University research programme *Classical Antiquity: Tradition and Transformation*, and we would like to thank the programme director, Professor Anders-Christian Jacobsen, for his immense support. We should also like to thank our colleagues, associate professor Troels Myrup Kristensen and associate professor Jakob Engberg, for their enthusiastic help as part of ASMA's editorial board. The anonymous peer-reviewers also receive our thanks for their valuable comments and corrections. The publication of these proceedings would not have been possible without the generous financial support from Aarhus University Research Foundation, for which we are grateful. We thank *Società Magna Grecia* for the permission to reprint the front cover illustration.

INTRODUCTION

HUGH BOWDEN

Concealing and Revealing in Ancient Greek Religion and Beyond

κρύψαντες γὰρ ἔχουσι θεοὶ βίον ἀνθρώποισιν.
The gods keep the means of life concealed from mortals.[1]

With these words Hesiod, near the start of his *Works and Days*, offers a view of the human condition. The consequence of this act of concealment by the gods is that men have to labour in the fields, drawing grain from the earth. This need to labour is what sets mortals apart from the gods. But this state of concealment is the result of previous events. Hesiod explains how Zeus concealed (ἔκρυψε) the means of life in anger at being deceived by Prometheus; he goes on to say that Zeus concealed (κρύψε) fire, but that Prometheus stole it back in a hollow fennel stalk, thus escaping the notice of Zeus. The response to this was the creation of Pandora, given as a gift to Epimetheus, Prometheus' brother. She opened a *pithos* containing (concealing) all the evils that can befall humankind, thus releasing (revealing) sickness and toil and misery into the world: and that is why the human condition is as it is.[2]

Following in the footsteps of J.-P. Vernant,[3] we may find further acts of concealment relating to this story by combining it with the account in Hesiod's *Theogony*. Here Hesiod explains Prometheus' deception of Zeus, when he concealed (καλύψας) the meat of a sacrificed ox inside its stomach, and concealed the bones beneath gleaming fat.[4] Hesiod then gives another account of the creation of Pandora, and contrasts her beautiful exterior with her evil nature – a further example of concealment.[5] J.-P. Vernant's analysis of these two passages demonstrates how concealment is presented as the fundamental element of the relationship between gods and mortal:

> The narrative logic operates by a process of inverted equation: for the gods in their dealings with men, both 'giving' and 'not-giving' = 'hiding'. The grammar of the

1 Hes. *Op.* 42. All translations are my own.
2 Hes. *Op.* 42-108. The myth of Pandora is the starting point for S. Bok's study of secrecy (Bok 1983, 3-4).
3 Vernant 1981.
4 Hes. *Theog.* 538-541.
5 Hes. *Theog.* 570-589.

> narrative also has a semantic function: for men good things are hidden in ills; and ills are either concealed within goods, or else invisible … [B]eneath all its forms and in all its diverse aspects, human life is set thanks to divine 'concealment' in a world of good and evil mixed, of ambiguity, of doubleness.[6]

We can explore this notion of concealing further by returning to the *Works and Days*. A few lines before the sentence quoted at the start of the article, Hesiod explains βίος as 'Demeter's grain'.[7] Every year grain has to be sown, that is buried in the earth, hidden from view, before it can later reappear on the stems of the wheat or barley that emerges in the spring. The image of grain concealed in the ground is also used in another early Greek poem, the *Homeric Hymn to Demeter*, when Demeter causes famine throughout the world: οὐδέ τι γαῖα / σπέρμ' ἀνίει, κρύπτεν γὰρ ἐυστέφανος Δημήτηρ ('nor did the earth send up seed, for fair-crowned Demeter had hidden it').[8] When Demeter relents the grain emerges once more, but implicit in the poem is the idea of the annual cycle of concealing and revealing of grain that is the basis of agriculture.

In the *Homeric Hymn* the myth that is linked to the cycle of the seasons is of course the Rape of Persephone. At the start of the poem Persephone is carried by Hades into the underworld, hidden from Demeter's view, and when she is finally allowed to return, she must still pass a third of the year ὑπὸ ζόφον ἠερόεντα ('down in the murky gloom'), that is, amongst the dead.[9] So here another aspect of the human condition, death, is associated with the same agricultural cycle: like the grain, the dead are concealed in the earth, although for mortals, unlike Persephone and the grain itself, there is no promise of rebirth.

Concealing and revealing have a significant place in the rest of the story in the *Homeric Hymn*. When Demeter learns that her daughter has been made wife of Hades with the full agreement of Zeus, she conceals her identity beneath a veil (καλύπτρα) and goes wandering over the earth.[10] When she comes to Eleusis, she is greeted by the daughters of the king, Celeus. In response to their questioning, she does not reveal her secret identity, but tells a story of being kidnapped, and then escaping unseen (λάθρη).[11] She is taken on as nurse to the son of Celeus and Metaneira, and in their palace, νύκτας δὲ κρύπτεσκε πυρὸς μένει ἠύτε δαλὸν / λάθρα φίλων γονέων ('At night she would conceal him like a brand in the heart of the fire, unseen by his dear parents'),[12] part of a process that would have given him immortality. When her secret actions are dis-

6 Vernant 1981, 53.

7 Hes. *Op*. 31-32.

8 *Hom. Hymn Dem*. 306-307, see also 452-453: ἔκευθε δ' ἄρα κρῖ λευκὸν / μήδεσι Δήμητρος καλλισφύρου ('The white barley was concealed by the plan of Demeter of the beautiful ankles').

9 *Hom. Hymn Dem*. 464, see also 482.

10 *Hom. Hymn Dem*. 93-95, see also 197.

11 *Hom. Hymn Dem*. 130.

12 *Hom. Hymn Dem*. 239-240.

covered by Metaneira, Demeter reveals her true identity;[13] then once Persephone has been restored to her, she teaches her Mysteries to the Eleusinians, rituals very much characterised by secrecy, as we will see.[14]

For poets in archaic Greece, it would seem, drawing attention to concealing and revealing is an important way of characterising what it means to be human in a world fashioned by the gods. The gods themselves are invisible, unless they choose to reveal themselves, as Homer suggests: τίς ἂν θεὸν οὐκ ἐθέλοντα / ὀφθαλμοῖσιν ἴδοιτ᾽ ἢ ἔνθ᾽ ἢ ἔνθα κιόντα ('Who could ever see with their eyes a god who does not want to be seen, as (s)he moves here and there?').[15] Human life was a negotiation with these invisible powers, and thus ideas of concealment were easy to associate with those areas and activities considered to be under divine control, including agriculture and death, and animal sacrifice and mysteries.

Can more modern studies of secrecy help us to develop this way of looking at the ancient world? At first sight it is not obvious that sociological approaches can. For example S. Bok in her 1983 study *Secrets: on the Ethics of Concealment and Revelation*, after recognising a relationship between secrecy and 'the sacred', determines to find a 'neutral definition' of secrecy, and she does not subsequently examine religion at all.[16] G. Simmel's seminal essay on "The Sociology of Secrecy and of Secret Societies" is similarly focused almost exclusively on human relations.[17] This is no doubt a reflection of the time when these works were written,[18] and the focus on secularisation that characterised the sociology of the later 20th century. Even when sociological approaches have been applied to the ancient world, they have considered 'religion' as a socially constructed means of human control, and secrecy as a means of reinforcing religious power, rather than as a way of making sense of the world as it was experienced.[19]

If however we turn from the contexts of secrecy to the way secrecy works, we can find that modern sociological analysis does point to valuable ways of thinking about secrecy in the ancient world. In a chapter on "The Sociology of Secrecy" that introduces her book *Legal Secrecy*, K.L. Scheppele offers a definition of secrecy: 'A secret is a

13 *Hom. Hymn Dem.* 275-280.

14 *Hom. Hymn Dem.* 473-479.

15 Hom. *Od.* 10.572-573.

16 Bok 1983, 6-9.

17 He does identify secrecy as a response of the early Christians to persecution, and then of 'paganism' to the rise of Christianity in the 4th century (Simmel 1906, 472), but his brief references to religious groups treats them in purely human terms (Simmel 1906, 477-81, 490-1). For more on G. Simmel, see Wright in this volume.

18 On G. Simmel see e.g. Hazelrigg 1969, 323. The importance of secret societies in Simmel's study was a reflection of his time: J. Conrad's novel *The Secret Agent*, which tells the story of a bombing organised by a secret anarchist cell, and its repercussions, was published the following year. See also, for an analysis of Simmel's work intended to relate it to ancient religion, Nedelmann 1995.

19 See e.g. Kippenberg & Stroumsa 1995, xiii: 'Obviously the knowledge of the gods which makes it possible to deal with them cannot be allowed to become an indiscriminate privilege granted to all and sundry. Hence religious secrecy'.

piece of information that is intentionally withheld by one or more social actor(s) from one or more social actor(s)'.[20] K.L. Scheppele is suggesting that secrecy is exclusively a characteristic of information, and that therefore it must be examined as a feature of communication. Developing this approach further M. Calinescu, in a study of secrets in literary texts, offers his own suggestive definition: 'Secrecy is a significant link in the chain of communication, temporarily or permanently occulted by the decision of an individual or a group'.[21] Secrecy understood in this way has been a concern of anthropologists as well as literary critics,[22] and it can help us think about the ancient world.

Hesiod's βίος is clearly not 'a piece of information' – it is grain, something absolutely material – and the other things that are concealed or revealed in the myth are similarly things experienced, not things communicated: the ills in Pandora's *pithos*, or Persephone, or the bodies of the dead. But Hesiod's poems are not descriptions of the real world. They, and the *Homeric Hymns*, recount myths that reveal the truth about what it is to be human, and that truth is that our understanding of the world is temporarily or permanently occulted by the decision of the gods.[23] The stories lay bare the power relations between gods and mortals: the world is controlled by an invisible and powerful secret society – the gods – who keep information from mortals, and thereby prevent mortals from living the blissful life they might otherwise experience.

If the separation of mortals from gods was absolute, this situation would be difficult to endure. However, in the ancient Mediterranean world there were ways of penetrating the veil that hides the divine from the human.[24] The gods might communicate with mortals through divination, although as we will see, continuing concealment is often an element in descriptions of divination. But direct contact with the gods was also possible through participation in forms of ecstatic ritual or through initiation into certain 'mystery cults'.[25]

Divination was precisely concerned with seeking information from the gods. Xenophon suggests:

> In such situations [i.e. at times of uncertainty] it is not possible to find anyone to give advice except the gods: they know all things and reveal them to those they wish to in sacrifices and omens and voices and dreams. It is reasonable to suppose that they are more likely to advise those who do not only ask what they should do

20 Scheppele 1988, 12.

21 Calinescu 1994, 443-4. On M. Calinescu, see also Hass in this volume.

22 See e.g. Piot 1993.

23 This is the message of Solon in Herodotus' account of his meeting with Croesus, Hdt. 1.32.1-5: ἐπιστάμενόν με τὸ θεῖον πᾶν ἐὸν φθονερόν τε καὶ ταραχῶδες … ἐκεῖνο δὲ τὸ εἴρεό με, οὔκω σε ἐγὼ λέγω, πρὶν τελευτήσαντα καλῶς τὸν αἰῶνα πύθωμαι ('My understanding is that the divine is always grudging and troublesome … about what you ask me, I cannot tell you until I have learned that you ended your life rightly').

24 Described as a mist (ἀχλύς) in Hom. *Il.* 5.127.

25 On the range of meanings of this term, see R. Gordon's entry in *OCD*[4], s.v. 'mysteries'.

when they are in need, but who also show concern for the gods, as well as they are able, in times of good fortune.[26]

In his historical works, Xenophon depicts divination as a sort of military intelligence-gathering. When a commander receives bad omens, these are often subsequently explained as reflecting practical aspects of the army's situation that were not known to the commander at the time.[27] But we find divination, and in particular the use of oracles, presented in a more complicated way in the works of other authors.

In most literary texts, oracular responses are usually presented as cryptic, which is to say that even after the god has spoken in response to an oracular consultation, the answer remains concealed, and can only be revealed through a subsequent act of interpretation.[28] Probably the best-known example of this is Herodotus' account of the Athenian consultation of the Delphic Oracle in 481 BC, when Xerxes' invasion of Greece was imminent. Herodotus presents the response to the Athenians' request for guidance as initially wholly negative, but then moderated by a reference to 'the wooden wall', a cryptic phrase whose correct meaning (the Athenian fleet) was identified by Themistocles.[29] Until relatively recently the dominant scholarly view had been to see the ambiguity of such cryptic answers as a historical phenomenon. It was argued that by giving ambiguous answers, oracles refocused questions, and allowed communities to formulate policy by gaining assent for a particular interpretation of the response.[30] This orthodoxy has however come increasingly under question, as scholars have acknowledged the extent to which cryptic answers are a phenomenon of narrative.[31] The inclusion of cryptic responses, and especially stories where consultants fail to interpret the answers they are given correctly, are a way of showing that communication between gods and mortals will always have the potential for occlusion.[32]

Concealment was itself a particularly appropriate subject for stories involving oracles. A particularly graphic example is Herodotus' story of the Corinthian tyrant Periander consulting the oracle of the dead in Thesprotia. Periander wanted to know where a deposit of money had been concealed, and summoned up the ghost of his wife Melissa. She refused to reveal the information because the grave goods with which she had

---

26 Xen. *Hipp.* 9.9: τὰ οὖν τοιαῦτα οὐδ᾽ ὅτῳ συμβουλεύσεταί τις οἷόν τε εὑρεῖν πλὴν θεῶν· οὗτοι δὲ πάντα ἴσασι καὶ προσημαίνουσιν ᾧ ἂν ἐθέλωσι καὶ ἐν ἱεροῖς καὶ ἐν οἰωνοῖς καὶ ἐν φήμαις καὶ ἐν ὀνείρασιν. εἰκὸς δὲ μᾶλλον ἐθέλειν αὐτοὺς συμβουλεύειν τούτοις, οἳ ἂν μὴ μόνον ὅταν δέωνται ἐπερωτῶσι τί χρὴ ποιεῖν, ἀλλὰ καὶ ἐν ταῖς εὐτυχίαις θεραπεύωσιν ὅ τι ἂν δύνωνται τοὺς θεούς.

27 For a detailed discussion, see Bowden 2004.

28 For an analysis of oracles in narrative, see Wood 2004. F. Kermode's 1979 book, *The Genesis of Secrecy*, begins with a discussion of divination and interpretation (Kermode 1979, 1-5). On other ways in which secrecy was a feature of oracular sanctuaries, see Friese in this volume.

29 Hdt. 7.139-143; Bowden 2005, 100-7.

30 See e.g. Maurizio 2001, esp. 41-6; Flower 2008, 188-210.

31 See e.g. Naerebout & Beerden 2012; Beerden 2013, esp. 20 n. 7.

32 See the story of Croesus of Lydia: Hdt. 1.46-91, esp. 91.

been buried had not been burned, and so were of no use to her. She demonstrated her veracity by revealing a secret of her own – that Periander had had sex with her corpse. Only when Periander had provided her with grave goods – by stripping the clothes from the married women of Corinth, and burning them – did she reveal the location of the deposit.[33] The story involves a sequence of concealings and revealings of increasing unpleasantness: the deposit concealed from Periander; his wife, concealed in her tomb but now revealed by the oracular process; her concealing her knowledge of the deposit, but revealing Periander's secret act of sexual depravity; his outrageous revealing of the naked bodies of the Corinthian women; and finally Melissa's revealing of the location of the deposit. But this gruesome story serves wider purposes. What the divinatory process, and the narrative as a whole, reveals above all is the evil of Periander, and by extension of tyranny as an institution.[34]

While divination was a way of discovering from the gods certain pieces of information that would otherwise remain hidden, initiation, or participation in ecstatic cult activity, was a way of breaking down entirely the boundary between the mortal and the divine, and therefore a way in which mortals could, in some way, join that secret society of the gods.[35] In Apuleius' *Metamorphoses* the narrator gives an account of his initiation into the cult of Isis; the description may be an imaginative construction with no relation to any specific ritual, but it can be taken as a possible representation of the experience of a participant. At the height of the ritual Lucius describes how

> I reached the boundary of death, and set foot on the threshold of Proserpina, and then I returned, carried through all the elements; in the middle of the night I saw the sun blazing with bright light; I approached the gods below and the gods above face to face, and worshipped them from nearby.[36]

The fullest exploration of this ecstatic cult activity is found in Euripides' *Bacchae*, written at the end of the 5th century, which depicts the arrival of the god Dionysus in Thebes to introduce his cult there.[37] The language of the play is full of concealing and revealing. The god enters in disguise,[38] and announces that he is planning to reveal himself.[39] In their song of praise to the god, the chorus refer to the story of Dionysus being hidden in the thigh of Zeus.[40] Later in the play Pentheus, the king of Thebes, disguises himself

---

33 Hdt. 5.92γ.

34 See Gray 1996 for further interpretation of this episode.

35 On these cults in general, see Burkert 1987; Bowden 2010.

36 Apul. *Met.* 11.23: *Accessi confinium mortis et calcato Proserpinae limine per omnia vectus elementa remeavi, nocte media vidi solem candido coruscantem lumine, deos inferos et deos superos accessi coram et adoravi de proximo.*

37 On the play in general, see Seaford 1996.

38 Eur. *Bacch.* 53-54.

39 Eur. *Bacch.* 22 (ἐμφανὴς), 42 (φανέντα), 50 (δεικνὺς ἐμαυτόν) etc.

40 Eur. *Bacch.* 98 (κρυπτὸν).

and plans to hide in order secretly to watch the Bacchants.[41] Inevitably he is revealed to the Bacchants, and he is killed by his own mother, who only later recognises him.[42] Of course, we should not be surprised at this in a play about Dionysus himself, as he is the god of masks.[43] In ancient Greek theatre masks simultaneously concealed and revealed – hiding the actor, but making clear the identity of the character being played.

As an example of an initiatory festival in the Greek world we may consider the Eleusinian Mysteries. The *Homeric Hymn to Demeter*, discussed above, offers an aetiology for the festival.[44] It is not clear how far, if at all, elements of the story of Demeter and Persephone were re-enacted as part of the festival,[45] but it is certainly the case that acts of concealing and revealing were central to the rituals. The word referring to a person about to be initiated is *mystēs*, related to the verb *muō*, meaning 'to close the eyes', while someone who has experienced the Mysteries is an *epoptēs*, 'one who has seen'. That the mysteries were something explicitly to be 'seen' is repeated in a number of texts from the 6th and 5th centuries, as well as later.[46] The climax of the ritual probably involved the revelation of something – possibly an ear of wheat or barley – to the initiates.[47]

The fact that we cannot be certain what the rituals actually involved is also a consequence of deliberate concealment: anyone who revealed what went on at the Eleusinian Mysteries faced the threat of severe punishment from the Athenians. This feature of the Mysteries has led scholars in the past to assume that there was some actual secret knowledge revealed to initiates.[48] It is now recognised that this was not the case; rather, the stress on the need for secrecy was a way of characterising the relationship between mortals and gods that the Mysteries established.[49]

A final aspect of Eleusinian cult can bring us back to our starting point. The poet ends the *Homeric Hymn to Demeter* by describing the gift the two goddesses offer to those they love: they send Ploutos (Wealth) to their house, who gives to mankind ἄφενος (abundance).[50] And we may see this as a revelation of a sort, because if a man

---

41 Esp. Eur. *Bacch.* 955-956: κρύψῃ σὺ κρύψιν ἥν σε κρυφθῆναι χρεὼν / ἐλθόντα δόλιον μαινάδων κατάσκοπον ('You will conceal yourself with the concealment with which you should be concealed, going as a deceitful spy of the maenads').

42 Eur. *Bacch.* 1280-1284.

43 See e.g. Segal 1997, 13-4.

44 Parker 1991; Bowden 2010, 26-48.

45 As is suggested by Clinton 1993, 118-9.

46 See e.g. *Hom. Hymn Dem.* 280-282; Pind. *fr.* 137a (Snell); Soph. *fr.* 837 (Radt).

47 Hippol. *Haer.* 5.8.39-40; Clem. Al. *Protr.* 2.

48 See Martin 1995, 117-21, for a discussion of the context in which such ideas arose in the study of religion in the period of the Enlightenment.

49 See Bremmer 1995, 72: 'It is the very holiness of the rites that forbids them to be performed or related outside their proper ritual context. It is also important to note that these 'emic' explanations do not suggest a valuable propositional element in the Mysteries. Unlike many gullible moderns seem to think, there was no esoteric wisdom to be found in the ancient Mysteries'. See also Burkert 1995.

50 *Hom. Hymn Dem.* 488-489.

has ἄφενος, then it follows that he has escaped from the condition Hesiod describes in the passage at the start of this introduction: βίος is no longer hidden from him. The revelations of the Eleusinian Mysteries bring with them, for those favoured by the goddesses, the revelation of the secret of life.[51]

My aim in these brief descriptions has not been to describe the rituals of ecstatic and initiatory festivals themselves, but to note how they are described. As with accounts of the consultation of oracles, the language is rich with notions of concealment and revelation. Even if these rituals did lead participants into direct encounters with the gods, such meetings cannot be described in ordinary terms. The effect of the way the language characterises the encounter might be compared to the effect of stroboscopic lighting, which reveals a scene for a moment and then conceals it again, disorienting the viewer and making the whole experience difficult to take in.

This introduction has turned to some of the earliest European literature to explore the significance of ideas of secrecy in a number of texts and religious contexts. The idea of secrecy, 'information deliberately withheld', can be seen in these works as a way of talking about areas of life where human knowledge must fail, such as the nature of the gods or death. In exploring the subject in this way I have been treating religious ideas as 'natural'; that is to say that they emerge from human experience, and are shaped to a significant extent by cognitive processes that are innate rather than socially determined.[52] 'Concealing and revealing' are not therefore something to be seen as having a function in religion distinct from their role in life more generally. This is something that will be further revealed in the chapters that follow.

Secrecy has recently re-emerged as a topic of great international concern. At the same time as the Aarhus seminar on which this book is based was being organised, the American whistleblower Edward Snowden was in the process of revealing large quantities of secrets about the practice of the intelligence agencies of the United States of America and of the United Kingdom.[53] This followed the revelations provided by Julian Assange through Wikileaks.[54] Such major news events can encourage oversimplistic assessments of the role of secrecy in society. This volume, amongst many other things, may serve to offer a rather broader perspective on what secrecy is, and what it has meant.

---

51 On further cultic activities related to Persephone, see Saxkjær in this volume.

52 On this, see e.g. Boyer 1994; Geerz 2013. In the context of this volume it is important to recognise Aarhus University as one of the leading centres for research into religion and cognition, through its Religion, Cognition and Culture research unit. For an alternative, sociological approach to secrecy in ancient religion, which sees 'religions' themselves as agents, see Kippenberg & Stroumsa 1995, esp. xxiv: 'The various ways in which religions have defined and made use of secrets reveal the practical options offered by the various religions to their believers, and the attitudes expected from them'.

53 On Snowden, see e.g. Harding 2014.

54 On which, see e.g. Leigh & Harding 2011.

Acknowledgements

I would like to take this opportunity to express my gratitude to Eva Mortensen and Sine Grove Saxkjær for inviting me to participate in the Secrecy Seminar of the research programme *Classical Antiquity: Tradition and Transformation* at Aarhus University on 6 September 2013, as well as to all the members of the research group who gave papers on the day, or contributed papers to this volume. The contents of this introduction are intended, in a small way, to reflect back some of what I learned from my participation, and are offered in return for the hospitality and scholarly companionship I encountered in Aarhus.

SECRECY IN NARRATIVES

ERIN JEANNE WRIGHT

Simmel, the Cycle of Secrecy, and the Socio-Spatial Dimension of Concealing and Revealing in the Gospel of Mark[1]

The first part of this paper considers how secrecy in antiquity can be understood as a form of social communication and interaction, as viewed through the lens of G. Simmel's social theory of secrecy. The second part will consider how the social construct of secrecy – i.e. the cyclical act of revealing, concealing and keeping hidden – is represented in ancient Christian narrative. Using the Gospel of Mark as primary text, we will focus in particular on the socio-spatial dimension of secrecy and how secrecy functions as a communicative strategy in narrative.

While secrecy – both in the modern and ancient worlds – is often considered only in terms of the concealment of certain information, it is perhaps more accurately considered a form of social communication and interaction. According to the social theory of secrecy, it has as much to do with the revealing of information as with its concealment. This cycle of controlled revelation – encompassing the acts of revealing, concealing and keeping hidden – can be leveraged by both individuals and groups to strengthen social bonds, construct social identities and protect group interests. Sociologist G. Simmel even goes so far as to claim that secrecy is 'one of the greatest achievements of humanity'.[2]

In the following, we will approach the study of secrecy in antiquity using G. Simmel's foundational social theory of secrecy, going on to consider how this theory can be applied to patterns of revealing and concealing in ancient narratives.[3] As G. Simmel's theory is complex and lacks a clear methodological presentation, we will take a focused approach and consider only the most relevant theoretical points for understanding secrecy in an

---

1 The content of this paper is based in part on my PhD project, *Secrecy as Communication: Simmel, the social theory of secrecy, and the literary shape and function of secrecy narratives in the Gospels of Mark and John* (working title), Aarhus University, expected 2015.

2 Simmel 1906, 462.

3 For an overview of secrecy in antiquity, see De Jong 1995.

ancient context, including: (i) a general introduction to G. Simmel and his theory; (ii) defining secrecy as a universal sociological form; (iii) outlining the three-part cycle of secrecy; and finally, (iv) considering the socio-spatial dimension of secrecy. Based on this overview of G. Simmel, we will then turn to a consideration of the socio-spatial dimension of secrecy in the Gospel of Mark, including examples of how the cycle of secrecy can be replicated in narrative. In conclusion, we will return to the question of secrecy in the ancient world, and how Mark's narrative representation of secrecy reinforces our understanding of secrecy as a form of communication.

I. Simmel and the Sociology of Secrecy

G. Simmel (1858-1918), a German social theorist, was the first to propose a social theory of secrecy in his essay "The Sociology of Secrecy and of Secret Societies" (1906).[4] While contemporaries like E. Durkheim found fault in G. Simmel's methodological approach,[5] one could postulate that his argumentative strategy – illuminating statements with examples transcending time and space, from merchant commerce, to Spartan war strategy, to the English Parliament under George III – has a certain modern appeal considering the current trend toward an increased emphasis on interdisciplinary studies in the humanities and social sciences.[6]

G. Simmel's early academic interests were influenced by 'Völkerpsychologie', and he thusly establishes his study of secrecy in terms of social interaction. According to G. Simmel, the social construct of secrecy has everything to do with our construction or understanding of the 'other'.[7] Using examples of reciprocal social relationships, G. Simmel aligns our expectation of truthfulness in relation to the intensity of the relationship: thus, the more intimate the relationship, the more revelation of personal information is increasingly relevant and expected.[8] However, he also points to the dualistic nature of social relationships: that the positive condition (i.e. reciprocal knowledge) must in fact presuppose the negative condition of 'reciprocal concealment', i.e. 'the limitation of the knowledge of one associate by another'.[9]

---

4 Simmel 1906.

5 See e.g. Durkheim 1964, 359, quoted in Frisby 2002, 142. For more on G. Simmel and his contemporaries, see also Frisby 2002, 139-45.

6 Furthermore, G. Simmel in more recent years has begun to be seen as the founder of modern sociology in general. As D. Frisby points out, already in the 1890's G. Simmel was 'establishing sociology as an independent discipline' – preceding M. Weber by a decade (Frisby 2002, xiii). Indicative of this renewed interest is the relatively recent publication of several English translations of some of his more major works that have been circulating only in German for over a century.

7 Simmel 1906, 442.

8 Simmel 1906, 451.

9 Simmel 1906, 448.

Secrecy as a Universal Sociological Form

G. Simmel conceptualises secrecy as 'a universal sociological form'.[10] In other words, secrecy is a social construct with no predetermined content, and as such is not influenced by this content; it functions in the same way, regardless of the secret itself.[11] Therefore, secrecy in antiquity need not reflect a contemporarily recognised or institutionalised form of secrecy (e.g. mystery cults, esoteric doctrine, etc.) in order to be recognised as secrecy in this more universal sense. What is culturally influenced is what becomes the secret itself, which is largely informed by the social 'rules' surrounding sanctioned revelation and concealment. Thus, while these rules can be expected to vary geographically and temporally, secrecy can be identified based on certain formal criteria regardless of the cultural context in which it is operating.[12]

Understanding secrecy as a social construct also helps to shed light on the often problematised relationship between secrecy and ethics.[13] S. Bok points out the paradox of secrecy: that that which proves the morality or ethical soundness of a secret is only possible through its revelation, thereby enabling the blanket negative valuation of all activity which remains concealed.[14] Thus, we find that secrecy is often characterised as 'the concealment of something which is negatively valued by the excluded audience, and in some instances by the perpetrator as well'.[15] G. Simmel, however, speaks directly to this characterisation: thus, in understanding secrecy as a universal sociological form, one must accept that it 'as such, has nothing to do with the moral valuations of its contents'.[16]

The Cycle of Secrecy

Turning now to the formal characteristics of secrecy, G. Simmel points to its cyclical nature: 'throughout the form of secrecy there occurs a permanent in- and out-flow of content, in which what is originally open becomes secret, and what was originally con-

10 Simmel 1906, 463.

11 Simmel 1906.

12 Simmel 1906, 441.

13 The ethics of secrecy plays an important role in the reception history of secrecy in the gospels, particularly in research on the so-called 'messianic secret' in Mark (see n. 30). This is enforced, for example, by both the post-Reformation view of Catholic secrecy, and even earlier in the Patristic reception of the so-called 'esoteric traditions' in early Christianity (Stroumsa 1996, 1-2). Considering this negative valuation of secrecy in early Christian tradition, the portrayal of Jesus in the gospels as someone who operates in secret, and who actively conceals what is now considered to be a universal message, is theologically problematic.

14 Bok 1982, xvi. This impression of a de facto equating of immorality with secrecy is further augmented by the fact that immorality is, generally speaking, concealed behaviour (Simmel 1906, 463).

15 Warren & Laslett 1977, 44.

16 Simmel 1906, 463. For more on secrecy and ethics in G. Simmel, see Simmel 1906, 444-8, 463-5. For a comprehensive consideration of the ethics of secrecy, see Bok 1982.

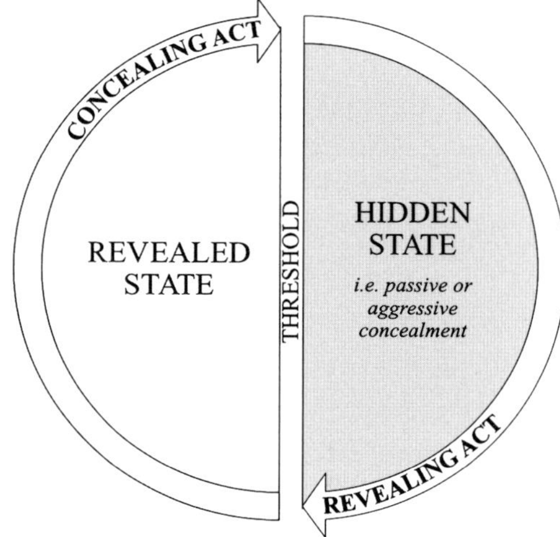

Fig. 1. *A visualisation of the three-part cycle of secrecy, demonstrating how concealing and revealing acts 'move' information between states of hiddenness and revelation (copyright Erin J. Wright).*

cealed throws off its mystery'.[17] B. Nedelmann (1995) elaborates on this idea from G. Simmel, called the 'Interaktionstriade' – what I refer to as 'the cycle of secrecy' – which has three moves or actions: (i) revealing (Enthüllen), (ii) concealing (Verbergen) and (iii) keeping hidden (Geheimhaltung).[18] These moves can be deconstructed as follows (Fig. 1):

(i) Revealing. The stage or move of revealing can take the form of an action or a state. The act of revealing secret information can be communicated through speech or action (including writing), or a combination of the two (i.e. a simultaneous 'telling and showing'). Conversely, the cycle of secrecy can be suspended in a state of revelation – i.e. the information remains in the public domain, whether permanently or temporarily. The revelation of secret information differs from a simple telling in that it is often delivered with an appended enjoinment to secrecy, or concealing act.

(ii) Concealing. The stage of concealing differs from the others in that it is the only part of the cycle that exists solely as an action: e.g. a concealing speech act.[19] A concealing act is the caveat that indicates the special status of this information. It can either precede the revealing act (e.g. "Don't tell anyone, but …"), or follow the revelation (e.g. "… but promise you won't tell anyone").

(iii) Keeping Hidden. Like the stage of revealing, keeping hidden can be an action or a state. It can be more difficult to identify, however, as it can be as simple as doing or

17 Simmel 1906, 467. As we will see in our later consideration of the cycle of secrecy in the Gospel of Mark, it is this 'in- and out-flow of content' that lends itself so well to the construction of suspense in the narrative.

18 Nedelmann 1995. 'Geheimhaltung' is perhaps more accurately translated as 'secrecy', however in order to reduce confusion (i.e. secrecy as one of the three parts of secrecy), I instead will refer to this part as 'keeping hidden'.

19 The act of putting on a disguise could also be considered a 'concealing act'.

saying nothing (passive concealment).[20] However, when confronted with the 'intent to discover', keeping hidden can also take an active form (aggressive concealment).[21] It is the various social techniques that can be employed to protect a secret – such as lying – on which G. Simmel focuses most of his attention.[22] While G. Simmel discusses this almost exclusively in the context of secret societies, certain elements of this can also extend to more general group dynamics and the construction of identity.

The Socio-Spatial Dimension of Secrecy

An important consideration for studying secrecy in antiquity is the socio-spatial dimension of secrecy. Put simply, for a communicative act to be an act of secreting, certain basic social and spatial requirements must be met. Considering first the spatial dimension of secrecy, in order to successfully conceal, private space must be available for the controlled revelation of information (i.e. to avoid being overheard or spied upon).[23] As for the basic social requirements, we have a second 'Interaktionstriade'.[24] Thus, in order for a telling to be considered secreting, there is a minimum social requirement of three parties: (i) a secret teller, (ii) a secret hearer, and (iii) someone from whom the secret is being concealed.[25] While this 'Interaktionstriade' is the minimum requirement, secrecy is of course used to control the revelation of information within much larger social groupings, for example organised secret societies.

Social groups engaging in secrecy employ an arsenal of techniques or strategies to protect their shared hidden knowledge, similar to secrecy at a more individualistic level. In such cases, the acts of revealing, concealing and keeping hidden are often highly

20 Passive concealment is typified by the absence of action; i.e. not revealing information to others, whether intentionally or unintentionally. An important take away from this is that not all forms of secrecy require intentionality. However, as G. Simmel explains, intentionality becomes a significant factor when one is confronted by a calculated attempt to discover. This 'intent to discover' becomes a sort of catalyst, and 'thereupon follows that purposeful concealment, that aggressive defence, so to speak, against the other party' (Simmel 1906, 462). Thus, while social relationships naturally abound in passive concealment, G. Simmel asserts that it is this aggressive form of concealment, in reaction to the intent to discover, that is 'secrecy in the most real sense' (Simmel 1906, 462).

21 See above.

22 On lying, see Simmel 1906, 445-7.

23 It is also worth noting that, in the modern world, we have certain advantages for accessing private space; as G. Simmel points out: 'modern life has elaborated a technique for isolation of the affairs of individuals, within the crowded conditions of great cities, possible in former times only by means of spatial separation' (Simmel 1906, 468-9). In the Gospel of Mark, for example, spatial separation is often used as a narrative tool for creating private space for controlled revelations within the storyworld. For other studies on space in relation to secrecy, see Munkholt Christensen and Krag in this volume.

24 Nedelmann 2002. The three-part cycle of secrecy, discussed above, is the other 'Interaktionstriade'.

25 Of these three parties, the third – someone from whom information is concealed – is arguably the most important, as it is this external interest in the concealed information that distinguishes secrecy from privacy. For more on this distinction, see Warren & Laslett 1977.

organised and ritualised. This group secrecy can be viewed from two perspectives: (i) *inter*group secrecy, i.e. group secrecy in relation to its greater social context (e.g. other social groups), and (ii) *intra*group secrecy, i.e. the internal characteristics and structure of the group itself, (e.g. internal hierarchy, initiation rituals and oral teaching).

Considering first intergroup secrecy, the existence of a secret society or any group engaging in secrecy presupposes a pre-existing, developed society within which it operates, and from which it conceals.[26] This juxtaposition between secret societies and the rest of society can be thought of in terms of an insider-outsider dichotomy: in regular society, which grows organically, 'whoever is not excluded is included'. Thus, unless outsider status is indicated (e.g. lepers or 'untouchables'), one belongs to the ranks of insider. From a non-organic, organised in-group perspective, however, we have the inverse: 'whoever is not expressly included is excluded'.[27] However, while intergroup secrecy acts as a defensive barrier between the in-group and outsiders, G. Simmel also points to the delicate balance required for keeping this information contained within the group.[28]

Thus, while intergroup secrecy is a defensive measure against outsiders, intragroup secrecy is a strategy of internal defence, i.e. protecting against the danger of betrayal. While this internal structure of secret societies can be quite elaborate, there are a number of qualities that can also be observed in more general group secrecy – the type of secrecy we observe in the gospel narratives – including (i) reciprocal confidence between members, (ii) a hierarchical structure,[29] (iii) the oral communication of secret knowledge and (iv) the potential for intragroup conflict.[30]

As we will see now in turning to the Gospel of Mark, we find elements of both intergroup and intragroup secrecy in the narrative.

II. Secrecy in the Gospel of Mark

The social construct of secrecy is observable in all four of the canonical Christian gospels; however, it is a particularly dominant theme in the Gospel of Mark. Often referred to collectively as the 'messianic secret', Mark repeatedly – if inconsistently – portrays Jesus as engaging in various secret activities (e.g. secret healings, teachings and miracles), including the active concealment of his messianic identity.[31] Ever since W. Wrede first

26 Simmel 1906, 483-4.

27 Simmel 1906, 490.

28 Simmel 1906, 473.

29 For a complex example of such a hierarchical structure, see G. Simmel's description of the Czech secret order, Omladina (Simmel 1906, 478-9).

30 Notably lacking in the group secrecy observed in the gospel narratives are (i) pledges or oaths for the entrance of new group members and (ii) established rituals. Thus, what we find in the gospels is closer to 'transitional secrecy' than a secret society proper (Simmel 1906, 471-2). For a comprehensive overview of G. Simmel on secret societies, see Simmel 1906, 470-98.

31 See Wrede 1901. For a recent and succinct summary of W. Wrede and subsequent scholarship on secrecy and concealment in Mark, see Watson 2010, 2-12.

proposed that the messianic secret in Mark was a dogmatic invention, as opposed to a historical recounting of events, the majority of research concerning secrecy in Mark has focused on historical questions; i.e. did Jesus conceal his messianic identity, or is this a later invention?[32]

While this historical line of questioning is important from a theological perspective, it overlooks other basic yet essential functions of secrecy in the Markan narrative. More specifically, Mark uses the moves of secrecy – revealing, concealing and keeping hidden – to create suspense and delay the denouement, effectively slowing the plot's forward momentum toward the climactic revelations of Jesus' identity (Mk 9.2-7; 14.62).[33] In doing so, Mark leverages this social construct to communicate essential information to both the reader and certain characters within the storyworld, while still maintaining the delicate balance between knowing and not-knowing in the storyworld. It is this communicative function of secrecy that is our focus here.

Thus, for our purposes, we will set aside historical questions and take instead as starting point Mark as a completed literary text. As we have learned from the consideration of G. Simmel above, secrecy entails both a spatial and social dimension: i.e. private space and at minimum three participants (a secret teller, a secret hearer and someone from whom the secret is concealed). Thus, we will begin with a brief consideration of the socio-spatial construction of the Markan storyworld: a narrative landscape divisible between public and private space, a socialscape divided between insiders and outsiders, and an in-group characterised by an internal hierarchy that privileges some members over others. Following this, we will take up examples of how Mark draws on these socio-spatial elements in his storyworld to reproduce the social construct of secrecy in a narrative context, and how these function as communicative forms.

Markan Landscape: Public and Private Space

In keeping with the spatial requirements for secrecy in an ancient context, Mark often prefaces secret activity with a movement into private space and away from outsiders (e.g. Mk 3.13; 4.10; 5.40; 7.17, etc.). Thus, it helps to imagine the landscape of the Markan storyworld as roughly divided into public and private spaces.[34] Generally, this division adheres to the ancient social distinction between the public and private spheres.[35] Activities like public teaching (e.g. Mk 1.21-22; 1.39; 6.6; 11.17-18) and conflict with religious authorities (e.g. Mk 2.6-12; 2.15-28; 3.1-6; 7.1-13) often belong to the public sphere or *polis*. Spatially, this includes urban areas – e.g. inside cities, marketplaces, etc. – and

32 Some notable exceptions include those who prefer a literary approach (see e.g. Kermode 1979, Tolbert 1989, MacDonald 1998), and those who take a social scientific approach (see e.g. Theissen 1995, Malina 2001, Pilch 1992).

33 See Tolbert 1989, 229-30; see also MacDonald 1998, 153.

34 In my dissertation, I further argue for a 'third space' (or 'group space') within the Markan storyworld. This space borrows from these ancient conceptions of the public and private, while attributing to them a new authority, social hierarchy and special group activities.

35 For more on this distinction, see Slater 1998.

public institutions like the Temple in Jerusalem (Mk 11.11-19, 11.27-13.1; cf. 14.49) and synagogues in the Galilee (Mk 1.21-29; 1.39; 3.1-5; 6.2-6).

Similarly, private activities within urban areas are largely confined to the *oikos*, the private domicile or household (e.g. Mk 1.29-31; 5.38-43; 7.17-23; 9.28-29, 33-50; 10.10-11). Mark further extends private space outside of urban areas to include naturally remote and uninhabited areas (ἔρημος τόπος, Mk 1.35-38, 45; 6.31-44), spaces associated with the divine (e.g. mountains, Mk 3.13-19; 6.46; 9.2-13; 13.3-37; 14.26-49) and forbidden or taboo spaces (e.g. among the tombs, Mk 5.2-5). It is these private spaces in which Mark sets secret teachings and other Jesus-group activities central to the plot.[36]

Markan Socialscape: Identifying Insiders and Outsiders

As discussed above, secrecy can be used in an organised group context to protect group interests and enforce an insider identity in contrast to outsiders.[37] In terms of the social requirements for secrecy, then, the concealed revelation of information takes place between two insiders – the secret teller and secret hearer(s) – with certain outsiders excluded.[38] There are multiple group identities represented in the Markan storyworld, representing both public identities (e.g. Pharisee, leader of the synagogue, tax collector, etc.) and private identities (e.g. family member, slave, etc.).

Depending on the perspective of the various characters, any one of these groups could be considered an 'in-group'.[39] However, given that the Gospel of Mark is centred on the speech and actions of Jesus, it is the individuals that form a group around him that we will consider insiders in the Markan storyworld.

This leaves the remaining characters and social groups in the storyworld as de facto outsiders. While not all outsiders are central to the plot, Mark paints certain out-groups in the storyworld as antagonists who repeatedly come in conflict with Jesus and his followers (e.g. 2.1-12; 2.15-17; 2.18-22; 2.23-28; 3.1-5, etc.), the most important of these being the various Jewish authorities, including the scribes, the Pharisees, the chief priests, the elders, the Herodians and the Sadducees.[40]

The Markan in-group – i.e. the group that gathers around Jesus – can be observed engaging in both inter- and intragroup secrecy. In terms of intragroup secrecy (i.e. internal social strategies to prevent betrayal), Mark constructs an in-group characterised by its hierarchical structure and the controlled, oral communication of teachings. Entry into the in-group is quite simple: an insider in the Markan storyworld is one who follows

36 For an in-depth study of space in Mark, particularly in relation to mythic significance, see Malbon 1986.

37 In the context of the Gospel of Mark, see Watson 2010, 24-6.

38 In terms of intergroup secrecy, the implication is that the outsider is a member of a different social group (an out-group), while in terms of intragroup secrecy, an outsider is more likely a less privileged member from within the in-group.

39 Like in the real world, one is not limited to a single social identity – for example, one can be a Jew, a father and a leader of the synagogue. However, in Mark, the Jesus-group identity tends to supplant other group identities (especially the religious and familial).

40 For more on Jesus' adversaries and conflict stories, see Hultgren 1979.

Jesus in a literal, spatial sense (e.g. Mk 1.18, 20; 2.14, 15; 3.7; 5.24; 6.1, etc.).[41] However, all insiders are not created equal.

Within the in-group exists a hierarchy of members – with Jesus at its top – which is measured by the level of access an insider is granted to various exclusive group activities (Fig. 2).[42] For example, the apostles – Jesus' twelve named disciples – form the core in-group and are thus the most privileged: they are granted the authority to exorcise demons, heal, teach and preach repentance (Mk 3.14-15; 6.7-13), they participate in the institution of the Lord's Supper (Mk 14.22-26; cf. 14.17), and they receive several exclusive teachings (Mk 4.10-34; 9.35-50; 10.32-34; 10.41-45; 14.17-21; 14.27-31).[43] This hierarchy extends even further among the twelve, with Simon Peter, John, James and sometimes Andrew, even further privileged among this core in-group (e.g. Mk 1.16-20; 1.29-34; 5.37-43; 9.2-8; 13.3-36; 14.33, etc.).[44] Peter is further singled out among these four, and is arguably the most developed character aside from Jesus (Mk 1.36-37; 8.29, 32-33; 9.5, 38-41; 10.28, 35-45; 11.21; 14.29, 37, 54, 66-72; 16.7).[45]

Aside from the twelve apostles, Mark references several other Jesus followers who are excluded from the inner-circle, but who in any case witness similar events (i.e. miracles, healings and exorcisms) and hear similar teachings as the apostles. Thus, on several oc-

41 E.S. Malbon (1983) argues for such an emphasis on followers and followership over disciples and discipleship in relation to the Jesus in-group in Mark.

42 The misunderstanding of Jesus' disciples (e.g. Mk 8.14-21) and their related conflict with Jesus is a commonly noted theme in Mark (particularly in connection with the messianic secret) and could be interpreted as evidence against their privileged position within the storyworld (Collins 2007, 386-8; Best 1986). However, the understanding of the disciples is primarily a theological problem. From a literary perspective, and in the context of the social theory of secrecy, being witness to revelation does not imply understanding, nor does membership within the Markan in-group appear to require it (it is following, not understanding, that identifies the insider; see Malbon 1983; Hurtado 1996, esp. 25-7; Longenecker 1996, 1-5). Furthermore, one of the qualities of intragroup secrecy outlined by G. Simmel is the potential for intragroup conflict, in which case the misunderstanding of the disciples functions to reinforce group identity as opposed to challenging it.

43 E. Best (1986) argues against distinguishing 'the twelve' as a privileged inner circle within 'the disciples' (Best 1986, 160), while still recognising that 'Mark distinguishes to some extent between the twelve and the disciples' (Best 1986, 157). While Mark does not make the distinction between groupings entirely explicit, I do believe that from a narrative perspective the references to 'disciples', 'the twelve and those who were with them' (Mk 4.10), 'the twelve', the Four/Three (Peter, James, John and Andrew), and Peter represent a clear narrowing of audience, even if the difference between groupings are neither fully developed nor consistently applied. Furthermore, the most important emphasis relies on the distinction between the top (Peter, James, John and Andrew) and the bottom (the crowd) of the internal hierarchy, as opposed to the more ambiguous middle (the disciples, the twelve). It is also worth remembering that the internal hierarchy of the in-group is irrelevant when the intended contrast is with members of external social groups.

44 On the greater authority of Peter, James, John and Andrew among the twelve named disciples, see Collins 2007, 218-20.

45 For more on Peter in Mark, see Best 1986, 162-76.

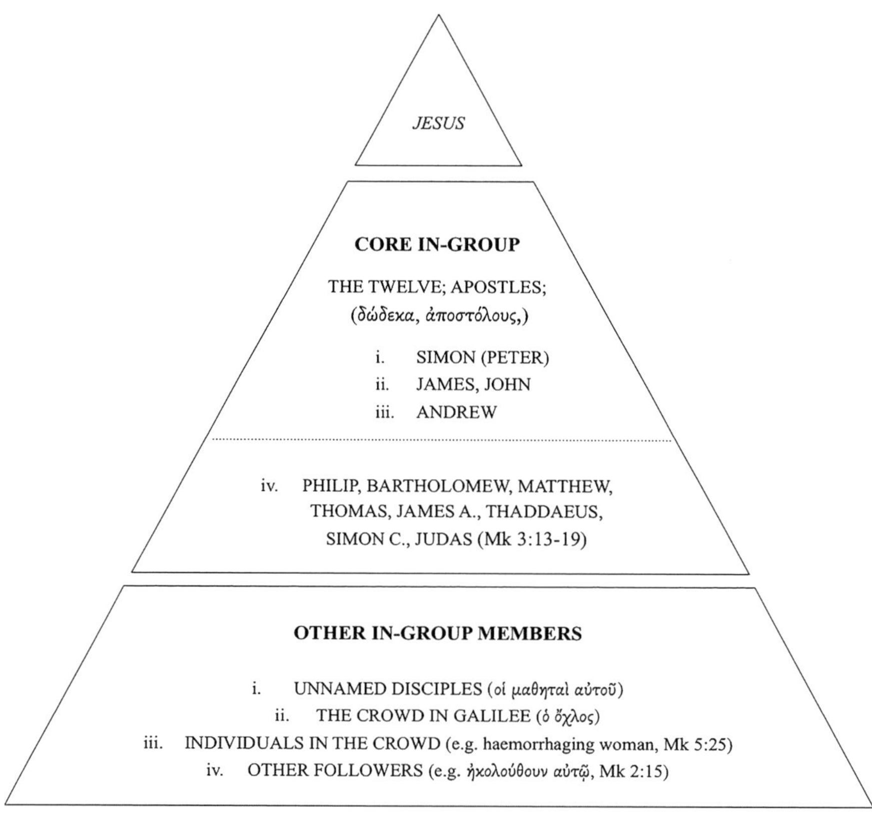

Fig. 2. *Hierarchy of the Markan in-group (copyright Erin J. Wright).*

casions, Mark makes general references to large crowds of followers,[46] both named and unnamed disciples (sometimes equatable to the twelve), as well as a number of named and unnamed individual followers;[47] it is these characters who make up the rest of the Markan in-group.

Mark and the Cycle of Secrecy

With a basic understanding of the public-private and insider-outsider dichotomies which characterise the Markan storyworld, we can now turn to consider specific examples which illustrate how Mark manipulates these socio-spatial elements to reproduce the cycle of secrecy. Thus, in the following we will consider two examples that demonstrate how Mark uses secrecy to communicate information both within the storyworld and to the reader: (i) the juxtaposed healings of the haemorrhaging woman and Jairus' daughter (Mk 5.21-43); and (ii) the transfiguration miracle (Mk 9.2-10).

46 See e.g. ὄχλος πλεῖστος, Mk 4.1; ὄχλος πολὺς, Mk 5.21, 24; 6.34; 9.14; 12.37; πολλοῦ ὄχλου, Mk 8.1; ὄχλου ἱκανοῦ, Mk 10.46; compare πᾶς ὁ ὄχλος, Mk 2.13; 4.1; 9.15; 11.18, 32.

47 See e.g. Levi (2.14), Jairus (Mk 5.22) and the haemorrhaging woman (Mk 5.25).

(i) *Healing the haemorrhaging woman and Jairus' daughter (Mk 5.21-43).* In this scene, Jesus is sought out by Jairus, one of the rulers of the synagogue, whose daughter is dying. Jesus concedes and performs a private healing miracle that revives the girl, who has allegedly died in the interim (Mk 5.37-43). On the way to Jairus' house is an embedded, more public healing of a haemorrhaging woman (Mk 5.25-34).[48] This juxtaposition between the healings – one performed amidst a large crowd, the other before an exclusive audience – helps illustrate the importance of the socio-spatial dimension for identifying the function of secrecy in narrative.

First, the healing of the haemorrhaging woman is performed in a heavily populated and urban setting: a great crowd (ὄχλος πολὺς) meets Jesus beside the sea (Mk 5.21) and 'presses into him' (συνέθλιβον αὐτόν) during the journey to Jairus' (Mk 5.24). Mark goes on to repeatedly invoke the presence of the crowd during the public healing (Mk 5.27, 30, 31). This heavily populated scene abruptly transitions to an exclusive healing scene. Upon arriving at Jairus' house, Jesus only allows the three most privileged core in-group members to follow him into the private space (Peter, James and John; Mk 5.37). Upon entering the house, Jesus further defines private space by expelling most of the mourning household members, only admitting the child's parents along with the three disciples (Mk 5.40). Jesus goes on to perform the healing act of raising the girl from the dead, a revelatory 'showing' of Jesus' abilities – and if not revealing his hidden identity, then at least gesturing toward it (Mk 5.41-42). This healing is immediately followed by a concealing act, with Jesus 'strictly charging them that no one should know this' (καὶ διεστείλατο αὐτοῖς πολλὰ ἵνα μηδεὶς γνοῖ τοῦτο; Mk 5.43). We can only assume that what follows is passive concealment (a state of hiddenness), as there is nothing further narrated.[49]

The concerted effort to conceal the healing of Jairus' daughter, in relation to the very public healing of the haemorrhaging woman, indicates toward the intrinsic difference in significance between the two healings: in one case Jesus inadvertently heals a medical condition (which is not necessarily observable to bystanders), while in the other Jesus raises someone whose death was witnessed by several people. It is clear that secrecy here is employed, at least in part, to protect group interests and Jesus' own autonomy within the storyworld, while further functioning to communicate certain vital information about Jesus' identity to only the reader and those present in Jairus' house.[50]

This juxtaposition of public and private is a repeated narrative strategy in Mark: following the initial establishment of the core in-group (the calling of the twelve), we

48 A.Y. Collins points to this narrative framing as an example of Markan style (Collins 2007, 276).

49 This could be considered significant in comparison to other instances in which Jesus' concealing command is ignored and the secret information does not remain a state of hiddenness, instead being revealed again and spread widely by others (see e.g. Mk 1.43-45; 7.36-37; compare Mk 1.24-28).

50 C.D. Marshall also suggests that this narrowing of audience between these public and private healings functions to underscore the particularly miraculous nature of the second healing (Marshall 1989, 91).

find a series of similarly juxtaposed public and private activities (e.g. Mk 3.22-35; 4.1-34; 5.21-43; 6.35-52; 7.1-23; 8.11-21; 9.14-29; 9.30-50; 10.1-16; 10.23-45; 11.12-25; 11.27-13.37; 14.22-42). In these examples, Mark narrates – for example – a more public teaching, followed by a movement into private space where a more exclusive and sometimes related teaching is delivered.

(ii) *The transfiguration miracle (Mk 9.2-10).* In this central scene, Jesus takes aside Peter, James and John, and performs the transfiguration miracle that explicitly reveals his messianic identity – information that has been largely concealed up until this climactic revelation.[51] This scene meets both the basic social and spatial requirements for secrecy. First, there are three implicit parties involved: Jesus (and 'a voice'; Mk 9.7) as secret tellers, the three most privileged disciples as secret hearers and all others as 'not-knowers', as implied by the instruction to tell no one what they have seen (διεστείλατο αὐτοῖς ἵνα μηδενὶ ἃ εἶδον διηγήσωνται; Mk 9.9). Furthermore, the scene takes place in an explicitly private space: Jesus takes the disciples up a 'high mountain' (εἰς ὄρος ὑψηλὸν[52]) where it is further specified that they are 'in private' (κατ' ἰδίαν[53]) and 'alone' (μόνους[54]). This triple emphasis on the private nature of the setting makes this the most explicitly private scene in the Gospel of Mark.

The scene clearly reflects the three moves of the cycle of secrecy. First, we have the revealing act in two parts: (i) an act of 'showing', i.e. Jesus' transfiguration before the three disciples (Mk 9.2-8), and (ii) an act of 'telling', spoken by an unidentified voice from a cloud (presumably God) who states "This is my beloved Son; listen to him" (Mk 9.7).[55] This particular revelatory scene is unique due to the presence of two 'secret tellers'; elsewhere in Mark, it is only Jesus who reveals directly to his followers.

The concealing act is also unique. While coming down from the mountain Jesus enjoins the three disciples to secrecy, instructing them "to tell no one what they had

51 Shortly before this transfiguration scene, Peter correctly identifies Jesus as 'the Christ' (ὁ χριστός) to an audience of Jesus and his disciples (Mk 8.27-29). Jesus responds to this with a negative affirmation of his identity ("tell no one"; Mk 8.30).

52 Mountains provide the setting for several private scenes in Mark, and only members of the core in-group are invited to join Jesus for private teachings and miracles in these spaces (ὄρος; Mk 3.13-19; 9.2-9; 13.3-37; compare 14.26-42). This Markan construction of mountains is consistent with the ancient conception of mountains as naturally isolated places associated with the divine. Mark further invokes the association between mountains and revelation found in the Old Testament (Foerster 1964-76, 475).

53 Mk 9.2; compare Mk 4.34; 6.31, 32; 7.33; 9.28; 13.3. O.J.F. Seitz (1949) argues that the phrase 'κατ' ἰδίαν' is an esoteric device introduced by Mark, and used as an editorial introduction to preface e.g. esoteric logia (Seitz 1949, 218).

54 Mk 9.2; compare Mk 4.10; 6.47; 9.8.

55 Καὶ ἐγένετο νεφέλη ἐπισκιάζουσα αὐτοῖς, καὶ ἐγένετο φωνὴ ἐκ τῆς νεφέλης · οὗτός ἐστιν ὁ υἱός μου ὁ ἀγαπητός, ἀκούετε αὐτοῦ (Mk 9.7).

seen, until the Son of man should have risen from the dead" (Mk 9.9).[56] While Jesus makes other enjoinments similar to this (e.g. Mk 1.44, 5.43, 7.36, 8.30; cf. 8.26), none of the other instances have a temporal clause. This conditional statement indicates that this information is not meant to remain permanently hidden, and that the cycle of secrecy is only temporarily suspended in a state of hiddenness. For the time being, Jesus is here depending on an aggressive form of concealment to maintain this hiddenness: relying on the hierarchy of the in-group and thus the reciprocal confidence that they will protect the secret for the sake of group interests.[57]

This scene demonstrates quite clearly how Mark employs the cycle of secrecy by drawing on the public-private and insider-outsider dichotomies of the storyworld, in turn functioning to control revelation while simultaneously communicating essential information to the reader and certain members of the core in-group. The overall effect is that the reader and the Three now approach the Passion events with this added insight into Jesus' identity, while still maintaining the level of not-knowing in the storyworld necessary to delay the denouement.

Conclusion: The Communicative Function of Secrecy

In both of the above examples, Mark indicates to the reader the importance of certain activities and information by drawing on the socio-spatial dichotomies of insider-outsider and public-private to recreate the universal sociological form of secrecy in the storyworld. This can be clearly observed in the narrowing of audience between the first and second healing in Mark 5.21-43, as well as in the repetition of privacy indicators in Mark 9.2-10 that precede the revelation to the Three. In the immediate narrative context, this framing strategy enhances and reinforces the significance of the secret activities in comparison to the more open activities that are narrated. In the greater narrative context, this repeated cycle of secrecy creates tension and suspense by maintaining the delicate balance between knowing and not-knowing, successfully advancing the plot toward the climactic revelations of Jesus' identity: both in private (Mk 9.2-7) and later in public (Mk 14.62).

We might return to G. Simmel here for further insight: 'Secrecy involves a tension which, at the moment of revelation, finds its release. This constitutes the climax in the development of the secret; in it the whole charm of secrecy concentrates and rises to its highest pitch – just as the moment of the disappearance of an object brings out the feeling of its value in the most intense degree'.[58] For G. Simmel, then, the 'climax' of the cycle of secrecy is found in its revelation, putting emphasis on its communicative function.

---

56 Καὶ καταβαινόντων αὐτῶν ἐκ τοῦ ὄρους διεστείλατο αὐτοῖς ἵνα μηδενὶ ἃ εἶδον διηγήσωνται, εἰ μὴ ὅταν ὁ υἱὸς τοῦ ἀνθρώπου ἐκ νεκρῶν ἀναστῇ (Mk 9.9).

57 This reciprocal confidence is affirmed by the Three, who keep their silence (Mk 9.10). This is significant in itself, as elsewhere Jesus' commands for silence are either ignored (Mk 1.43-56; 7.36-37) or else the result is not narrated (Mk 5.43; 8.26; 8.30; compare Mk 1.25-26, 34; 3.12).

58 Simmel 1906, 465.

Putting narrative aside, the implications here for the study of secrecy in the ancient world are multiple. Firstly, the social theory of secrecy can be applied to patterns of revealing and concealing that are not explicitly recognised as secrecy in their contemporary cultural context. Secondly, G. Simmel moves the emphasis of secrecy from content to form, effectively removing the negative ethical stigmatisation of that which is kept hidden. And finally, by emphasising the communicative nature of secrecy, its essential role in all social interaction comes into stark relief. Based on this centrality of secrecy to social relationships, then, one cannot help but agree with G. Simmel that secrecy is surely 'one of the greatest achievements of humanity'.[59]

59 Simmel 1906, 462.

UFFE HOLMSGAARD ERIKSEN

Hooked on Concealing: The Descent to Hell in Doctrine and Drama

This article examines how the doctrine of Christ's descent to hell was transposed into a sacred, dramatic narrative, in which secrecy and concealment play a pivotal role. After an outline of the development of the doctrine of the descent to hell, special attention is given to five authors from the 4th century AD, Ephrem the Syrian, Cyril of Jerusalem, John Chrysostom, Gregory of Nyssa and Ps.-Athanasius of Alexandria, who develop the idea of the descent as a 'divine deception', where God disguises himself in the flesh of Jesus Christ in order to deceive the Devil and Hell. In the final section two kontakia *by the Byzantine poet Romanus the Melodist are analysed in terms of how he transforms the doctrinal material into dramatic narratives that centre on concealment, secrecy and disguise, and re-enact the drama of redemption.*

In connection with the overall theme of this volume, my contribution deals with secrecy and concealment as both theological and narrative themes centred upon the motif of God in disguise. The motif of a god in disguise is well known from classical literature. One needs only to recall how the goddess Athena in the guise of Mentor guides and helps Telemachus find his lost father, Odysseus, in the famous epic by Homer.[1] Closely connected with this motif is the motif of recognition, both abundant in the Homeric epics and classical drama, and according to Aristotle a key element in a successful plot.[2] Disguise – the act of concealing an identity for some purpose – is often used in relation to this recognition motif, i.e. to keep something secret, whereas recognition is brought forth by disclosing the hidden identity.

In the Bible and early Christian literature, disguise and recognition play an important role.[3] Indeed, according to the dominant view among early Christian authors, the true Christian is one who believes that Jesus Christ is God, that the hidden and invisible

1 Athena appears in several other guises throughout the *Odyssey*, but most often takes on the guise of Mentor from Hom. *Od.* 2.267 onwards right until the very last verses of Hom. *Od.* 24.545-548.

2 See Arist. *Poet.* 1450a34, and especially in chapters 11 (1452a28-1452b8) and 16 (1454b18-1455a20).

3 For a recent study of the use of recognition scenes with special focus on the Gospel of John, see Larsen 2007.

God is revealed in the visible human Jesus. Not being able to recognise or acknowledge the identity of both God and human in Christ is viewed by the early Christian authors as heresy,[4] and the cause for this heresy is ultimately being deceived by the Devil.

In this article, I present and analyse how the motifs of disguise and recognition were applied in the development of the doctrine of the 'descent to hell', and especially how God uses disguise to deceive the Devil, who himself is the ultimate deceiver. First, I outline the development of the theme from the Bible to the full, narrative accounts in Late Antiquity. Second, I look at how Christian authors during the 4th century AD[5] in particular applied two metaphors – the 'gastronomic' and the 'piscatorial' – to describe the deception of the Devil, the descent to hell and the resurrection. Finally, I examine more closely how these metaphors and ideas were transposed into dramatic narratives in the hymns of the Byzantine poet, Romanus the Melodist.

The Descent to Hell – From Doctrine to Drama

In the *Apostles' Creed*, which is recited at Sunday services and used in baptisms in most Western churches, it is said that Jesus Christ was 'crucified, dead, and buried: He descended into hell'.[6] The second article of faith in the *Apostles' Creed* is in fact not more than a condensed outline of the basic narrative in the gospels. It is surprising then, that none of the gospels mention a descent to hell as such. In the early Church, however, several scriptural passages from both the Old and the New Testament were interpreted as referring to a descent to hell in the development of the doctrines that later came to define orthodoxy. A brief overview of some of the most important text passages will provide the background on which the doctrine of the descent to hell was formed.

In the cultural and religious context in which the texts later canonised as the New Testament were written, the souls of the departed were believed to go to the realm of the dead, Hades (Ἅιδης) in Greek or Sheol in Hebrew.[7] Thus, in keeping with this,

4 Although heresy, especially in the form of Arianism and later Nestorianism, is crucial as a motivation for the development of the narratives on the descent to hell and the theory of divine deception, I have chosen not to go further into this interesting topic, as my focus here lies on secrecy and concealment and how these ideas are transposed into dramatic narratives. For an excellent study of the connection between the descent to hell, divine deception and heresy, see Constas 2004, to which this article is much indebted. See also my dissertation, Eriksen 2013, 208-12, 238-46, for a more detailed analysis of these motifs and themes in the *kontakia* of Romanus the Melodist.

5 Throughout this article, all references to years are AD.

6 Here quoted from the *Book of Common Prayer*, available online http://www.churchofengland.org/prayer-worship/worship/book-of-common-prayer/the-order-for-morning-prayer.aspx (accessed 14 May 2014); see Kelly 1960, 368. The Latin text, on which translations into the vernacular of the Protestant Churches are based, dates back to the 7th-8th centuries (Kelly 1960, 398). Before the 7th-8th centuries, different versions existed, but the origins of the *Apostles' Creed* can be traced back to around the beginning of the 2nd century (Kelly 1960, 100-30).

7 It falls beyond the scope of this article to give a broader presentation of the history of hell in the cultural and religious context in which Christianity rose and from which it was influenced. For

Christ's soul must too have gone to Hades. Two important allusions to such a descent to hell are found in the Gospel of Matthew. The first is the Jonah-Christ typology to which I will return in the second part of this article. The other is Matthew 27.40, where the dead rise again from their graves and walk around, which was interpreted as the purpose of the descent; that is to free the dead from their imprisonment. The liberation of the captives in hell was further substantiated by Old Testament passages such as Psalm 107.10-16, where the prisoners are freed from their chains and the Lord 'shatters the bronze gates and crushes the iron bars'.[8] This 'harrowing of Hell' as it has been called in the English tradition also marks the victory over death, which the apostle Paul triumphantly proclaims in his first letter to the Corinthians.[9] The only instance in which a descent to the netherworld is mentioned directly is in the first letter of the apostle Peter. Here, the apostle tells that Christ 'was put to death in the flesh, but made alive in the spirit, in which also he went and made a proclamation to the spirits in prison (ἐν φυλακῇ)',[10] which also refers to the common understanding of the dead as prisoners in hell.

The development of the doctrine of the descent to hell is complicated, as opinions varied among the Church Fathers as to where hell was located and, in particular, why Christ descended. Some, like Irenaeus of Lyon (c. 130-200) and Ignatius of Antioch (c. 35-117) followed the first letter of Peter and saw the purpose of the descent of Christ to be to preach the gospel to the patriarchs, prophets and other Old Testament saints who had not heard the gospel preached in their lifetime.[11] Others, such as Clement of Alexandria (c. 150-215) saw a more universal approach in that the purpose of Christ was to preach for all souls in hell, including pagans.[12] Clement and his pupil Origen of Alexandria (c. 185-254), as well as Hippolytus of Rome (c. 170-235) and the anonymous author of *The Ascension of Isaiah* claimed that not only had Christ descended to preach the gospel, he also set free the prisoners kept captive in hell and brought them back to

---

a very concise introduction, see Bauckham 1992. 'Hell' is the English translation of the Greek word 'Hades' in both the New Testament and the Greek Old Testament, the Septuagint (LXX) – which in turn is a translation of the Hebrew word 'Sheol'. Strictly speaking, the English word 'Hell' should be used when referring to the Greek 'Tartaros' or Hebrew 'Gehenna'. But for sake of ease, I have used the English word throughout this article, as the most common reference to the descent is referred to as the descent to 'hell' in the English translation of the *Apostles' Creed* and research literature.

8 Ps 107.16.

9 1 Cor 15.54-55. Paul quotes Hosea (Hos 13.14): 'Death has been swallowed up in victory. / "Where, O death, is your victory? / Where, O death, is your sting?"' (κατεπόθη ὁ θάνατος εἰς νῖκος. ποῦ σου, θάνατε, τὸ νῖκος; ποῦ σου, θάνατε, τὸ κέντρον; *NTNA*). All English translations of quotes from the Bible derive from the *NRSV*, unless otherwise indicated. The victory over death and hell is furthermore found in Matth. 16.18; Apc 1.18, 20.14.

10 See 1 Petr 3.18-19. The idea that Christ went to the dead to preach the gospel is repeated in 1 Petr 4.6.

11 See Iren. *Adversus Haereses* 4.27.2; Ignatius *Ad Magnesios* 9.2.

12 Clem. Al. *Strom.* 6.6.

paradise.[13] The plundering of hell later became more elaborated and dramatised, as we shall see.

The first steps toward a more dramatic rendering of the descent are found in Origen's commentary on the Gospel of Matthew. In explaining to whom it is that Christ gives his life as a ransom for all, Origen states that the ransom is given to the Devil. But by accepting the soul of Christ in hell as a ransom, the Devil is actually deceived:

> the Devil it was who had us in his power until he accepted the soul of Jesus as a ransom for us and thus allowed himself to be deceived (ἀπατηθέντι), as he thought he could lord it over that soul and did not see that he would never be able to keep a hold on it by his own effort.[14]

The Devil cannot keep the soul of Christ imprisoned because Christ is 'free among the dead' (ἐν νεκροῖς ἐλευθέρου).[15] Thus Origen applies here the concept of deception which is later expanded by Gregory of Nyssa to be a willing act of God: a divine deception, to which I will return in the second part of this article.

Based on these doctrinal discussions, mostly found in letters or commentaries on the Bible, the longer narratives on the descent to hell were developed by the 4th century featured in extra-canonical Gospels, homilies and hymns.[16] It is also in this century that the descent is treated as a doctrinal issue, for instance in the *Fourth Formula of Sirmium* in 359.[17] Likely in the same century, the descent is also inserted as a confessional doctrine in the Aquilean version of the *Apostles' Creed*, on which Rufinus made

---

13 Clem. Al. *Strom.* 6.6; Orig. *Homiliae in Exodum* 6.6 (*PG* 12.336B); Hippol. *De Antichristo* 26, 45; *Ascenion of Isaiah* 9.16-17, 10.8-14.

14 Orig. *Commentarium in evangelium Matthaei* 16.8. The Latin translation in *PG* has 'decepto' for 'ἀπατηθέντι', see *PG* 13.1398B-C. The English translation is slightly altered and adapted from Daniélou 1955, 272-3. Only God was allowed to use deception, whereas the Christian should refrain from deception and hypocrisy, especially when praying, see Christensen in this volume. God's use of deception was justified as an act of restoration (ἀποκατάστασις) reversing the Devil's deception of Adam and Eve in the Garden of Eden, compare Greg. Nyss. *Oratio catechetica magna* 26 and Constas 2004, 142-5; 155.

15 See Ps 87.6, which Origen applies to Christ.

16 This short presentation of the theme is based on Bauckham 1992; see esp. 145-59 for the most important sources. For an elaborated treatment of the subject, see Kelly 1960, 378-83; Bernstein 1993. For an easy introduction to the main sources from the Old Testament passages to the *Gospel of Nicodemus*, see Toit 2007. Here, the important passages in the main sources are quoted in English and thus Toit's article provides a small compendium of the development of the theme of the descent to hell, although there are some mistakes on p. 113. Toit seems to quote from Hippol. *De Antichristo* 26, 45, Orig. *Commentarium in evangelium Matthaei* 16.8 and Orig. *Commentarii in epistolam ad Romanos* 5, but actually cites a summary given by M. Peel in his article on the descent in the *Teachings of Silvanus*, see Peel 1979, 42-5. For a recent treatment of the descent with a focus on the Eastern tradition, see Alfeyev 2009.

17 See Kelly 1960, 288-90.

a commentary in 404.[18] Thus, before the 4th century the descent into hell was not an officially recognised doctrine, or at least not part of any creed. The different version of the *Apostles' Creed* that eventually reached a unified formulation in the 7th and 8th centuries also included the descent.

In the 5th and 6th centuries the descent was further elaborated in the second part of the so-called *Gospel of Nicodemus*,[19] in the *Questions of Bartholomew*,[20] and in homilies attributed to Eusebius of Alexandria (or John Chrysostom), Epiphanius of Salamis[21] and not least in the hymns by Romanus the Melodist, to which I will turn in the last section of this article. In these narratives, often told in dialogue form with a quarrel between personifications of Hell and the Devil, the idea of 'divine deception' plays an important role as a part of the plot.

A final step in the development was turning the descent to hell into a ritual in the end of the 6th century; or at least, this is the earliest account of such a ritual. The chronicler John Malalas (c. 491-578) describes in his *Chronography*[22] how the restored Hagia Sophia in Constantinople was inaugurated in 562 in a kind of ritual drama, which symbolised the descent to hell by chanting Psalm 24.7-10 (23.7-10 LXX):

> (7) Lift up your heads, O gates! and be lifted up, O ancient doors! that the King of glory may come in. (8) Who is the King of glory? The Lord, strong and mighty, the Lord, mighty in battle. (9) Lift up your heads, O gates! and be lifted up, O ancient doors! that the King of glory may come in. (10) Who is this King of glory? The Lord of hosts, he is the King of glory.

These verses were from the 4th century onwards interpreted as Christ entering the gates of hell.[23] In a later ritual, perhaps dating back as early as the 6th century, a deacon would hide behind the doors of a church about to be inaugurated and play the role of

---

18 Rufin. *Commentarius in symbolum apostolorum* (*PL* 21.335-86).

19 The second part is known as the *Descencus ad Inferos*. The two parts have traditionally been linked together, even though the first part (*Acta Pilati*) is most probably written no later than the 4th century, whereas the *Descensus ad Inferos* is most likely written in the 5th or 6th century, see Elliott 1993, 165; see also *ODB*, vol. 2, 1472, s.v. 'Nicodemus, Gospel of'.

20 This work is difficult to date precisely. J.K. Elliot suggests somewhere between the 2nd and 6th centuries, see Elliott 1993, 652. A short presentation of the text with at focus on the descent to hell is found in Frank 2009, 218-9.

21 See four homilies by Ps.-Eusebius of Alexandria (who is considered an imagined author by scholars): *De Adventu et Annuntiatione Joannis apud Inferos*; *De Proditione Judae*; *In Diabolum et Orcum*; and *In Sancta et Magna Parasceve, et in Sanctam Passionem Domini*; and a homily attributed to Epiphanius of Salamis *In Divini Corporis Sepulturam*. For a brief summary and overview of these homilies as well as questions concerning the dating of them, see Grosdidier de Matons 1967, 269-73, and Carpenter 1970, 228-9, who builds her treatment on Grosdidier de Matons.

22 Ioh. Mal. 18.143.

23 See Stiefenhofer 1909, 91-2; Puchner 2002, 322. This ritual has been used as a consecration ritual in both Western and Eastern churches since the Middle Ages. The verses play a prominent role

the Devil. A bishop outside the church would assume the role of Christ and then chant verse seven "Lift up your heads…". The deacon would respond from behind the closed doors with verse eight "Who is the King of glory?" and the bishop and the congregation would answer "The Lord, strong and mighty, the Lord, mighty in battle". Contrary to the Western church, the Byzantine church never developed any liturgical plays or dramas, but in this ritual is a kernel of drama or theatre, which most likely is based on the patristic exegesis of the verses of Psalm 24.[24] Thus we see a development from doctrinal disputes into more elaborate narrative and dramatic accounts, from which the descent is eventually adapted for ritualistic re-enactment.

The Crook on the Hook

From this outline of the development of the theme of the descent to hell, I will now turn to the idea of 'divine deception', which involves concealment. As mentioned, this motif was frequently applied to expositions of the theme of the descent, especially in order to explain exegetical and theological difficulties, not least the seemingly outrageous idea that God could suffer, die and go to the realm of the dead.

Two striking metaphors were frequently used and reused in homilies and hymns, both related to deception. One is what Archbishop Hilarion Alfeyev has dubbed 'gastronomic',[25] while the other could be called 'piscatorial'. The gastronomic metaphor is used to depict Hell swallowing something he cannot digest and therefore has to regurgitate; the piscatorial metaphor depicts Hell as a fish being deceived by Christ as the bait on the hook of the cross. Often the two metaphors are combined so that Hell disgorges his captives because he has swallowed the bait, which he cannot digest. In both instances, Hell is being deceived by appearances: what appeared to be good food turns out to be an emetic; what appeared to be a good piece of human flesh turns out to be the indigestible God. We find these metaphors especially in the hymns and sermons of Ephrem the Syrian,[26] John Chrysostom, Gregory of Nyssa and a homily attributed to Athanasius.[27] The metaphors might seem far-fetched or overly pedagogical, but in fact they rely on exegesis of the Old Testament.

The earliest use of the gastronomic metaphor is found among others in the works of John Chrysostom and Ephrem the Syrian. In one of his homilies on 1 Corinthians,

in the *Gospel of Nicodemus* 21.1 and in the homily *In Sancta et Magna Parasceve, et in Sanctam Passionem Domini* (*PG* 62.723) by Ps.-Eusebius of Alexandria. See also Winling 2003, 18-31 on the interpretation of the psalm by the Church Fathers.

24 See Puchner 2002, 322-3; 1979, 125-8.

25 Alfeyev 2009, 65.

26 See esp. the *Nisibene Hymns* (Carmina Nisibena). See Brock 1983, 14-5 and his translations no. 3, 6, 7, 10, 14, 15, 16 that have dialogues between Satan and Sheol. See also Alfeyev 2009, 70-3, 106-32.

27 Greg. Nyss. *Oratio catechetica magna*. Probably written in 385. See Constas 2004, 142-9.

Chrysostom applies the analogy of regurgitation to explain how hell was emptied of its prisoners:

> … as they who take food which they are unable to retain, on account of that vomit up also what was before lodged in them; so also it happened unto death. That body, which he could not digest (τὸ σῶμα,ὅπερ οὐκ ἦν ἱκανὸς κατεργάζεσθαι), he received: and therefore had to cast forth (ἐξέβαλεν) that which he had within him.[28]

As we shall see, the verbs ἐκβάλλειν (cast out/throw up) or the less euphemistic ἐξεμεῖν (vomit forth/disgorge) are central in determining the sources to this gastronomic metaphor, which is only yet an analogy in Chrysostom's homily. In Ephrem the Syrian's *Hymn on the Unleavend Bread*, the analogy is now turned into a metaphor: 'With the Living Lamb, Sheol's hunger / disgorged back the dead, against its nature'.[29] Seemingly satisfying his hunger with Christ, the Living Lamb, Hell ('Sheol' in Hebrew and Syriac) is forced to spew out the dead who until now have been captives in his belly. The question is of course where this image of Hell as a creature with a mouth and a belly comes from?

In Cyril of Jerusalem's (c. 313-86) *Catechetical Lectures* 14.17 the answer is given explicitly; however, in Cyril's lecture it is not Hell who swallows and vomits the dead, but Death who at the resurrection would 'throw up those it had swallowed up' (ἐξεμέσῃ τοὺς καταποθέντας ὁ θάνατος).[30] Cyril teaches how Christ likens himself to the prophet Jonah in the Gospel of Matthew.[31] As Jonah descended in the belly of the fish for three days and three nights, so too shall Christ voluntarily descend to Death, the 'spiritual fish',[32] Cyril explains.

The image of Hell as a creature with a mouth and a stomach is thus constructed from two important passages in the Old Testament: Isaiah 5.14, where Hell is depicted as having a large appetite and opening its mouth (διήνοιξεν τὸ στόμα, LXX) for the people of Jerusalem; and Jonah 2.1-3.10, where Jonah is swallowed by the fish, resting in its belly for three days and three nights[33] and then cast out again (ἐξέβαλεν).[34] From the belly of the fish, Jonah prays to God and says "from the belly of Hell (ἐκ κοιλίας ᾅδου) You heard my crying, my voice".[35] Thereby, the connection between the fish with its mouth and belly and Hell lay near at hand. As we have seen demonstrated in Cyril's

28 Chrys. *Homilia in Epistulam i ad Corinthios* 24.7 (*PG* 61.204). Translation by H. Alfeyev (2009, 65).

29 Stanza 11, English translation by S. Brock (1983, 38).

30 Cyril of Jerusalem *Catecheses ad illuminandos* 14.17.

31 Matth. 12.40.

32 οὗτος δὲ κατῆλθεν ἑκουσίως ὅπου τὸ νοητὸν τοῦ θανάτου κῆτος, Cyril of Jerusalem *Catecheses ad illuminandos* 14.17.

33 καταπιεῖν τὸν Ιωναν·καὶ ἦν Ιωνας ἐν τῇ κοιλίᾳ τοῦ κήτους τρεῖς ἡμέρας καὶ τρεῖς νύκτας, Jon 2.1 LXX.

34 Jon 2.10 LXX.

35 Jon 2.3 LXX.

Fig. 1. *The fish literally spewing out the prophet Jonah. Miniature from the Menologion of Basileos II, an illuminated Byzantine manuscript containing the vitae of the saints for each month in the liturgical year, c. AD 1000 (image from Wikimedia Commons http://en.wikipedia.org/wiki/Menologion_of_Basil_II#mediaviewer/File:Menologion_of_Basil_008_page.jpg, accessed January 2015).*

lecture, this exact passage in Jonah is used typologically in Matthew 12.40, where Jesus says that he will stay in 'the heart of the earth' (ἐν τῇ καρδίᾳ τῆς γῆς)[36] for three days and nights. The belly of the fish, which is already the 'belly of Hell' in Jonah, becomes the 'heart of the earth' in Matthew. The combination of Isaiah 5.14, Jonah 2.1-3 and Matthew 12.40 therefore obviously lends itself to an image of Hell with a belly, swallowing the dead and Christ, and eventually regurgitating him after three days and nights, in the same way as the fish swallowed and later spewed out Jonah ((Fig. 1).

The gastronomic metaphor and the image of Hell might even have had a deliberate comic twist: G. Frank finds that there might be thematic parallels between characters with stomach-aches in Roman satire and the general philosophical critique and mockery of gluttonous people, resounding in the apostle Paul's letters where he condemns the ones for whom 'god is the belly'.[37]

Now, concerning the piscatorial metaphor, this is elaborated elegantly by Gregory of Nyssa (c. 335-95) in his *Catechetical Discourse* and in the homily *On the Passion and the Cross* attributed to Athanasius of Alexandria (c. 298-373). Here, further Old Testament passages are combined to depict the descent to hell and the resurrection. Job 40-41, Psalm 104.26 (103 LXX) and Isaiah 27.1 all tell about dragging the old dragon (the Devil) with a 'fish-hook' (ἄγκιστρον).

In his *Catechetical Discourse*, Gregory of Nyssa explains how God deceived the deceiver, the Devil, by using Christ in human flesh as bait (δέλεαρ): '… the deity was hidden under the veil of our nature, so that, as with ravenous fish, the hook of the

36 Matth. 12.40.

37 Phil. 3.19; Frank 2009, 223-4.

deity might be gulped down along with the bait of the flesh'.[38] To deceive the Devil, God uses concealment and hides under the human flesh.

Germinating in Gregory's *Catechetical Discourse,* we find what N. Constas calls a 'dramatic theory of atonement' containing a 'typological reversal'.[39] Although Gregory does not present the idea of 'divine deception' in either a dramatic or narrative form (but rather in an expository, oratorical style), he has constructed the essential elements in the plot of the descent to hell that we shall see turned into a dramatic narrative in the *kontakia* of Romanus.

The dramatic rendering becomes even more apparent in the homily by Ps.-Athanasius. In his exposition of the divine deception, Ps.-Athanasius applies a very interesting adaptation of Homer's *Odyssey*. Here, the preacher likens the Devil to Irus, a minor character in the *Odyssey*.[40] Irus is a bragging beggar who normally sits outside the house of Odysseus, which has been taken over by suitors in the latter's absence. However, Odysseus returns to his house in Ithaca disguised as an old beggar seeking hospitality. Faced with another beggar as a competitor, Irus challenges the apparently old man to a wrestling match thinking that the old man is weak. This challenge is a mistake with devastating consequences for Irus, as he is beaten to a pulp and thrown out of the house by Odysseus in disguise. In the same way, the Devil has become 'another Irus' whose ignorance, boasting and apparent richness was turned upside down by Christ:

> [...] the devil, having arrogantly presumed against the Lord, has now become another Irus, cast forth from the universe, and trampled upon by all ... and the dragon who boasted that he was rich has been stripped of all, and he is now a naked and impoverished Irus, utterly despoiled.[41]

Ps.-Athanasius casts God as an Odysseus, who has hidden himself in order to deceive the villain. It is an interesting adaptation of a highly dramatic scene in the *Odyssey* involving disguise, reversal and – in the case of Irus – non-recognition, as Irus does not recognise the beggar as Odysseus. In the dramatic narratives of Romanus, however, the recognition is pivotal and fatal for the evil one below.

The Drama of Redemption in the Hymns of Romanus the Melodist

Romanus the Melodist (c. 485-560) was a composer of many of the type of Byzantine hymns called *kontakia*.[42] Often, his *kontakia* contain dramatic retellings of the biblical

---

38 Greg. Nyss. *Oratio catechetica magna* 24. Translation by N.P. Constas (2004, 143).

39 Constas 2004, 143.

40 Hom. *Od.* 18.45-135.

41 *PG* 28.233.12-14, 28.236.11-13. Translation by N.P. Constas (2004, 152).

42 A *kontakion* is a certain kind of hymn, which came to be used in the Byzantine liturgy from the 5th century and onwards. It normally consists of 1-3 initial stanzas (proems) and 18-24 stanzas that all end with the same refrain, which often highlights the over-all theme of the hymn. In a *kontakion*,

narratives with himself as the narrator who introduces biblical characters engaged in monologue or dialogue, not unlike the epics of Homer.

Approximately 60 *kontakia* are considered by scholars to be genuine, i.e. written by Romanus. About one fourth of his *kontakia* are related to the Paschal Week, especially the crucifixion, the descent to hell and the resurrection. In the following, I will focus on two *kontakia* that construct the tension and plot around the gastronomic and the piscatorial metaphors.

In *On the Victory of the Cross*, which was written to be performed on Good Friday, Hell and the Devil discuss the consequences of the crucifixion. The first stanza opens with Hell lamenting in pain and agony. The cross that Pilate has fixed on Golgotha has pierced Hell like a lance:

> who has fixed (ἐμπήξας) a nail in my heart?
> ... I feel pain in my inners, my stomach hurts.
> My senses! My breath quivers,
> and I am compelled to vomit forth (ἐξερεύξασθαι)
> Adam and Adam's race.[43]

Although the cross is not described as a fishing rod in this *kontakion* and the piscatorial metaphor not applied, there is a connection between the cross and Hell's sudden urge to vomit 'Adam and Adam's race', a metonymy for all dead people held in his custody.

However, the Devil finds Hell's lament ridiculous and tries to convince him that nothing is wrong, as it is all part of his plan. He made the cross and caused the Jews to crucify Christ (second stanza). In the following stanzas (three to nine), they argue back and forth about what has happened in alternation. Hell tries to warn the Devil by directing his attention to what is happening: the sky is covered, the rocks shattered, the veil in the temple rent and the dead risen from their graves (here Hell 'reports' the events in Matthew 27.51-52). This, however, does not convince the Devil either. It is only when Hell in stanza nine tells the Devil that Christ pardons one of the thieves crucified next to him and takes him to Paradise[44] that the Devil begins to realise his mistake. The Devil runs up and is bewildered that Christ pardons a thief. He sees Christ crucified

---

the poet will often expound a certain biblical passage in the same way as in a prose homily, but following the poetic rules of the genre; that is, recurring rhythmic patterns in every stanza and an acrostic, which is formed from a combination of the initial letter in each stanza. In Romanus' *kontakia*, the acrostic most often reads 'by the humble Romanus'. For a recent introduction to Byzantine hymnography, see McGuckin 2008. For an in depth history of Byzantine music and hymnography, see Wellesz 1961, esp. 179-97 about the *kontakion*.

43 SC 38, stanza 1.5.7-10. Translation by author. I refer to the French edition of the *kontakia* in five volumes in the series *Sources Chrétiennes*, abbreviated SC followed by the number of the hymn in that edition and the abbreviation st. for stanza.

44 Luke 23.42-43.

and stabbed in the side with blood and water coming out.[45] The water gushing out suddenly makes the Devil realise that Christ is divine:

> … I saw the Tree at which you shuddered.
> crimsoned with blood and water.
> And I shuddered, not, I tell you, at the blood, but at the water.
> For the former shows the slaughter of Jesus,
> but the latter, his life, because life has gushed
> from his side. For it was not the first
> but the second Adam who carried Eve,
> the mother of all living, again to Paradise.[46]

In this compressed expression, the Devil realises that whereas the blood refers Christ as human, the water is the 'living water' that is so prominent a metaphor for Christ as God in the Gospel of John.[47] Being the second Adam, Christ goes down to Hell and brings Eve back to Paradise as the first human, as she was the first human to fall in the Garden of Eden;[48] being the 'mother of all living' she acts as a *pars pro toto* for all humankind. In this way, the water is what reveals that the divine was concealed in the human Jesus Christ.

In *On the Resurrection V*,[49] which is in many ways similar to *On the Victory of the Cross*, it is Adam who discusses with Hell. In the first half of the story, just before the crucifixion, Adam is suffering in Hell, burning and waiting for water to quench his thirst. He warns Hell that Christ will arrive soon in the underworld to destroy the power of Hell. However, Hell does not believe Adam. Hell thinks of himself as the mightiest king, who reigns over the patriarchs, prophets and even Adam, the first of all humans. Adam rebukes Hell for being a loud braggart who is but a simple guardian of the prison of the dead until the real king arrives. Adam was deceived by Hell,[50] but Adam warns: "the one you think you suppress as a human / that one you shall swallow (καταπίῃς) as a mortal, but you shall throw him up (ἐξεμέσεις) as God".[51] In the scheme of deceiving Hell, we see that the secret is already revealed to Hell beforehand: the human, Christ, who Hell thinks of nothing but a 'helper' (βοηθός)[52] of Adam, is really God. But that does not convince Hell.

In stanza six, Romanus recounts the crucifixion narrative as told in the Gospel of

45 John 19.34.

46 SC 38, st. 11.4-11. Translation by E. Lash (1995, 154-63).

47 See John 4.10, 7.38.

48 See Gen 3.20.

49 SC 44.

50 An allusion to the snake in the Garden of Eden. The snake is most often associated with the Devil, whereas the snake and Hell are identified here.

51 SC 44, st. 5.7-8. Translation by author.

52 SC 44, st. 4.2.

Matthew and offers a subtle interpretation of the events. When Christ gives up the spirit, Romanus says that the sun, the moon, and the stars did not dare to watch it and therefore *hid* their lights (κατέκαλυπτον τὸ φέγγος),[53] the mountains thought about escaping, and the veil in the holy temple was rent. There is a deliberate play on concealing and revealing here as consequences of the crucifixion, however not to keep something secret, but because of exposure or too much disclosure: the sun, the moon and the stars cannot stand watching the death of their Creator, whereas the veil in the temple, that kept the holy of holies as a well-guarded secret, is now fully exposed.

Then, in the following stanza Romanus combines the piscatorial metaphor with the gastronomic:

> But Christ, who is Life, went to lead (ὑπᾶξαι) Death on:
> Hell received Christ as any earth-born.
> He swallowed the heavenly bread like bait,
> and was wounded by the hook of the divinity.
> Hell shouted aloud with painful cries:
> "I am pierced in the stomach, the one I swallowed I cannot digest".[54]

And therefore he is forced to throw up Christ and all his believers. In stanza nine, Romanus puts the Jonah-typology in the mouth of Hell himself: "Just as Jonah was thrown up (ἐξέμεσε) from the fish on the third day, / so shall I throw up Christ and all those who belong to Christ".[55] Cyril of Jerusalem's catechetical instructions and Gregory of Nyssa's elaborate theory of divine deception with the fishhook are here transposed into a drama in Romanus' *kontakia*. Although Romanus does not quote verbatim from Cyril or Gregory, the typological exegesis, the motif of deception, and the gastronomic and the piscatorial metaphors were all borrowed and reused from a tradition beginning in the 4th century. In the hands of Romanus, the metanarrative of redemption as constructed by Gregory and Ps.-Athanasius is turned into a dramatic narrative, in which the deceit is experienced and voiced by the Devil, Hell or Death. This renders the Devil, Hell and Death as suffering, seemingly tragic characters, whose inability to recognise God in the human Jesus Christ has fatal consequences, and whose lament over their defeat turns them into comic and ridiculous characters. Romanus also states explicitly in another *kontakion* that ridiculing the demons and the Devil in the Church is good:

> We know how to injure them,
> it is when we make a comedy (κωμῳδοῦμεν) of their fall:
> Certainly, the Devil mourns when the 'triumph' of the demons
> is made into a tragedy (τραγῳδῶμεν) by us in the churches.[56]

---

53 SC 44, st. 6.6.

54 SC 44, st. 7. Translation by author.

55 SC 44, st. 9.1-2. Translation by author.

56 *On the Man Possessed with Devils*, SC 22, st. 2.4-7. Translation by author.

Even though Romanus uses the terminology from drama metaphorically – that is, the *kontakia* were not performed as theatre with actors impersonating the characters – it reveals the purpose of his dramatic narratives. Besides explaining doctrinal truths about redemption that he borrows from the tradition, the dramatisation also enacts these truths; i.e. the performance brings about what it says. As narrative re-enactments of the descent to hell, where God deceives the Devil or Hell to swallow the bait concealing the hook of divinity and thereby to regurgitate all the prisoners, the *kontakia* not only unfold a dramatic theory of atonement, but disclose and reveal the drama of redemption.

Conclusion

In this article, I have argued for a gradual development from doctrine to drama – and even a kind of theatre – concerning the descent to hell. The descent to the realm of the dead as such is only briefly mentioned in the New Testament, but as a consequence of the death of Christ, his soul was also believed to go to hell as any other human being's soul after death. Through exegesis of Old Testament texts and typologies, the early Christian authors developed the doctrine of the descent into the 'gastronomical' and 'piscatorial' metaphors. The idea of 'divine deception' found in Gregory of Nyssa's *Catechetical Discourse* and Ps.-Athanasius' homily *On the Passion and the Cross*, which adapts a dramatic non-recognition scene from the *Odyssey*, adds to the doctrine of the descent a dramatic micro-narrative, where concealing, secrecy and disguise play a crucial role. This narrative is expanded and dramatised in the hymns of Romanus the Melodist, who turns the doctrine into a full-fledged comic scene, where the Devil and Hell are mocked because of their ignorance; the divine nature of Christ remains hidden for them, concealed by the flesh of his human nature. Retelling a narrative about how the God in disguise reveals his divinity after the descent to hell, Romanus shows how concealing and revealing can be used as important plot devices to mock the enemies' defeat and thereby re-enact a drama of redemption.

EVA MORTENSEN

Remembering or Concealing Mythical and Historical Events in the Cityscape of Early Roman Ephesus

The cityscape of early Roman Ephesus incorporated and referenced narratives from the city's past. But there are some gaps in the stories being told. Do these gaps in the narratives demonstrate an intentional concealment of segments of the city's history? This article discusses the meanings of these narrative lacunae using a combination of the archaeological record and the literary sources.[1]

The past played an enormously important role for the cities of western Asia Minor, as they maintained, shaped and redefined their identities with the onset of Roman rule. City patrons gave the past a prominent position in the monuments they constructed, as they attempted to show both inhabitants and visitors the heritage and political, social and religious values of the cities they lived in. Incorporated into the urban fabric were both mythical stories as well as references to important historical events. However, it was not usually the entire story that was presented: a story could be altered so that parts of it were left out or concealed. Stories and myths (especially founding myths) were shaped and adapted so that they suited the specific needs of the contemporary city – in diplomatic negotiations or in the quest for status, titles and money.[2] Some stories were emphasised and received a place in the history of the city and in the cityscape, while other stories were (deliberately?) lost.

An attentive person taking a walk through the public city centre of Ephesus in the early Roman period would have been taking a walk through the history of the city. On the so-called Curetes Street,[3] the main street connecting the two agoras, there were a variety of monuments that referenced the city's past and seemed to conceal very little

1 I am most grateful to my colleague Anna Collar for discussing the article with me and for correcting my English. Any errors herein are entirely my own.

2 See e.g Jones 1999; Patterson 2010; Mortensen 2015.

3 I use the modern name of the street, given by the excavators. In antiquity it may have been termed *Embolos* or *Plateia*. For a discussion, see Thür 1995c, 85-6.

of the city's history. Both glorious and not so glorious events received a place in this public space. But even though the street could be considered as an avenue of memories with what was apparently a fairly comprehensive summary of the city's past, not all aspects of the different stories and events were represented. Some parts of the stories were discarded and other and 'better' parts were invented.

In this article, I will explore three monuments through which some elements of the past received a place in the urban landscape of Ephesus, and some did not. The aim is to determine whether some aspects were concealed deliberately – that is, kept secret from inhabitants and/or visitors. I begin with a short overview of the historical background of Ephesus and its urban layout. This is followed by an outline of the theoretical framework, drawn from study of memory and the branch of literature focused on gaps in narratives. Within this framework, it is possible to explore and compare the archaeological record and the literary sources to reveal some of the intentions behind the decisions about which parts of the past should be remembered and displayed, and which should be kept from the public gaze. The last part of the article analyses how the past was displayed in the cityscape and how ancient viewers might have understood the city.

Historical Background

The harbour city of Ephesus is a good case for exploring 'the intentions' behind the appearance of the city, since a huge part of the city's public centre has been excavated and published, and this work has revealed a cityscape with an abundance of sculpture, inscriptions and monuments.[4] In this article, I will focus on the period from c. 133 BC, when the province of *Asia* was established, to the end of the Augustan era in AD 14, because this was a period of major change during which the city had to re-negotiate its identity. The 150 years under consideration will be referred to as the early Roman period.

Prior to Roman supremacy, the area had been controlled by alternating foreign powers – Seleucids, Ptolemies and Attalids. With Roman control, the area was thus subjected to yet another foreign power, and war and instability continued to trouble the region. On several occasions the people of Ephesus had taken sides in various power struggles. Aristonicus, the illegitimate son of the Attalid ruler Eumenes II mounted a resistance against the Romans, and it was Ephesus which seems to have provided the fleet that defeated him in the sea battle off Cyme (c. 133-131 BC).[5] Half a century later, the Ephesians expressed their disgruntlement over Roman taxation by welcoming Mithridates VI, which led to the massacre of Romans and Italians in the province in what has become known as the 'Ephesian Vesper' (88 BC). The city was fined heavily for its misdeeds,[6] although the fine was eventually reduced. However, when the triumvirs defeated Brutus and Cassius (42 BC), Mark Antony took up residence in Ephesus

4 For an overview of the excavation activity, see e.g. Wiplinger & Wlach 1996.

5 Strabo 14.1.38. See Dreyer 2005, 55-8.

6 App. *Mith.* 22-3, 61-2.

with Cleopatra, and together they drained the city's finances.[7] Two years after Octavian won the battle at Actium in 31 BC, he stayed in Ephesus for some months in order to reorganise the province. Around this time, Ephesus became the provincial capital, and although it is tempting to connect this with the reorganisation of 29 BC, there is no concrete evidence to confirm this connection.[8] With the *pax augusta* the cities in western Asia Minor finally experienced a period of peace and stability.

In addition to attracting tourists to the sanctuary of Artemis, Ephesus became a *conventus* – one of the judiciary districts where the governor or his representative held trials, which would also have attracted large crowds.[9] Additionally, the city developed into an important transit centre through which money, grain and officials were transported.[10]

The Cityscape of Ephesus

The city of Ephesus had been located between Panayırdağ and Bülbüldağ at least since Lysimachus moved the city in the early 3rd century BC.[11] The scarce remains of the Hellenistic period reveal a city laid out according to a rectangular street grid.[12] In the 3rd century BC, building activity as well as inscriptions suggest the existence of a gymnasium in the upper city, and an agora with warehouses (later to become the *Tetragonos Agora*) in the lower city.[13] It is not clear whether the theatre and stadium existed in this period.[14] The old processional road cut across the regular layout of the orthogonally planned city, but since it was considered sacred, it was allowed to wind through the grid and connect upper and lower city. The rivers in the area around Ephesus were always prone to silting, and marshland had started to extend into the coastal area. This marsh area was filled up with mud, sand accumulated on the shore of the bay, and the harbour was moved further west.[15] In the early Roman period, we see an increase in building activity, and monumentalised public centres evolved around the existing monuments and squares (Fig. 1):

In the upper city there was an open space enclosed on the north, east and south sides by porticoes, and to the north, sacro-political buildings started to be built that

7 Plut. *Luc.* 23; Dio Cass. 48.24.2; Joseph. *AJ* 15.89. Laale 2011, 149-50, 162-3, 165-7; Magie [1950] 1975, 427-9.

8 Raja 2012, 57, 84-5.

9 Magie [1950] 1975, 171-2.

10 Cic. *Att.* 5.13; *Verr.* 3.83. Kirbihler 2007, 28.

11 For evidence of an earlier settlement in this area, see Kerschner, Kowalleck & Steskal 2008, 118, 122.

12 Groh 2001; 2006.

13 See e.g. Scherrer 2001, 66-7, 71; Engelmann 1993b, 288-9; Thür 2004, 222; Scherrer & Trinkl 2006, 13-9.

14 See e.g. Hofbauer 2002; Scherrer 2001, 71.

15 Kraft, Brückner & Kayan 2005; Zabehlicky 1995, 206-12.

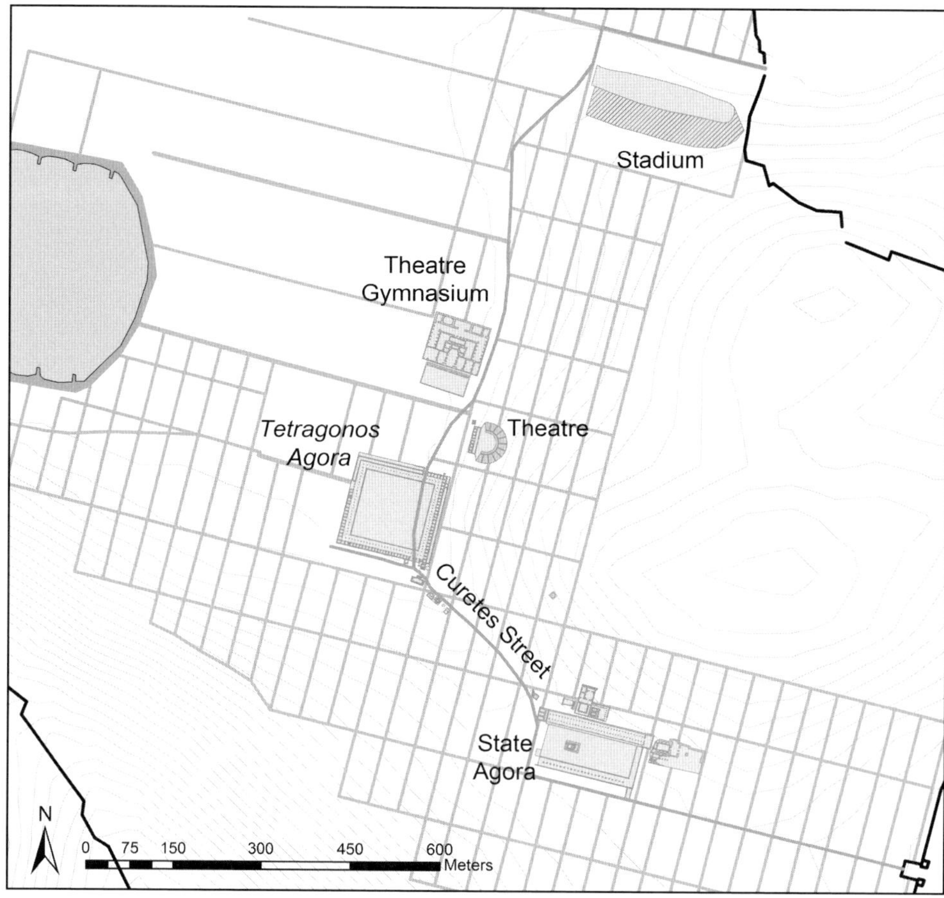

Fig. 1. *Map of Ephesus in AD 14 (map by author).*

would eventually define the space as the State Agora.[16] In the lower city, the *Tetragonos Agora* was refurbished, with the erection of two-storied stoai around an almost square (*tetragonos*) area, and the renovation of the gates used to access the agora.[17] The most impressive was the South Gate, which was also the northern backdrop of the *Triodos* square upon which stood a trapezoid podium, possibly an Artemis altar.[18] To the north of the *Tetragonos Agora* was a theatre and the so-called Theatre Gymnasium, further

16 See e.g. Steskal 2010, 77-8 (prytaneion); Bier 2011, 81-5 (bouleuterion); Scherrer 1990, 98-101; Alzinger 1999, 390 ('temenos').

17 Scherrer & Trinkl 2006, 19-29.

18 *I.Eph.* 3059. See Thür 2005; Knibbe 1991, 7-8. For an alternative interpretation, see Engelmann 1993a.

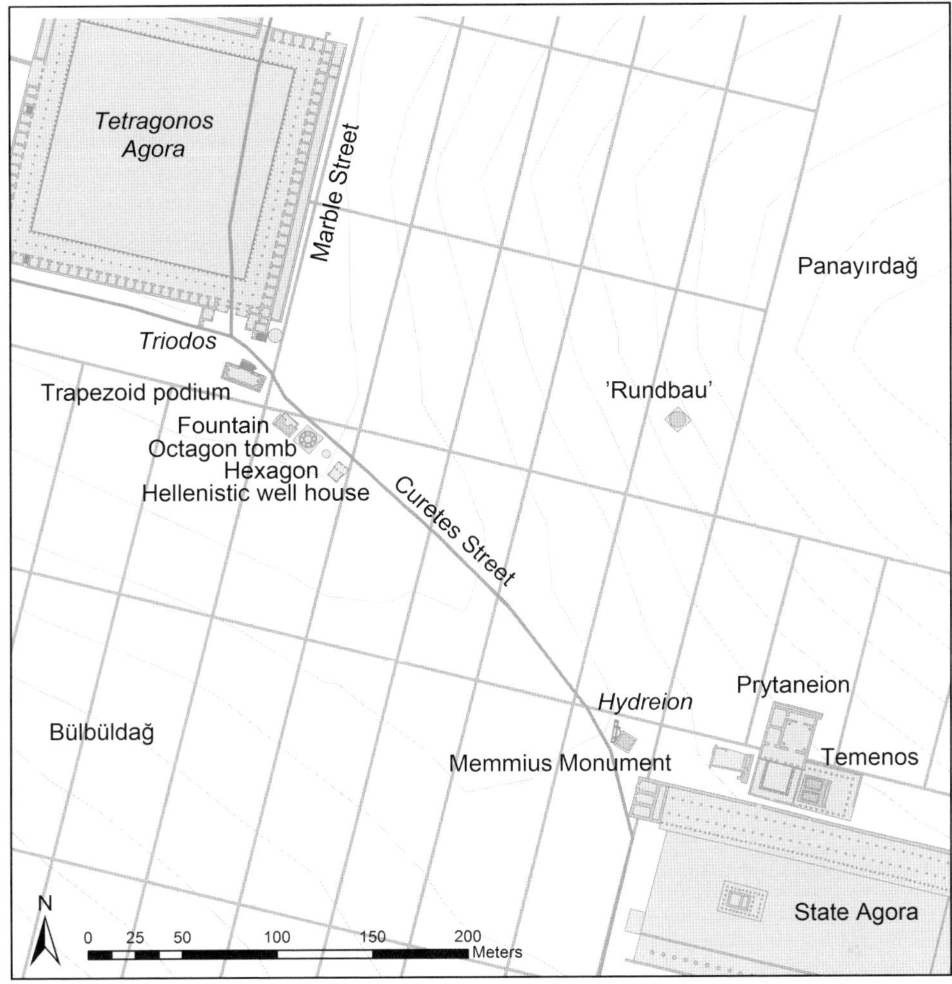

Map of so-called Curetes Street and environs in AD 14 (map by author). **Fig. 2.**

north the stadium, and at this time colonnades were built along the street connecting theatre and stadium.[19]

Curetes Street, part of the original processional way, led people through the city and connected the two agoras. Prior to the Hellenistic period the street had been lined with tombs,[20] a method of self-representation and memorialisation, and this tradition continued: the monuments constructed on the street during the early Roman period reflect past memories and illustrate various episodes and narratives of the city's history. The monuments erected include a fountain, an octagonal tomb, a hexagon probably displaying an honorary statue, the so-called monument of Memmius, a fountain called

19 Knibbe 1985, 73-6.

20 Langmann & Knibbe 1993, 51-3.

the *Hydreion*[21] and a round building.[22] The last-mentioned building towered above the street on Panayırdağ, its position rendering it highly visible from the street (Fig. 2).

Narrative Gaps in a Remembered Past

Any kind of exploration of the minds and intentions of ancient people as they were confronted with the cityscape of Ephesus – either as patrons or viewers – requires a theoretical and methodological framework from which to start. Both visualising narratives through monuments in the cityscape and writing the history of a city are practices of memory, and with both methods, the past was remembered in a tangible and concrete form, which facilitates the scholar's process of deduction as to which cultural memories were shared within an ancient society.[23] Memories and information were inscribed and stored for posterity.[24] However, in the process of selecting the stories to be remembered, some were also left out, and with time, probably forgotten.[25] My intentions are to review those episodes that were remembered and received a lasting place in the urban landscape, and to explore the gaps within these remembered narratives.

The gaps in the narratives on display in the city provide us with knowledge about intentions with regard to the remembering or concealing of the past in the cityscape; and in order to reveal the rejected parts of the stories (for whatever reason they were rejected or hidden), the literary sources are invaluable. They often tell a different story from that of the actual cityscape, and a comparative analysis of the material and literary evidence can help identify gaps. Although, of course, ancient authors also hide and adapt information, they may still help inform us of gaps in the stories visualised in the cityscape.

'Gaps' or 'blanks' in narratives have been a subject within the study of literature for some time.[26] A narrative has certain gaps, which could be viewed as withheld information and concealment of meaning (perhaps even secrets),[27] and the author of the narrative will assume that the readers, when confronted with the gaps, will use inference in order to comprehend the narrative.[28] Filling in the narrative gaps is automatic as the reader uses memories and life-experiences for drawing inferences.[29] Constructing these

---

21 *I.Eph.* 435.

22 For the monuments not discussed further in the article, see e.g. Thür 1990 (octagon); 1999 (octagon, hexagon); Scherrer 2000, 96, 122, 124 (octagon, hexagon, *Hydreion*).

23 Cultural memory: how a group, through a common interpretation and adaptation of a common past, defines themselves and creates their identity (Assmann 1988).

24 Regarding practices of memory, see e.g. Connerton 2004. For memory practices in relation to the material record, see e.g. Rowlands 1993; Price 2002; Van Dyke & Alcock 2003, 3-5.

25 Alcock 2002, 17, 23, 32-5.

26 See e.g. Iser 1978, 182-203; Kermode 1983, e.g. p. 109; Calinescu 1994; Gerrig 2010. See also Hass in this volume.

27 For secrets, see Calinescu 1994.

28 Gerrig 2010, 20.

29 For a short review, see Gerrig 2010, 20-4.

gaps of concealed information moves beyond the collective and includes or excludes people depending on their level of knowledge in the given situation. An analogy may be drawn between the process of interpreting literary narrative gaps and the study of narratives in the cityscape.

Patrons, Viewers and Concealing Information

The stories or narratives from the past, chosen to decorate the cityscape also have 'authors' and 'readers', who would definitely have made inferences as they were confronted by the narratives. Depending on the identity of the reader (viewer) and the person's reasons for being in Ephesus (for instance, as resident or visitor with a religious, mercantile and/or official purpose), different experiences of the narrative and the city would present themselves.[30] The viewers would understand the narrative differently and each would draw their own inferences as to the gaps in the narratives – or perhaps not even realise that gaps were present. Furthermore, their movement through the city would create spatial narratives that differed from viewer to viewer, thus providing each with different preconditions for understanding the gaps.[31]

It must be kept in mind that the cityscape was shaped in order to tell the story that the authors (patrons) wanted to tell. The patrons behind the monuments in early Roman Asia Minor could be individuals, associations, as well as a city in general, and it could be Ephesians and foreigners alike. But no one could make improvements or additions to the public city centre without consulting the citizens first, and many inscriptions provide us with information about the negotiation process between patron, *boulē* and *dēmos* as it was decided whether a monument or benefaction should be accepted by the community.[32] The power of the patrons as creators of the cityscape was thus ascribed and accepted by the citizens, and the citizens thereby also took part in shaping their public space of the city. How much impact the patron had on design, decorative elements and the final result in general could, however, be dependent on production processes, the availability of the raw material, civic pressure and the 'visual codex' governing what would generate meaning for the viewers, whoever that might have been.[33]

The narrative gaps found in the monuments may therefore also exist for different reasons. They could be part of the 'visual codex', which meant that even with a gap in the story, it would still be interpretable by almost every ancient viewer; they might represent choices made by the *dēmos* and not the patron; they may have been accidental, for instance, the available space for a decorative frieze was smaller or higher up than anticipated, thus presenting the patron with a choice of rearranging whatever was planned for the frieze; or perhaps the workshop hired to do the job had limita-

30 See e.g. J. Elsner's (1995) comprehensive work on ancient viewers and different ways of interpreting Roman art.

31 On movement creating narratives, see Tilley 1994, 28-9; 2010, 29.

32 Nijf 1997, 113-6; Zuiderhoek 2009, 106-7; 2013.

33 See e.g. Birk & Poulsen 2012, 7-10.

tions that conflicted with the desires of the patron. Those patrons that commissioned the monuments and authored the stories (with or without gaps) presumably hoped that their endeavours would ensure themselves and their city a place in posterity. In this scenario it seems likely that those stories that were most likely to achieve this aim would be the ones chosen for public display.[34] Moreover, the choice of story relied on the space available – there is obviously a difference in presenting a story scene-by-scene or as one scene (a synoptic narrative).[35] When the story is compressed, choices have to be made, and these reveal the values of those responsible for the monument: values regarding the focus of the story and values regarding posterity, in effect making some information available while concealing other information.[36]

No matter how narrative gaps were generated, whether it had to do with preferences of the patron, workshop limitations, civic pressure, ignorance or the available space to tell the story, the gaps comprised hidden information that could be decoded only if the viewer was able to close them by processes of inference. However, whether narrative gaps could also be read as intentional concealment is unclear. In order to explore the potential of monuments for concealing and revealing aspects of the city's history, I have chosen to focus on three monuments: two on Curetes Street, the so-called heroon of Androclus and the so-called Memmius Monument, and the round building located above the street on Panayırdağ.

The Mythical Founder Androclus

I begin with the heroon of Androclus and the story of the city's foundation. We know about Androclus' deeds from three different authors: Strabo, Athenaeus and Pausanias. Strabo tells us:

> He [Pherecydes] says that Androclus, legitimate son of Codrus the king of Athens, was the leader of the Ionian colonisation, which was later than the Aeolian, and that he became the founder of Ephesus (14.1.3). The city was in ancient times round the Athenaeum, which is now outside the city near the Hypelaeus, as it is called (14.1.4). The city of Ephesus was inhabited both by Carians and Leleges, but Androclus drove them out and settled most of those who had come with him round the Athenaeum and the Hypelaeus, though he also included part of the country situated on the slopes of Mt. Coressus (14.1.21).[37]

Pherecydes was a 5th-century BC genealogist and mythographer, fragments of whose systematic work on genealogies of gods and heroes have been preserved in the works

34 See e.g. Foxhall 1995.

35 See e.g. Saxkjær 2013, 186.

36 Gordon 1990, 203.

37 Translation by H.L. Jones. All translations of ancient literary sources are from Loeb Classical Library.

of other ancient authors such as Strabo,[38] who was active in the age of Augustus and thus in the period studied here.

Another source on the founding of Ephesus is Athenaeus. Although Athenaeus lived in the late 2nd/early 3rd century AD, he is important in the present context because his source is Creophylus, the earliest writer on the subject of Ephesus, who in the 5th century (or earlier?) composed a local history of the city.[39] His version of the founding is as follows:

> Creophylus, in Chronicles of the Ephesians, says that the founders of Ephesus, after suffering many hardships because of the difficulties of the region, finally went to the oracle of the god and asked where they should place their city. And he declared to them that they should build a city 'wheresoe'r a fish shall show them and a wild boar shall lead the way.' It is said, accordingly, that some fishermen were eating their noonday meal in the place where are the spring to-day called Oily (*Hypelaeus*) and the sacred lake. One of the fish popped out with a piece of live coal and fell into some straw, and a thicket in which a wild boar happened to be was set on fire by the fish. The boar, frightened by the fire, ran up a great distance on the mountain, which is called Trecheia, and when brought down by a javelin, fell where to-day stands the temple of Athena. So the Ephesians crossed over from the island after living there twenty years, and for the second time settled Trecheia and the regions on the slope of the Coressus (8.361).[40]

The 2nd-century AD geographer Pausanias also has some valuable information on Androclus' life. Despite the fact that Pausanias lived later than the period under study, his statements may reflect narratives as they were observed and viewed in the cityscape some years after they were originally constructed. He writes:

> But Androclus the son of Codrus (for he it was who was appointed king of the Ionians who sailed against Ephesus) expelled from the land the Leleges and Lydians who occupied the upper city (7.2.8).... Androclus helped the people of Priene against the Carians. The Greek army was victorious, but Androclus was killed in battle. The Ephesians carried off his body and buried it in their own land, at the spot where his tomb is pointed out at the present day, on the road leading from the sanctuary past the Olympieum to the Magnesian gate. On the tomb is a statue of an armed man (7.2.9).[41]

These different statements have been discussed several times, especially with regard to the exact location of the Ionian settlement – a debate revolving around toponyms of

38 *Neue Pauly* (K. Meister), s.v. 'Pherecydes'.
39 *Neue Pauly* (K. Brodersen), s.v. 'Creophylus'.
40 Translation by C.B. Gulick.
41 Translation by W.H.S. Jones.

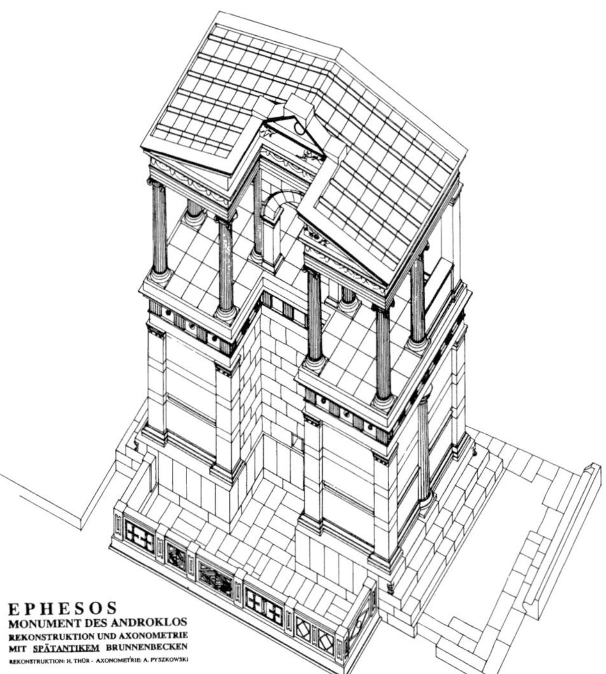

Fig. 3. *Reconstruction of the so-called heroon of Androclus (courtesy of H. Thür).*

mountains and city quarters.[42] Presuming that these tales of Androclus would have been those flourishing in Ephesus at least from around the 5th century BC until the end of the 2nd century or the beginning of the 3rd century AD, when Athenaeus was active, the shared memory of the city in the early Roman period would certainly include Androclus. The story of the founding, however, was already appearing in two versions in the 5th century BC. Androclus is not mentioned by Athenaeus (and Chreophylus), and the wild boar is not mentioned by Strabo (and Pherecydes).

How then was the story of Androclus expressed in the cityscape? By the 2nd century AD, Androclus would have been almost impossible to avoid in Ephesus. Inscriptions, statues and other forms of decoration relating to the legend of Androclus abounded.[43] But for the early Roman period, we only know of one monument that displayed the story of the founder.

This monument, also functioning as a fountain, is the so-called heroon of Androclus erected in the first half of the 1st century BC.[44] It is located near the *Triodos* and the *Tetragonos Agora* and oriented towards Curetes Street. The monument could be approached from two sides, from the *Tetragonos Agora* and the so-called Marble Street and from the upper part of Curetes Street. The octagonal tomb, which was built next to it

42 For a review of the debate, see Kerschner, Kowalleck & Steskal 2008, 16-8.

43 Rathmayr 2010; Thür 1995a; Fontani 2002.

44 Regarding the date, see Waldner 2009, 283-93.

around 50-20 BC,[45] would have 'hidden' the heroon, which stood a little lower than the octagon and was a little more secluded from the street (Fig. 2). Thus over time, a 'correct way' to approach the monument was created, from the northwest instead of the southeast.[46] It is not possible to ascertain from the preserved remains whether it was a heroon, 'just' a fountain with a commemorative frieze, or a sort of meeting place for those involved in the worship of Androclus.[47]

The architectural fragments of the monument have been assessed together to make a reconstruction of how the monument once looked (Fig. 3). It consisted of two storeys rising c. 12 m high on a Π-shaped ground plan, with a water basin in front (enclosed anew in the Byzantine period with decorated plates). The marble-covered core of the lower storey was decorated on both side wings with Doric half-columns and corner pilasters with three rosettes on the capitals. Above these was a frieze with triglyphs and metopes decorated with rosettes, flowers and *phialai*. The upper storey was open to the north, west and east, with Ionic columns on the side wings and an arch in the middle. On these columns, arch and the southern back wall rested the entablature and the roof. The entablature was decorated with a garland frieze with heads of bulls and deers, while half-gables on the side wings continued the frieze that ran across the middle part on decorated plates. The middle was crowned by a gable decorated with a round shield.[48] The garland frieze and the metopes gave the monument a sacral character, whereas the fountain aspect places it in the profane sphere.[49]

The interpretation of the monument as a heroon for Androclus is based on the reliefs decorating the upper frieze. The reliefs depict battle scenes widely separated and with an empty background, warriors on foot, a *biga* chariot with charioteer and a warrior on horseback with his cloak billowing behind him (Figs. 4 and 5). Later representations of Androclus on Antonine coins and on a Hadrianic relief[50] from the so-called temple of Hadrian located across the street, where he is represented just like the warrior on horseback, led H. Thür to suggest that this monument was a heroon of Androclus.[51]

In the relief on the fountain, Androclus on horseback is alone, presumably hunting for the wild boar, which would have been depicted in the now missing lower right corner (Fig. 4). This assumption is made because of the Hadrianic and Antonine representations of Androclus that include a wild boar.[52] Among the other battle scenes, there is a fallen naked warrior with two enemies towering above him (Fig. 5). Could this be a depiction of Androclus' death as described by Pausanias? And could the battle scenes be

45 See e.g. Thür 1990.

46 On 'correct ways' to approach monuments, see Tilley 1994, 28-9.

47 That this monument is identical to the tomb of Androclus, mentioned by Pausanias, has been suggested by H. Thür (1995a, 102). H. Engelmann (1996) argues against this interpretation.

48 For a comprehensive description of the monument, see Thür 1995a, 80-8.

49 Thür 1995a, 102.

50 Quatember 2010, 388-91.

51 Thür 1995a, 80-102; 1995b, 159-77.

52 Thür 1995b, 171-2.

Fig. 4. *Androclus hunting for the wild boar? (photo: ÖAW – H. Thür. Courtesy of the Österreichisches Archäologisches Institut).*

depictions of those fights the Ionians had with the native population as they colonised the area?[53] If these interpretations are correct, this monument outlines the foundation story: Androclus killed the wild boar, he and his men fought the native population, and he eventually died in battle.

But did Androclus kill the wild boar? Not according to any of the literary sources. The stories of Ephesus' foundation fused at some point in history, but whether this had happened before the early 1st century BC, when the fountain was built, is difficult to confirm. Androclus and the wild boar appear together for the first time in the Hadrianic/Antonine period, and the first instance of Androclus as a hunter with his hunting dog, is from the C. Laecanius Bassus Nymphaeum dated to AD 79/80.[54] Thus, from the late 1st century AD onwards, the Ephesians presumably regarded Androclus as the killer of the wild boar (unnamed in Creophylus/Athenaeus), but beforehand this connection may not have been made. Androclus' victim in the relief on the 'heroon' could just as

53 Thür 1995a, 99; 1995b, 172-3.

54 Rathmayr 2011, 138, 141-2.

A depiction of Androclus' death? (photo: Th. Römer. Courtesy of the Österreichisches Archäologisches Institut). **Fig. 5.**

easily be reconstructed as an enemy in battle. His iconography here would then have been reused to depict him in the scene with the wild boar at a later date.

If this were the case, the version of the founding story on the monument would agree with Strabo and Pausanias – that of Androclus and the Ionians fighting natives. That Pausanias in particular did not connect Androclus with the wild boar, even though he was active in the period after which Androclus was perceived as a hunter, could indicate that he had seen other narratives in the cityscape – with a focus on Ionians fighting natives. Although recorded by Pherecydes in the 5th century BC, the wild boar, the fish and the fishermen were hidden in the early Roman cityscape.

With this frieze, it would not have been possible for the viewer to infer that another version of the foundation story existed. Neither a visual codex nor the lack of available space can explain the missing story. Accepting that the horseman is a warrior, all of the six preserved reliefs display different scenes of battle. Had the patron(s) wished the alternative foundation story to be represented, some of these battle scenes could have been exchanged with scenes from the other story. In other words, the alternative foundation myth was concealed and only later brought up in the cityscape. The warrior on horseback, who came to represent Androclus and the fusion of the stories, would eventually bridge the gap between the two narratives. In addition, the topographical settings, Mt. Coressus, Athenaeum and Hypelaeus, important to the foundation story, are not depicted. These places would have made it easier for the viewer to decipher the narrative of the frieze. The fact that the monument also functioned as a fountain could potentially make the connection with the Hypelaeus spring, mentioned by both Strabo and Athenaeus, and thus it may be that the shape of the monument itself helped to close the narrative gap regarding the physical setting of where the story once played out.

It is not known who commissioned the monument, but no matter who was behind it, the monument and its decoration, that favoured one version of the foundation story over another, would have been accepted by the *dēmos*.

Mithridates VI of Pontus and the Revenge of Sulla

Further up Curetes Street another story from Ephesus' history was encountered. This concerned L. Cornelius Sulla, whose relation to Ephesus is connected with the Mithridatic Wars and is described by Appian:

> He [Mithridates] proceeded to Magnesia, Ephesus, and Mitylene, all of which received him gladly. The Ephesians even overthrew the Roman statues which had been erected in their cities – for which they paid the penalty not long afterward (*Mith.* 21). The Ephesians tore away the fugitives, who had taken refuge in the temple of Artemis, and were clasping the images of the goddess, and slew them (*Mith.* 23). The Cappadocian faction, both men and cities, were severely punished, and especially the Ephesians, who, with servile adulation of the king, had treated the Roman offerings in their temples with indignity. After this a proclamation was sent around commanding the principal citizens to come to Ephesus on a certain day to meet Sulla. When they had assembled Sulla addressed them from the tribune as follows: (*Mith.* 61). "… You, on the other hand, when Attalus Philometor had left his kingdom to us in his will, gave aid to Aristonicus against us for four years, until he was captured and most of you, under the impulse of necessity and fear, returned to your duty. Notwithstanding all this, after a period of twenty-four years, during which you had attained to great prosperity and magnificence, public and private, you again became insolent through peace and luxury and again took the opportunity, while we were preoccupied in Italy, some of you to call in Mithridates and others to join him when he came. … I shall only impose upon you the taxes of five years, to be paid at once, together with what the war has cost me, and whatever else may be spent in settling the affairs of the province. I will apportion these charges to each of you according to cities, and will fix the time of payment. Upon the disobedient I shall visit punishment as upon enemies" (*Mith.* 62).[55]

55 Translation by H. White.

The greed and oppression of the Roman tax collectors had made it easy for Mithridates to persuade the cities of western Asia Minor to rise against the Romans.[56] Sulla's revenge on the cities that accepted Mithridates would not have been a proud moment for the inhabitants of Ephesus. And yet, the Ephesians came face to face with the revenge of Sulla every time they walked from one agora to the other.

At the upper end of Curetes Street was a monument dedicated to C. Memmius, known through the Latin building inscriptions to be the maternal grandson of Sulla.[57] It was constructed in the third quarter of the 1st century BC, and thus before the period of Augustus' reconciliation policy.[58] It is not known whether the monument functioned as an honorary monument, a grave or a cenotaph.[59] On a foundation and a four-stepped *crepidoma* were two storeys rendering the monument c. 20 m high. The lower storey consisted of a square core with arched niches on three sides, and pilasters on each side of the niches decorated with a caryatid standing on the orthostate blocks. The corners of the lower storey had fluted half-columns flanked by smooth pilasters, also resting on the orthostate. The appearance of the upper storey is, however, contested. A. Bammer reconstructed it as an *attica* decorated on three sides with the relief plates that were found by the monument,[60] but U. Outschar suggests that a peristyle enclosed a relief-decorated core on three sides (Fig. 6).[61] These relief plates, whose exact number are not known, are c. 2 m high and each represent a figure. One figure is a *togatus*, presumably representing Memmius himself.[62] The other reliefs depict men wearing short *exōmis*, cloak and belt and in the background or in their hands are attributes such as short sword, ship's bow or altar and torch or trumpet-like instrument. These figures could be interpreted as the mythical heroic ancestors of Memmius (Fig. 7).[63] A Greek inscription found by the monument possibly mentions Mnestheos, the eponymous ancestor of the Memmii, thus giving validity to this interpretation.[64] W. Alzinger suggests that more *togatus* reliefs existed, representing Memmius, Sulla and the father of Memmius,[65] and A. Bammer interprets the sculptural decoration as symbolising the political situation of Sulla's revenge for the 'Ephesian Vesper': Vitruvius has described how caryatids had their origin in representing the subdued women of Caryae, a state which chose the

---

56 Plut. *Vit. Luc.* 7.5. See e.g. Kirbihler 2007, 22; Madsen 2010.

57 *I.Eph.* 403. It cannot be ruled out that there also existed a Greek inscription with the same content, Tuchelt 1979, 110. See also Torelli 1988, 422. On the identity of C. Memmius, see Torelli 1988, 409-12.

58 Outschar 1990, 85.

59 Alzinger & Bammer 1971, 86-7, 91-2.

60 Alzinger & Bammer 1971, 42-79; Bammer 2007.

61 Outschar 1990.

62 Outschar 1990, 84.

63 Torelli 1988, 418-22. For other interpretations, see Alzinger & Bammer 1971, 106-7; Scherrer 2000, 96.

64 Bammer 2007, 59; Torelli 1988, 422; *SEG* 57.1111; Verg. *Aen.* 5.114-123.

65 Alzinger & Bammer 1971, 106-7.

Fig. 6. *U. Outschar's reconstruction of the so-called Memmius Monument (courtesy of U. Outschar).*

Persian side and therefore was punished by the Greeks.[66] The caryatids holding the arches would thus represent the subdued Ephesians carrying Sulla.[67]

Would this have been obvious to the ancient viewer? In order to decode the overall message, if indeed this was the overall message, these gaps had to be closed with a com-

66 Vitr. *De arch.* 1.1.5.

67 Bammer 2007; 1972-5.

Two reliefs from the Memmius Monument displayed in a cubistic representation of the monument (photo by author). **Fig. 7.**

bination of knowledge of architectural history and the story of the women of Caryae with the events surrounding the Mithridatic Wars. However, perhaps the patron(s) of this monument employed only 'symbols' that could be easily deciphered by the ancient viewer, thus staying within the frames of the visual codex. If not, the contents of the inscriptions would be a reminder of the misdeeds of the Ephesians and Sulla's revenge – whether the viewer was Ephesian or foreign.

It is not known who was responsible for constructing the monument and for highlighting a narrative about Roman superiority and Ephesian subjection, but it was presumably Memmius' family or other Romans based in the city, since it is highly unlikely to have been prompted by the *dēmos*. Furthermore, a private or association-based dedication should be anticipated because of the Latin building inscriptions, which in this period do not appear on monuments in Asia Minor set up by the *dēmos*.[68] The *dēmos*, however, would have had to authorise the erection of the monument and release the plot of land, which in this case would probably have meant that a large sum of money had been paid by whoever dedicated the monument.[69] Though the story told by this

68 Tuchelt 1979, 110-1. See also Kader 1995, 218; Torelli 1988, 409-17.

69 Tuchelt 1979, 111.

monument revealed Ephesian faithlessness and Roman revenge, it was nevertheless accepted by the Ephesian people as part of their cityscape.

The monument, oriented towards the square in the upper end of Curetes Street, was prominently placed, almost at the junction of three streets, and thus viewers could approach it from three different sides; from Curetes Street, from the sacro-political area of the State Agora and from the street and square on the western side of the State Agora (Fig. 2). No matter how the monument was encountered it would, however, reveal the same information – with caryatids in the lower storey and with one *togatus* and a number of heroic figures on each of the sides of the upper storey. Perhaps a Greek inscription would have provided the viewer with the names of the figures – though it may not have been present on all three visible sides. This inglorious part of the Ephesian past was uncovered and ready to be read, the only part that was concealed was the Ephesians' regret of their atrocities, summed up in two decrees written in 86/5 BC, at the time when the Ephesians prepared themselves for war against Mithridates. The decrees accentuate loyalty to Rome and blame Mithridates' deception and their own panic for earlier misdeeds.[70] It must be assumed that this gap in the narrative was intentionally created by the patron(s), who only wished to present their version of the story. It would be interesting to know how far from the Memmius Monument the marble stele with the two decrees was displayed, but unfortunately the decrees were not found *in situ*.

Thrasyllus, Aristonicus and P. Servilius Isauricus

High above Curetes Street on the southern slope of Panayırdağ is the circular memorial monument referred to as the 'Rundbau'. It was c. 12 m high, and consisted of two round storeys on a square foundation. The lower storey had Doric half-columns and entablature; the upper consisted of an Ionic *monopteros* with vegetal decoration on the volutes of the capitals. Between the columns of the *monopteros* and the core was room for sculptures, and consoles found by the monument may have carried sculpture. It is unclear how the very top of the monument is to be reconstructed, but perhaps it carried a tripod, a statue or a trophy of some kind. Its date ranges between the latter half of the 2nd century and the 1st century BC.[71] There are different interpretations as to whom or what it was set up to commemorate: perhaps P. Servilius Isauricus (consul with Caesar in 48 BC and governor of *Asia* in 46-4 BC),[72] perhaps the victory over Aristonicus, or perhaps it was a renewal of an old *tropaion* commemorating the defeat of the Athenian military commander Thrasyllus.[73] Presumably the missing top part could have told us something more about the person or event that this monument was meant to commemorate.

70 *I.Eph.* 8; Chaniotis 2013, 19-20.

71 See e.g. Alzinger 1974, 37-40; Benndorf, Niemann & Heberdey 1906, 143-80; Kader 1995, 215-6.

72 Broughton 1952, 298.

73 Servilius Isauricus: Keil 1964, 116 followed by Halfmann 2001, 23. Defeat of Aristonicus: Benndorf, Niemann & Heberdey 1906, 165. Defeat of Thrasyllus: Alzinger 1974, 40.

The suggestion that this 'Rundbau' was a renewal of an old *tropaion* is based on the location of the monument, which corresponds with the location of a *tropaion* mentioned by Xenophon:

> … Thrasyllus sailed to Ephesus; and having disembarked the hoplites at the foot of Mount Coressus, and the cavalry, peltasts, marines, and all the rest near the marsh on the opposite side of the city, he led forward the two divisions at daybreak. The defender of the city sailed forward to meet the attack. … All these contingents [the Ephesians and their allies] directed their first attack upon the hoplites at Coressus; and after routing them, killing about a hundred of them, and pursuing the rest down to the shore, they turned their attention to those by the marsh; and there also the Athenians were put to flight, and about three hundred of them were killed. So the Ephesians set up a trophy there and a second at Coressus (*Hell.* 1.2.7-9).[74]

Thrasyllus was an Athenian military commander who campaigned in Ionia in 410 BC.[75] He was defeated by the Ephesians and their allies, and to commemorate this event the Ephesians erected two trophies,[76] one by the marsh and one on the mountain called Coressus. Coressus also figured in the foundation legend and it is the name of a quarter in the Roman city. The definitive placing of the mountain and the city quarter in the topography of Ephesus is not certain,[77] however, the mountain may be Panayırdağ, and the *tropaion* could have been on the site of the 'Rundbau' in the early Roman period – however, if the date (based on stylistic criteria) of the 'Rundbau' is to match this interpretation, it can only be a renewal of the *tropaion*.

That the 'Rundbau' should commemorate the defeat of Aristonicus or Servilius Isauricus is also conjectural, based only on the fact that the monument was constructed in the early Roman period – perhaps when Aristonicus had been defeated or perhaps when or just after Servilius Isauricus was governor of *Asia*. It is unclear which side the Ephesians supported with regard to the usurper Aristonicus, whose mother was the daughter of an Ephesian lyre player.[78] We have already heard from Appian that Sulla denounced the Ephesians for their support of Aristonicus,[79] on the other hand, Strabo, who is closer in date to the events, states:

> Now he [Aristonicus] was banished from Smyrna, after being defeated in a naval battle near the Cymaean territory by the Ephesians, but he went up into the

74 Translation by C.L. Brownson.

75 Pesely 1998.

76 The event (not the trophies) is also found in Dio. Sic. 13.64.1.

77 See e.g. Kerschner, Kowalleck & Steskal 2008, 15-8.

78 Plut. *Vit. Flam.* 21.6. Magie [1950] 1975, 148, 1034-5 n. 2.

79 App. *Mith.* 61.

interior and quickly assembled a large number of resourceless people, and also of slaves, invited with a promise of freedom, whom he called Heliopolitae (14.1.38).[80]

Ephesus may have erected a monument to celebrate the defeat of Aristonicus and to flatter their new Roman rulers, but such a monument is mentioned neither in literary sources nor in inscriptions.

That Servilius Isauricus was honoured in Ephesus is known from inscriptions that mention a combined cult for him and Dea Roma.[81] The inscriptions are dated to the 1st and 2nd centuries AD,[82] establishing that his cult outlasted him considerably. He was honoured in several cities in Asia Minor. In Pergamum, he is credited for having restored 'the ancestral laws', and he may have done the same in Ephesus in order to receive the high honour of a shared cult with Roma.[83] He may also have donated a stoa in the northern part of Ephesus, since two inscriptions (from the 2nd-3rd century AD) mention a 'stoa of Servilius'.[84] Although it seems obvious that he would have received an honorary monument in the city that honoured him for more than a century, he cannot be directly connected with the 'Rundbau' itself.

We thus know that the event surrounding the defeat of Thrassyllus was commemorated in the cityscape, but we cannot be sure that this memorial still existed (even in a renewed form) in the early Roman period. Likewise, we have no direct evidence that the defeat of Aristonicus was visible in the early Roman city. The popular governor Servilius Isauricus may have made a place for himself in the cityscape by donating a stoa, but the 'Rundbau' cannot with any certainty be connected to him either. The monument was set up to commemorate some event or some person, but it is not possible to ascertain what or who: we cannot deduce who was responsible for the erection of the monument – we cannot bridge this gap. The surviving building decoration likewise provides no clue as to the purpose of the monument.[85] The ancient viewer would perhaps have been able to bridge the gap we cannot, if the missing top part depicted something connected with the possibilities outlined here – or indeed, something else. An inscription could also be anticipated, but in order for the monument to tell its story to anyone other than the Ephesian inhabitants (who would probably know its purpose anyway), it should have been possible to understand it from where the visitors would have seen it, on Curetes Street. If they chose to move closer to the monument, then also the sculpture that may have been displayed within the *monopteros* could have revealed more about the narrative connected with the event or person commemorated here.

80 Translation by H.L. Jones.

81 *I.Eph.* 702, 3066.

82 Kirbihler 2011, 256, 270. See also Robert 1948, 40-2.

83 Magie [1950] 1975, 417. See also Kirbihler 2011, 269.

84 *I.Eph.* 445, 454b. Knibbe 1985.

85 Kader 1995, 216.

Remembering and Concealing

Studying the past presents the modern scholar with two types of narrative gaps. We are confronted both with the gaps made deliberately by ancient people, and with gaps caused by deterioration or created through circumstances of preservation. As we have seen, the latter has a huge influence on how we understand the monuments: for instance, could the missing corner of the relief with the warrior on horseback (Fig. 4) reveal how Androclus was perceived and how the story about the foundation was remembered in the early Roman period? Could a Greek inscription have made the message of the Memmius Monument clearer? And could the missing top part of the 'Rundbau' have been a clue to the meaning of the monument?

Exploring the ways narratives were used to remember as well as to conceal allows us to study the gaps created deliberately in antiquity. Regarding the founding of the city, only one side of the story was shown in early Roman Ephesus. In this period of transformation it was important for the city to claim a leading role among the Greek cities of Ionia. One way of doing this was to emphasise Androclus, an Athenian prince and leader of the colonising expedition: in other words, Ephesus was the leading city then as now, with strong ties to Athens, cementing their origin in mainland Greece.[86] Androclus' death, also shown on the monument, would remind viewers of Ephesus' magnanimity in helping their fellow Ionians. Androclus embodied important diplomatic relations, and he was remembered at the expense of the other version of the founding myth.[87] Could this even be said to have been secrecy – that is, intentional concealment of information?[88] Since the literary sources ensure the information was not blocked, it cannot be classified as secrecy proper, as the concealed information could reach the readers of the narrative. That the 'secrets' are somehow shared and collective (the group sharing them, being those familiar with the literary sources, either by first hand reading or by communication) makes access difficult to control. But the gaps are still concealed information not appearing in the cityscape. The gaps could be said to be modes of silence, perhaps even of deception, which in this specific case may lead us to view them as secrecy.[89]

The Memmius Monument, on the other hand, exposed the misdeed of the Ephesians. The symbolism in the monument may or may not have been immediately understood, but the presence of Sulla and his chastisement of the Ephesians would be inferred, and thus the story of the 'Ephesian Vesper' would be remembered. The patrons of the monument were presumably Memmius' own family or other Roman citizens, and as those that had once been treated wrongfully they were interested in underlining the superiority of the Romans. It was the preferences of patron(s) that caused the intentional concealment of the other side of the story – the Ephesians' regret. We cannot know who or what was honoured with the 'Rundbau', but it could be one of the possibilities

86 See e.g. Ng 2007, 232; Hall [1997] 1998, 52.

87 See also Mortensen 2015.

88 For definitions of secrecy, see Bok 1982, 5-9. See also Bowden and Wright in this volume.

89 On silence and deception in relation to secrecy, see Bok 1982, 6-7.

outlined above. It was surely placed where it was in order to be seen high above the busy streets. An interpretable top part could reveal some of the story it was intended to tell, but it may not have been the entire story, and was possibly not understood by everyone. In this instance a gap caused by the preservation circumstances overshadows the possibility of drawing further conclusions regarding possible narrative gaps.

In conclusion, a cityscape is a manipulated image: one that shows the past and the present of the city, but that is adapted to remember or to conceal a specific story. As we have seen, concealment could have happened for different reasons, and with an analysis of three different monuments some of the intentions behind the choices made by the patrons, individuals or the *dēmos*, have been uncovered. In the early Roman period, a period of huge transformations, the past and the present were employed differently – in order to remember as well as to conceal.

WRITING TO REVEAL OR TO CONCEAL?

TRINE ARLUND HASS

A Secretive Muse: Hidden References in a Neo-Latin Eclogue

In this article, I examine a Renaissance eclogue written by a young Danish medical student in an attempt to suggest that – to paraphrase H. Bloom – the secret hidden in one text may actually be another text.[1] *I take M. Calinescu's principles of secrecy in literature as a referential framework for this hypothesis. Before turning to literary theory, I first explore humanistic bucolic poetry as a particularly relevant focal point for the consideration of secrecy in literature.*

The Secretive Nature of Bucolic Poetry

Cum semper odiosa fuerit, nunc capitalis est veritas. Crescentibus nempe flagitiis hominum, crevit veri odium, et regnum blanditiis ac mendacio datum est. Id me sepe dixisse, interdum etiam et scripsisse memini; sed dicendum sepius scribendumque est. Non ante fletus desinet quam dolor. Ea me pridem cogitatio induxit, ut Bucolicum carmen, poematis genus ambigui, scriberem, quod paucis intellectum plures forsitan delectaret. Est enim nonnullis corruptus adeo gustus ingenii, ut eos notus sapor, quamvis idem suavissimus, offendat, ignota omnia, licet asperiora, permulceant.

Though truth has always been hated, it is now a capital crime. It is a fact that the hatred of truth and the kingdom of flattery and falsehood has increased in proportion to the growing sins of mankind. I remember often having said this, and sometimes even writing it, but it ought to be said and written more often. The lament will not cease before the grief. This idea led me some time ago to write the *Bucolicum Carmen*, a kind of cryptic poem which, though understood only by a few, might possibly please many; for some people have a taste for letters so corrupt that the well-known savor, no matter how sweet, offends them, while everything mysterious pleases them, no matter how harsh.[2]

1 Bloom 1973; Calinescu 1994, 449.

2 Petrarch *Epystole sine nomine, praefatio*. Text from Dotti's edition (Petrarca 1974). Translation by N.P. Zacour in Patterson 1988, 43. This work contains critique of the papal court in Avignon, which is why Petrarch has obscured the names of his recipients. The papal court is also criticised

In this passage of his preface to *Epystole sine nomine* – a collection of letters intended for public circulation – Francesco Petrarca (1304-74) clearly asserts that the true meaning of the eclogues in his *Bucolicum Carmen* was only intended to be accessible to a section of his readership. Those readers who could not grasp this true meaning and the underlying critique, he claims, could simply enjoy the pleasant text.

It is no coincidence that Petrarch chose to hide his secrets in bucolic poetry. There are several indications that Petrarch's conception of bucolic poetry was formed by Vergil and the readings of Vergil presented by the late antique commentaries, especially the writings of Servius.[3] In his preface to his commentary on the eclogues, Servius emphasises the secretive layer of meaning in Vergil's *Eclogues*:

> *[I]n qua re tantum dissentit a Theocrito: ille enim ubique simplex est, hic necessitate compulsus aliquibus locis miscet figuras, quas perite plerumque etiam ex Theocriti versibus facit, quos ab illo dictos constat esse simpliciter.*
>
> In this respect alone he differs from Theocritus: for Theocritus is simple in every respect, while Vergil, forced by necessity, in various places mixes in figures that are even for the most part cleverly made out verses by Theocritus which people in general agree to be uttered in a simple manner by him.[4]

This quotation demonstrates that Vergil's poems were thought to contain an allegorical level of meaning, suggesting that his charming, idyllic poems about shepherds and unrequited love were actually comments on contemporary political and personal issues. This secretive layer of higher meaning is what sets his poems apart from those of his model, the idylls of Theocritus, and makes Vergil's poetry more complex. When such complex poetry is used as a model for other poets, as it was by Petrarch, writing bucolic poetry involves composing a text with two layers, one accessible to all and another with a secret meaning accessible only to a particular audience – or, to use secrecy terminology, to intentionally withhold and conceal information.[5]

The poetics of the pastoral genre were not formalised by the classical poetics and are not mentioned in Horace's *Ars Poetica* or in the poetics of Aristotle. Rather, pastoral genre characteristics developed over time through imitation. Since Vergil was the normative model, not only for Petrarch and bucolic poetry, I would like to take his poetry and the authoritative reading of it in the late antique commentaries as a starting point for a consideration of norms and standards of this genre in the Renaissance.

Bucolic poetry involves a greater variety of secrets than allegory. Some secrets are

---

in *Bucolicum Carmen*, but, since the critique is veiled in allegory, it does not incriminate its recipients in quite the same way. For more information on *Epystole sine nomine*, see Martinez 2009.

3 A decisive piece of evidence is that Vergil's texts are surrounded by Servius' commentaries in Petrarch's codex of the Vergilian works. For more information on this, see Hass 2013.

4 Servius Honoratus 1887, preface. Unless otherwise stated, translations are mine.

5 Scheppele 1988, 12; Calinescu 1994, 444.

intended to remain secrets until the author provides the 'key' for their disclosure, while other secrets can be disclosed through careful reading and study. In the Servius quotation above, we see how the text of Theocritus quite literally figures in Vergil's text in the form of loans. In Petrarch's time, it was a challenge for every writer to use and establish a connection with a poetic model whilst positioning the new text as a valid, independent work in its own right; in other words, it was important to establish a balance between dependency (on a model) and originality. Petrarch invites us to witness this balancing act. In the letter cited below, he asks his scribe, Giovanni Boccaccio, to revise a passage in his tenth eclogue because he has discovered that it resembles his model too closely:

> ... *Quod hodiernum erat, est decima pastorii carminis egloga, cuius quadam in parte ita scripseram: "solio sublimis acerno"; postmodum vero dum relegeretur, attendi simile nimis esse virgiliano carmini; ille enim ait in septimo divini operis: "solioque invitat acerno". Mutabis ergo et loco illius pones ita: "e sede verendus acerna". Omnino enim acernam esse sedem volui Romani Imperii, cum equus Troiani excidii apud ipsum Virgilium sit "acernus", ut sicut in theologicis lignum humane prius causa miserie post salutis, sic in poeticis non modo lignum idem genere sed arbor eadem specie sit redivivi Imperii materia que ruine fuit. Habes intentionis mee summam, nec opus est pluribus.*
>
> ... At issue today is the tenth eclogue of my pastoral poem where I had written in a certain section, "Solio sublimis acerno"; upon a later rereading of the verse, I noticed its close similarity to Virgil's words in the seventh book of his divine poem, "Solioque invitat acerno." Consequently, you are to change them and substitute the following, "E sede venerendus acerna." For I wished the Roman imperial throne to be of maple because in Virgil the Trojan horse is of maple; and thus, as in theology wood was the first cause of human misery and later of human redemption, so in poetry not only that same wood in general but that same tree in particular caused the ruin of the resurrected empire. There you have the gist of my thought, nor is there need of further explanation.[6]

In this passage – which can be found near the end of his letter – Petrarch finally reveals the concrete purpose of his communication: to explain to the scribe how the poem should be altered. Much of the earlier part of the letter contained Petrarch's meditations on imitation and the relationship between literary works in an imitative literary tradition. In this section, he explains that works with which he is more familiar are more likely to enter his own writings without his noticing, whereas works with which he is less familiar only enter his own text if he makes a conscious effort to include them. In my opinion, we can make two observations concerning secrecy from the above passage. Firstly, it is interesting how Petrarch's references to Vergil, Horace, Cicero and other writers remain secret to Petrarch himself until he re-reads and scrutinises his own work.

6 Petrarch *Familiares* 22.2.22-23. The text of *Familiares* is quoted from P. Stoppelli's edition of 1997. Translation by A.S. Bernardo (Petrarca 1985).

Secondly, this demonstrates that Petrarch, in a very concrete way, wishes to make the inspiration of his passage obscure to the reader; he actively conceals the reference so that what was at first a reference secret to himself now becomes more secretive to his reader. In this way, Petrarch establishes a balance between originality and dependency by striving for a decidedly original expression that still maintains a connection to its models. As his explanation shows, the meaning of maple wood requires the reference to Vergil. His famous formulation of the principle, stated just lines before the quotation, is *similitudo non identitas*,[7] likeness not identity – or, as A.S. Bernardo renders it, 'imitation not sameness'. Although most humanistic writers strive to live up to the principle of *similitudo non identitas*, few writers operate with as strict a conception of it as Petrarch.

Having outlined these aspects of bucolic poetry in general and Petrarch's bucolic poetry in particular, I will now use this as a point of departure to discuss secrecy in literature in general before examining a specific case of secretive bucolic literature.

Secrecy and Literature

In M. Calinescu's writings on secrecy in literary fiction, he claims there are two types of reading: sequential reading, where the reader is eager to know what comes next (usually typical of a first-time or one-time reader) and reflective re-reading, where a critical reader interprets a text.[8] According to Petrarch (even with regards to his own reading of his own poetry), it is only on such a critical, reflective re-reading that a reader can potentially access secrets hidden in a text. The reader's success depends on the type and purpose of the secret in question, since not all secrets are accessible to everyone (despite a thorough analysis). In his book *Rereading* from 1993, M. Calinescu considers the purpose of textual concealment. He lists four different types of secrets, which I will now discuss in turn.

The first secret is the communication of hidden meaning 'by way of equivocation or amphibolic speech',[9] which aims to make meaning inaccessible to outsiders.[10] This category would fit the secrecy described by Petrarch in *Epystole sine nomine* (quoted

7 *Quid ergo? Sum quem priorum semitam, sed non semper aliena vestigia sequi iuvet; sum qui aliorum scriptis non furtim sed precario uti velim in tempore, sed dum liceat, meis malim; sum quem similitudo delectet, non identitas, et similitudo ipsa quoque non nimia, in qua sequacis lux ingenii emineat, non cecitas non paupertas; sum qui satius rear duce caruisse quam cogi per omnia ducem sequi.* ('And so? I am one who intends to follow our forebears' path but not always others' tracks; I am one who wishes upon occasion to make use of others' writings, not secretly but with their leave, and whenever possible I prefer my own; I am one who delights in imitation and not in sameness, in a resemblance that is not servile, where the imitator's genius shines forth rather than his blindness or his ineptitude; I am one who much prefers not having a guide than being compelled to follow one slavishly.' Translation by A.S. Bernardo (Petrarca 1985)). Petrarch *Familiares* 22.2.20.

8 Kermode 1983, 133-55; Calinescu 1994, 445.

9 Calinescu 1993, 248.

10 Calinescu 1993, 247-54.

in the beginning of the present article); the double-coded message which entails that only certain readers can access the esoteric coding of the text while most readers can only reach the exoteric coding. One could assume that this is the secrecy intended in Petrarch's satiric critique of the Papal Curia in *Eclogues* 6 and 7.

The second type of secret is described as 'didactic', since it makes meaning accessible to a reader who meets certain conditions, i.e. a reader who has a certain background or experience. In the presentation of this category, M. Calinescu briefly raises the potentially problematic issue of references in older texts that appear secretive to readers today but may not have done so to readers at the time. The same could be said of references in texts from a different cultural perspective. However, M. Calinescu continues to claim:

> At any rate, from the perspective of a reader sensitive to nuances of secrecy and hiddenness, virtually all of the great classic texts of literature, from Homer to Joyce, contain such secrets, whether intended by their authors or credibly attributed to them by generations of interpreters.[11]

This is certainly true of Classical texts, as the tradition of allegoric readings of Vergil's *Eclogues* clearly demonstrates. However, irrespective of whether these secrets appear differently to original and modern readers, didactic secrets differ from the first type of secret (described above) since, in principle, they are accessible to anyone who undertakes to educate or initiate him- or herself.

The third category of secret is the 'playful' secret. This can be difficult to distinguish from what M. Calinescu calls the 'enigma' or 'riddle', which are used to structure or vary the narrative. M. Calinescu suggests a tentative distinction between 'intertextuality', which challenges the reader to identify references to other texts, and 'textual gaps' in the narrative information, some of which are filled later in the texts and others left unfilled. At this point, I would also like to suggest that playful secrets could be hard to distinguish from didactic secrets; for example, is the purpose of the secretive meaning of *acerna* in Petrarch's tenth eclogue playful or didactic? It certainly requires an educated reader with a high degree of familiarity with Vergil to grasp it; however, if the reader fulfills these criteria, is it not a playful addition of meaning?

The fourth type of secret is pseudo-concealment. This involves imitating secrecy by simulating allegoric reference or a highly mannered style. M. Calinescu has no method to distinguish between alleged and true secrecy.

Having established a typology for analysing secrets in literature (including a relevant final caveat), I will now continue to discuss the potential secrets in a line of Danish neo-Latin bucolic poetry.

---

11 Calinescu 1993, 249.

Secrets in a Refrain by Hans Philipsen Pratensis

In 1563, a Danish student of medicine, Hans Philipsen Pratensis, published a bucolic poem entitled *Daphnis*[12] in a collection of other poems in Latin and Greek (Fig. 1). This collection was composed to celebrate the wedding of a highly esteemed minister and writer of hymns, Hans Thomesen, to a charming and chaste young woman from Ribe, Magdalene Anchersen. Pratensis' wedding poem takes the form of a bucolic poem. It draws on Vergil's first eclogue for the expository position: two shepherds, Thyrsis and Lycidas, meet outside the city and discuss why soldiers and warships are gathering in the surroundings. Unlike in Vergil, the country is only on the verge of war, and there are no indications that either of the shepherds have been or will be implicated. However, given that Vergil's first eclogue and its traditional interpretation would have been familiar to a Latin reader, there is no doubt that these similarities, however vague they may appear to a modern reader, would have functioned as a playful secret to a reader at the time. Lycidas learns from another shepherd, Mopsus, that the reason for the present turbulence is that their dear Irenicus can no longer tolerate the provocative behaviour of another cowherd and the loss of garlands (*insignes corollas*, v. 79) given to him by his beloved Lycoris. It has been suggested by K. Friis-Jensen[13] that this cryptic explanation is actually an allegoric description of the cause of the Nordic Seven Years' War between Denmark and Sweden, which broke out in 1563, the same year as the poem was published. Irenicus is Danish King Frederik II and the masque is a wordplay: the Greek εἰρήνη mirrors the root of the name Frederik, the Danish *fred*, since both mean 'peace'. It follows by logical deduction that the unnamed cowherd must be Frederik's opponent, Swedish King Erik XIV. The garlands are the symbols of the three crowns used to symbolise the three members of the Kalmar Union (Denmark, Norway and Sweden), the insignia of which both kings claimed to have a right to display on their coat of arms. It could also be suggested that Lycoris, the giver of the crowns, is most likely Danish Queen Margarete (1353-1412), who, as regent of Denmark (and subsequently also of Norway and Sweden), united the three countries in the union.

I should emphasise that we are again in the realm of playful secrets from the intended reader's point of view: The riddle of the king's name is relatively easy to solve with only limited knowledge of Greek, and the war and its rhetoric must have been at the forefront of everyone's mind at the time. However, as readers estranged from the original

12 Full title: *Daphnis. Seu votum in Nuptias clarissimi viri M. Johannis Thomae Ripensis, Ecclesiae Hafniensis ad Sanctam Virginem pastoris, et honestissimae virginis Magdalenae, natae patre prudentissimo, Matthia Ancherio ciue Ripensi et alia epithalamia scripta ab Erasmo Catholmio, Erasmo Christierno Randrusiensi, et Canuto Bramtio Haderslebio.* The text is printed in Copenhagen by Laurents Benedikt. It is transmitted in two copies, one in Copenhagen University Library (accessible online through www.kb.dk) and one in the Uppsala University Library. I have had access to copies of both texts.

13 Friis-Jensen 1987, 100-2.

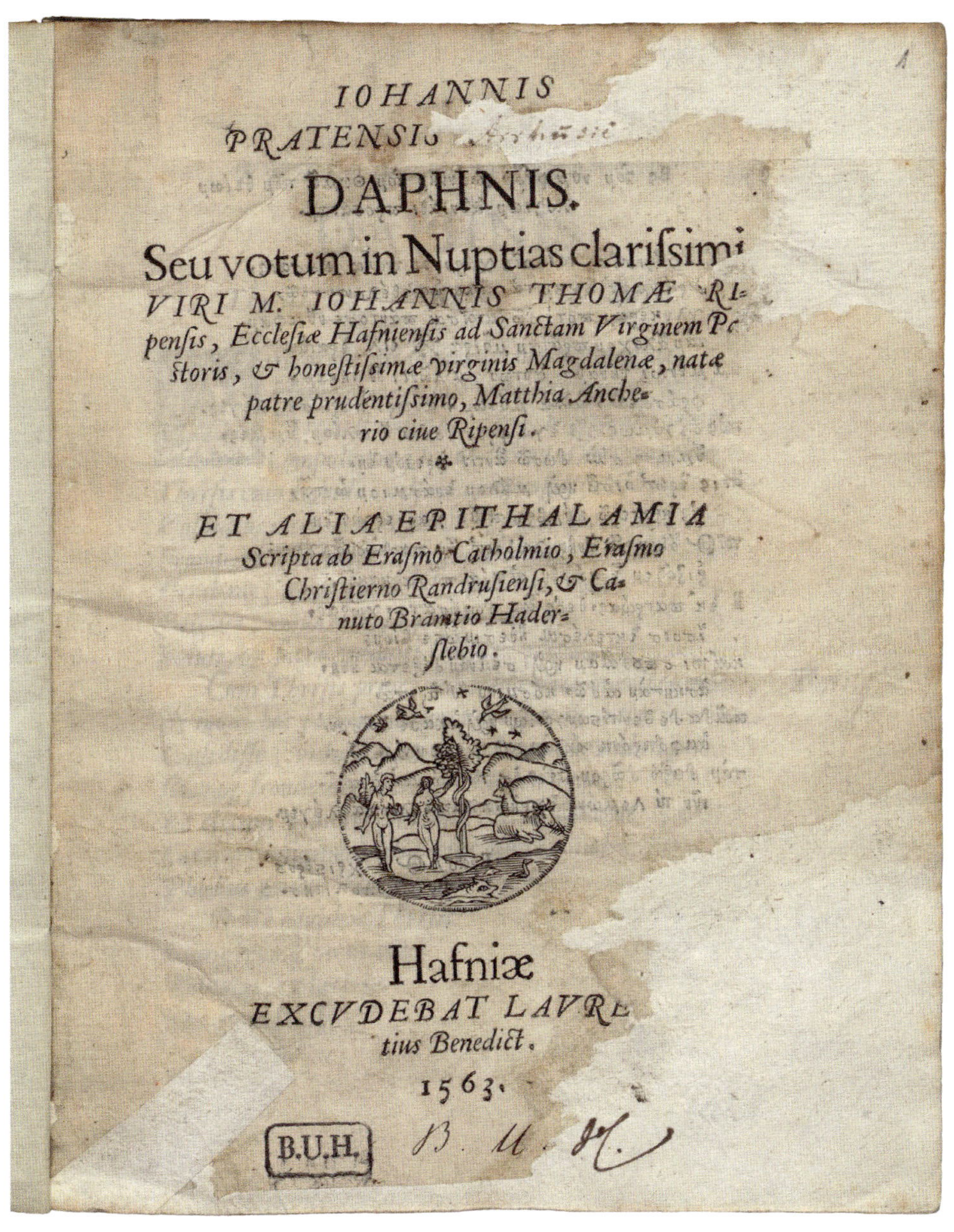

IOHANNIS
PRATENSIS
DAPHNIS.
Seu votum in Nuptias clariſsimi
VIRI M. IOHANNIS THOMÆ RI-
penſis, Eccleſiæ Hafnienſis ad Sanctam Virginem Pa-
ſtoris, & honeſtiſsimæ virginis Magdalenæ, natæ
patre prudentiſsimo, Matthia Anche-
rio ciue Ripenſi.

ET ALIA EPITHALAMIA
Scripta ab Eraſmo Catholmio, Eraſmo
Chriſtierno Randruſienſi, & Canuto Bramtio Hader-
ſlebio.

Hafniæ
EXCVDEBAT LAVRE-
tius Benedict.
1563.

Johannes Pratensis, Daphnis seu votum in nuptias (...) Johannis Thomae Ripensis (...) et Magdalenae (...) Ancheri[i] (...) et alia epithalamia (...), Hafniæ: excudebat Laurentius Benedict, 1563 (LN 1342). The Royal Library (Copenhagen), shelfmark G 14470 4° (image published with permission of The Royal Library of Copenhagen and ProQuest. Further reproduction is prohibited without permission. Image produced by ProQuest as part of Early European Books. www.proquest.com).

Fig. 1.

context of the texts, it is helpful to lean on K. Friis-Jensen's interpretation in order to enter the esoteric level of the text.

The war discussion is interrupted when a friend of Thyrsis and Lycidas, Moeris, appears on the scene. Moeris is cheerful. He is wearing a garland of myrtles and has a wine mug and flute around his neck. When asked why he is cheerful, he explains that he is on his way to Daphnis' wedding party. From this point on, the poem turns into an *epithalamium*, a wedding poem celebrating the groom, bride and their union. It is in the laudation of the bride and groom that we encounter the verse on which we shall focus in the remainder of this article. Here, Moeris introduces a refrain which is used by all three shepherds throughout the rest of the eulogy:

> *Dicite Valbiacum Musæ mihi dicite carmen*
> Sing, muses, sing me a Valbyan song[14]

Connecting the muses to the locality of Valby Bakke, a hill on the outskirts of Copenhagen, may seem odd to a modern reader, who knows that Valby is now an integrated part of the city zone. However, in Pratensis' time, Valby was a rural area and, as such, its association with a bucolic environment does not seem illogical. For Pratensis' intended contemporary reader, the location and its use in a bucolic context may have triggered a more particular association with another text. In 1560, three years before the publication of *Daphnis*, the theologian Erasmus Lætus wrote the first collection of bucolic poetry published by a Dane, *Bucolica* (Wittenberg 1560),[15] an ambitious and complex work consisting of seven eclogues of various lengths. In a prefatory letter written by Philipp Melanchthon, Protestant preceptor of Germany, Lætus dedicates his work to the king, Frederik II. Although the nature of this work remains largely secretive to today's reader, it is generally accepted by scholars[16] that one of the main ambitions of the allegorical work is to present King Frederik II as a Danish Augustus and the author as a Danish Vergil. In the last eclogue of Lætus' collection, this line of action culminates: the singer Phædrus, who most likely represents Lætus[17] and whose departure was lamented in the first eclogue, has finally returned to Denmark; he is standing on the city limit about to enter Copenhagen, and he is preparing to sing the praise of the new king, Faustus or Frederik II. The invocation introduces a *translatio musarum*, a 'transfer of the muses', from Greece to Denmark. This signals that the antagonist of the narrative, Phædrus, has finished his travels and that he is bringing Classical learning home with him. The argument is that, since Mount Helicon is occupied by the Turks, the muses may as well take residence in Denmark,

14 Pratensis 1563, vv. 139, 149, 161, 177, 189, 201, 210.

15 Lætus 1560.

16 See Friis-Jensen & Skafte Jensen 1984; Skafte Jensen 2004; Zeeberg 2008; 2010.

17 Zeeberg 2010.

and, more specifically, on Valby Bakke. In his introduction to this translation, Lætus invokes the muses as follows:

> *Dicite, Valbyaco diductum cespite carmen*
> Sing a song from the Valbyan hilltop[18]

The fact that Pratensis introduces a refrain invoking the muses in a manner resembling Lætus should be taken as an instance of esoteric communication: it was not unusual to place the muses in a local area (during this period, writers across Europe did so); however, although every learned European would have been able to read Pratensis' poem, only those who had read and were able to recall the collection of Lætus' poetry would have appreciated the refrain as a tribute to and confirmation of the translation of muses made in his work three years previously.

The poem's intended readership – which would have comprised the dedicatee, Hans Thomesen, and his circle, learned men from Copenhagen who were theologians (like Lætus) and oriented towards Wittenberg – would have most likely made this connection. In this way, Pratensis' text functions as a confirmation of the society to which the readership belonged; a society defined by its religious confessions as well as its education.

The reference to Lætus is not a secret of M. Calinescu's first type, since it is unlikely that the intention was to keep the meaning secret from selected groups. Quite the contrary; although it may have taken more effort for a non-local member of the intended readership to discover the secret – and thus have the potential to act as both a playful and a didactic secret – it could be viewed as a factor contributing to the construction of a Danish identity that grasping Danish literary secrets requires diligent re-reading.

Before introducing the refrain, Pratensis inserts two other variations of verses in which muses are invoked to sing Valbyan songs. The first helps to set the scene in the poem's introduction, and the second is found relatively close to the refrain. If we examine these three verses in more detail, we can see that the first two are much closer to Lætus' verse (they quote Lætus almost verbatim) while, in the third, the refrain has been altered fairly extensively. I will now quote Lætus and Pratensis' verses (respectively) and underline the parallels:

18 Lætus 1560, *Eclogue* 7.5. The similarity between Lætus' *Eclogue* 7.5 and Pratensis' refrain is discussed in Skafte Jensen 2004, 31; Skovgaard-Petersen & Zeeberg 2007, 257-9; Zeeberg 2010. It is the subject of Zeeberg 2008.

Lætus:
Dicite, Valbyaco diductum cespite carmen[19]
Sing a song from the Valbyan hilltop[20]

Pratensis:
Dic rogo Valbiaco diductum cespite carmen
Sing, I pray, a song from the Valbyan hilltop[21]

... Dicere Valbiacum diductum cespite carmen
... to sing a song from the Valbyan hilltop[22]

Dicite Valbiacum Musæ mihi dicite carmen
Sing, muses, sing me a Valbyan song[23]

By changing Lætus' verse gradually, Pratensis makes it more likely that his reader will unveil the secretive reference and recall the model even once the wording has developed into a more original expression.

P. Zeeberg has demonstrated that, by changing the phrasing of the verse, Pratensis preserves the allusion to Lætus whilst adding an allusion to Vergil:

> *Dicite Valbiacum Musæ mihi dicite carmen.*
> (v. 116 etc.)
> The most likely model for such a stanza-refrain pattern is Virgil's eighth eclogue. And indeed Pratensis' refrain is quite close to the first of Virgil's two refrains in this eclogue, namely:
>
> *Incipe Maenalios*[24] *mecum, mea tibia, versus.* [begin, my flute, Maenalian verses with me]
> (Ecl. 8.21 etc.)

19 P. Zeeberg writes about *diductum* in Zeeberg 2008 note 11: 'This line in Laetus is a reference to Vergil's sixth eclogue v. 4-5: '... *pastorem, Tityre, pinguis/pascere oportet ovis, deductum dicere carmen*'. The variant *diductum* instead of *deductum* can actually be found in one of the main mss. to Vergil (Palatinus). But whether Laetus knew it from an edition of the Virgil text we cannot tell. It is not attested in any of the 16th-century editions I have been able to consult. The two forms are often confused in medieval manuscripts (cf. TLL s.v. diduco). The meaning of *deductum* is here 'finely spun', a metaphor taken from the spinning of wool. In Laetus' poem *diductum* may either mean simply 'taken from' or perhaps 'dispersed from' with a reference to the poem being distributed to a wide audience.'

20 Lætus 1560, *Eclogue* 7.5.

21 Pratensis 1563, v. 21.

22 Pratensis 1563, v. 116.

23 Pratensis 1563, vv. 139, 149, 161, 177, 189, 201, 210.

24 A mountain in Arcadia.

The metrical pattern is the same: two dactyls and a spondee, two dactyls and a spondee – and indeed the same as in Virgil's model, the first Idyll of Theocritus. They both call for songs from a certain mountain. And the syntactic patterns are very close: an imperative followed by the name of the mountain as an adjective referring to the object (a poem/verse) which is placed at the end of the verse after the addressee of the imperative (the muses/the flute).[25]

P. Zeeberg's arguments for an added secretive reference to Vergil's refrain are convincing: there are many similarities and, as we have already seen, the intended readership would have expected references to Vergil. However, if we look more closely at the changes Pratensis has made to Lætus' verse, we notice that not all the alterations cohere with the Vergilian verse: Pratensis has changed the addressee and made his refrain an invocation of the muses, not of his own skill. This change is in part carried out by a repetition of the imperative *dicite* in the fifth foot of the verse. I would like to suggest that, through a critical, informed re-reading of the passage, it is possible to identify a resemblance between the pattern of repeated imperatives and another bucolic refrain; namely, that of Vergil's model, Theocritus' first idyll:

Ἄρχετε βουκολικᾶς, Μοῖσαι φίλαι, ἄρχετ' ἀοιδᾶς
Begin, dear Muses, begin the bucolic songs[26]

The Theocritean refrain has a metrical structure similar to both Vergil's and Pratensis' verse (as already stated by P. Zeeberg) and, besides the repetition of the imperative ἄρχετε, the imperative's addressees are the muses, just as in Pratensis' verse. Like Theocritus, Pratensis places them in vocative between two *caesurae* at the end of the third and beginning of the fourth foot. Furthermore, both Pratensis and Theocritus let the adjective bucolicos/βουκολικᾶς qualify the object of the imperative. Pratensis has *carmen*, song, in singular as his object, while both Vergil and Theocritus use plural; Vergil writes *versus*, verses, and Theocritus ἀοιδᾶς, songs – again semantically closer to Pratensis. The use of the imperative *dicite* may also be explained with reference to Theocritus; however, in order to establish this, we first need to re-read the text with neo-Latin translations of Theocritus in mind.

The first translation of the entire Theocritean corpus was made by German poet and humanist Helius Eobanus Hessus (1488-1540) and published in 1531 together with an edition of the Greek text edited by Joachim Camerarius (1500-74), both prominent figures at the time.[27] Here, the refrain of the first idyll reads:

25 Zeeberg 2008, 99. The translation of Verg. *Ecl.* 8.21 is my addition.

26 Theocritus *Idyll* 1.64, 70, 73, 76, 79, 84, 89, 94, 99, 104, 108, 114, 119, 122.

27 Theocritus 1531. For Hessus, see Hardin & Reinhart 1997, s.v. 'Eobanus Hessus'; Vredeveld 2004, xv-xvii.

Dicite bucolicos mea carmina dicite cantus
Sing my songs, sing bucolic tunes

As we can see, Hessus translates the Theocritean ἄρχετε as *dicite* in his version of the refrain. The translation follows the original quite accurately, the largest difference being the replacement of Μοῖσαι φίλαι with *mea carmina* and the translation of ἄρχετε, 'begin', as *dicite*, 'say' (or 'sing'). In my opinion, the fact that *dicite* is not a direct translation of ἄρχετε and that it occurs in a translation of the model (of the model) of Pratensis' refrain indicates that Pratensis selected this word intentionally for his version, especially considering Hessus' position in the learned society of 16th-century Germany. Hessus was part of the Melanchthonian circle and held various positions in academia and as a teacher (for example, at the Egidion gymnasium in Nürnberg founded by Melanchthon), but he was probably more famous as a poet and translator. Erasmus attributed the title *Ovidius Christianus* to him, a title inspired by Hessus' poems about holy women inspired by the *Heroides*.[28] However, Hessus established himself as a poet with the work *Bucolicon*, a collection of bucolic poetry published in Erfurt in 1509.[29] By his own testimony, this was the first collection of Latin eclogues published by a German writer, and, in his fifth eclogue, it is possible to identify a refrain with the repeated imperative *dicite*:

Dicite Pierides: certantes dicite Musae[30]

As observed by H. Vredeveld,[31] this might have originally been inspired by a translation of Theocritus' first seven idylls undertaken by Martino Filetico (first published in Rome by Eucharius Silber c. 1482).[32] Filetico lets the verse *Dicite, Pierides, pastorum dicite cantus* open Thyrsis' line in his translation (v. 64), but the repeated refrain is *Ite meae musae, faciles huc ite camoenae* (v. 104ff.). The metrical pattern of Filetico's verse and Hessus' own refrain are identical, although there are some differences between these and Hessus' translation of Theocritus'. The repetition of *dicite*, however, remains a shared feature.

Hessus writes many kinds of poetry, but he continues to return to the bucolic genre in various ways. Nineteen years after publishing *Bucolicon*, he reissues a revised edition of his bucolic poems, perhaps motivated by his declared adherence to Luther's protestant movement in 1521.[33] In the revised edition entitled *Bucolicorum Idyllia* (Hagenau 1528),[34] the eleven eclogues of the original edition, which culminated in a praise of the Holy Virgin, have been transformed into twelve idylls and five newly composed idylls

28 *Heroides Christianae*, 1514 (2nd edition 1532).

29 Hessus 1509.

30 Hessus 1509, *Eclogue* 5.61, 71, 81, 91, 101.

31 Vredeveld 2004, 490-1 (on Hessus, *Eclogue* 5.61).

32 Theocritus c. 1482.

33 *In evangelici Doctoris M. Lutheri laudem Elegiae* ('Elegies in Praise and Defense of the Evangelical Doctor Martin Luther', 1521).

34 Hessus 1528.

have been added, some with Lutheran content. In the new edition, he abolishes the refrain with *dicite*. By referring to the new poems as 'idylls' rather than 'eclogues', Hessus indicates a shift in focus from Vergil to Theocritus. This can also be seen in a school commentary to Vergil's *Eclogues* published in 1529, which focuses on Theocritean loans, and, of course, ultimately on his translation of 1531.

Since Hessus was generally well-known and continually returned to bucolic poetry, it is very likely that Pratensis and his community knew Hessus' writings. However, we cannot claim with certainty that a reader in the 1560s would have known both the 1509 and the 1528 version of Hessus' own pastoral poems. It is quite possible that he would have only been familiar with the reissued 1528 version, which is also the version featured in Hessus' *Opera Omnia* (Schwäbisch Hall 1539).[35] This also means that a 1560s reader would not have necessarily noticed that Hessus leaned on another translation in his acquiring of Theocritus, even if this explains the origination of the connection between *dicite* and ἄρχετε. However, it seems unlikely that a reader interested in bucolic poetry would not have used the popular[36] bilingual edition of Theocritus from 1531 as his standard edition of the *Idylls*. Given the bilingual nature of the edition, it is relevant to consider the aforementioned similarities between Pratensis' and Theocritus' refrains on the basis of both the original text and the translation.

Conclusion

On the basis of the observations and considerations presented in this article, I would like to suggest that there is another secret interwoven into Pratensis' refrain: a reference to Theocritus. With his alteration of Lætus' verse, it seems possible that he manages to allude to three bucolic authorities – Lætus, Vergil and Theocritus – in one single verse. If this is the case, it could be said that Pratensis sums up the canonic writers of the Classical tradition and places them besides his own local role model. In doing so, he places Lætus – and himself – into a prominent line of bucolic succession, but he also establishes a particular Danish lineage of tradition.

On this assumption, Pratensis' verse would be an example of a double, or perhaps even a triple, coding that works on several levels. Any reader at the time with knowledge of Latin would have been familiar with Vergil's *Eclogues*, which makes it likely that he would recognise a Vergilian reference in Pratensis' verse. It is also likely that a Latin reader from Denmark or the surroundings of Wittenberg University would have recognised the connection between Pratensis and Lætus. Theocritus never acquired the status of Vergil in this period, but it is reasonable to assume that his writings were known, especially among the Wittenberg milieu, where the importance of Greek was underlined and the principle of *ad fontes* was practiced.

The references to Vergil and Theocritus certainly require critical reading and re-reading from the modern reader, which might suggest that we should categorise them

35 Hessus 1539.

36 VD16 lists four editions published between 1531 and 1553.

as didactic secrets. It is not enough to know the model; one also needs to know its reception and tradition to disclose the secretive reference. However, Pratensis' verse works well on its own as a mere invocation of the Muses, and I acknowledge the possibility that my attempt to reveal a Theocritean secret may be a case of a later reader discovering secrets that the writer did not intend to hide in his text. At this point, we can appeal to M. Calinescu's pseudo-secret: How are we to tell whether this is a secretive reference or a phrasing that matches the style of the genre? When the venture is to disclose secrets kept from members of another society, we are left in a position where disclosures will be linked as much – or more – to probability than to certainty. As M. Calinescu clearly acknowledges in the title of his article of 1994, discussing secrecy in literature is to some extent identical to discussing intertextuality. We are faced with the same problems when suggesting parallels, and arguments take the same form. If our intention is to understand the text from the reader's point of view and to make informed assumptions against this backdrop, we have to attempt to reconstruct the horizon of expectations of the intended reader. What the concept of secrecy offers these ventures is the possibility of uncovering some of the psychological aspects connected to reading intertextuality. Secrecy does not provide us with solutions to problems such as whether a reference is intended by the writer or whether a reference is strictly linguistic or also draws on content, but it does provide us with a terminology to discuss the effects of intertextuality that have the potential to further our understanding of these complex texts.

SØREN SINDBERG JENSEN

Better to Reveal than to Conceal? Christian Attitudes to Secrecy in the Early Islamic Period

This article examines secrecy as topos in early Christian Arabic writings. Using the Arabic writings of the Christian theologian Ḥabīb ibn Ḫidma Abū Rā'iṭa at-Takrītī (c. AD 770-c. 835) as a case, it will compare the extent to which Christians in the early Islamic period emphasised the revelation or concealment of God's knowledge. A clarification of this issue will not only further our insight into early Christian Arabic writings, it should also pave the way for a better understanding of Christians living under Islamic rule in the early Islamic period.

As a result of the Arab conquests of the 7th century AD, territories in the Near East, where Christians made up the majority of the population, came under Arab rule. This gave rise to a situation where members of the emerging Islamic communities entered into dialogues and disputes with their Christian counterparts, resulting in the exchange and shaping of ideas between Islamic and Christian communities. This process accelerated when Christians started producing apologetic and polemical writings in Arabic in defence of Christianity during the 8th century AD.

These facts reflect a well-known yet for centuries often neglected historical reality. In the past four decades, however, the interaction between Christians and Muslims in the early Islamic period in the Near East has caught the attention of an increasing number of scholars. Many different studies have been carried out, resulting in an increase in our knowledge and understanding of this part of history. Many topics, however, have been omitted.

In this study, I will discuss secrecy as *topos* in early Christian Arabic apologetic literature.[1] The working hypothesis is that attitudes to secrecy can inform us in a broader

1 To the best of my knowledge, this will be the first attempt to integrate the study of secrecy into the field of early Christian-Islamic encounters in the Near East. For an overview of the history and sources of non-Islamic perceptions of early Islam, see Hoyland 1997. For a general introduction to the study of early Christian and Islamic encounters, in particular in the early 'Abbāsid period, see Griffith 2008. Studies focusing on a specific topic have avoided taking account of secrecy as *topos* in early Christian-Islamic encounters. Instead, they have been preoccupied with

sense about Christians living under Islamic rule in the 8th and 9th centuries AD. In particular, I will focus on the Arabic apologetic writings of the Christian theologian Ḥabīb ibn Ḫidmah Abū Rāʾiṭa at-Takrītī (c. AD 770-c. 835). Abū Rāʾiṭa wrote extensive apologetic treatises in Arabic and defended Christianity in ways which are similar to other Christian authors of the early Islamic period.[2] This makes him a suitable case for how Christians in the early Islamic period in general treated secrecy.[3] Secrecy, in the present context, is understood as attitudes towards God's knowledge: should it remain concealed or be revealed, and why?

The study falls into three parts: firstly, I will briefly introduce Abū Rāʾiṭa and his time. Secondly, I will investigate the relative relationship between revelation and concealment as *topoi* in the Arabic apologetic writings of Abū Rāʾiṭa,[4] identifying his attitude to secrecy. On this basis, thirdly, I will raise the question of how Abū Rāʾiṭa's attitudes to secrecy can be explained, by discussing his attitude to secrecy in relation to early Islamic thinking and contemporary Christian and Islamic apologetics.

Abū Rā'iṭa and His Time

Little is known about Abū Rāʾiṭa, besides a few well-established facts.[5] From his *nisba* (the part of his name indicating origin) we can deduce that he was from Tikrit in Mesopotamia. His native tongue was, most likely, Syriac, and we know that he was a theologian in the Syrian Orthodox ('Jacobite') church, although he probably did not hold any official position within the church. Tradition has it that he entered into indirect and direct dispute with the Christian theologian Theodore Abū Qurra, whom I shall return to below.

Living in one of the areas which had come under Arab control in the 7th century, Abū Rāʾiṭa and contemporary Christians were part of a multifaceted process of enculturation, which had started earlier but was certainly intensified after the ʿAbbāsid revolution in

---

other matters. Compare for instance T.W. Ricks (2013), who looks at the Trinity in early Christian Arabic writings; S.H. Griffith (2013), who deals with the Bible in early Islam; and D. Thomas (1994), who is concerned with the miracles of Jesus in Islamic polemical writings.

2 Griffith 2008, 45-106.

3 Admittedly, there is a risk that focusing on one author will compromise the extent to which the findings can be generalised. If nothing else, the case study will hopefully form the basis for further investigations of a larger number of sources.

4 Of Abū Rāʾiṭa's Arabic corpus I focus on two of his three lengthy apologetic writings: *A Risāla of Abū Rāʾiṭa t-Takrītī on the Proof of the Christian Religion and the Proof of the Holy Trinity (Risāla li-Abī Rāʾiṭa t-Takrītī fī iṯbāt dīn an-naṣrānīya wa-iṯbāt aṯ-Ṯālūṯ al-muqaddas)*, and *The Second Risāla of Abū Rāʾiṭa at-Takrītī on the Incarnation (Ar-risālat aṯ-ṯāniya li-Abī Rāʾiṭa t-Takrītī fī t-taǧassud)*, which I shall refer to as *The Proof* and *On the Incarnation*, respectively. Throughout, I quote from S.T. Keating's edition of the Arabic text and her translation, using her division of the texts into paragraphs (Keating 2006).

5 For a more elaborate account of what is known about Abū Rāʾiṭah, see Keating 2006, 1-55.

the mid-8th century.[6] For the Christians, the process involved the adoption of Arabic in the churches[7] and the familiarisation with Islamic doctrines and literature. Abū Rāʾiṭa's Arabic apologetic writings reflect this specific historical situation very well. He wrote texts in defence of the beliefs of his denomination against other Christians, as well as general defences regarding the reliability of Christian doctrines, especially the trinity and the incarnation in response to Islamic charges.[8] In the latter kind of texts, with which we are concerned here, he displays a profound knowledge of Islamic notions, makes allusions to passages of the *Qurʾān*, and, in addition, merges Aristotelian theoretical thinking with analytical terminology known among contemporary Arabic grammarians.

Secrecy in the Arabic Apologetic Writings of Abū Rā'iṭa

Concealment

It is remarkable how little attention Abū Rāʾiṭa pays to the question of concealment of God's knowledge. The only text in which the matter is treated to any great extent is *On the Incarnation,* in which it is a recurring issue. Part of the treatise follows the well-established structure of questions, raised against Christian doctrines, and how they should be answered.[9] Here, secrecy is part of a broader discussion of why God, according to Christians, had to incarnate himself to save man. Could he not just have saved man secretly? Abū Rāʾiṭa lets his counterpart formulate the problem in the following way:

> If they [the non-Christians] say: "Which of the two descriptions of God is more suitable and better ...: that He permitted their salvation without inconvenience [to Himself] or departure from His place, or that he carried this out Himself,

6 See Griffith 2005 for a concise examination of this process of 'enculturation' (esp. Griffith 2005, 94).

7 Some Christians made use of their knowledge of both Arabic and Greek/Syriac as translators, which made them vital contributors to the 'translation movement', i.e. the grand projects of translations into Arabic of Greek and Syriac classical literature, carried out in the early ʿAbbāsid period under the auspices of members of the Islamic elite (see Gutas 1998).

8 Keating 2006, 56-9.

9 Although the genre of the text can be said to be 'the Apologetical Treatise' (see Griffith 2005, 108-12), the question-and-answer aspect of the text echoes the genre of 'the Master and His Disciples', which was one of the other genres that flourished in the early Islamic period (see Griffith 2005, 101-5; 2008, 81-5). Although these dialogues most certainly should not be read as transcripts of actual dialogues, but should more likely be seen as the product of literary imagination, they probably do have some historical bearing in the sense that the charges raised against Christians and the answer to those charges, given in those texts, to some degree reflect the content of debates between Christians and Muslims in the early Islamic period. Thus, it is notable how well-known Christian teachings were to Muslim theologians at least from around AD 800 onwards (see Thomas 2003b).

> becoming incarnated and suffering what [He] suffered, being killed and death and other things that you have described?".[10]

To Abū Rā᾿iṭa, this question gives rise to a longer answer. For our present purpose, the end of the answer deserves a closer examination:

> Now if the salvation and deliverance of the servants from error was [done] by permission of [God] alone, secretly (*sirran*), without being manifest or the Savior being seen, then the muddle, confusion and collapse into destruction would necessarily be greater for them than if they had been left in their original [state of] ruin …
>
> And whom should [human beings] thank for their salvation if this had been obscure to them?[11]

Here, Abū Rā᾿iṭa's attitude to secrecy is, clearly, negative. Had God acted secretly and not incarnated himself into Christ, it would have caused more sufferings for Man. Moreover, Man would not know where to direct his thanks had God not made himself visible.

A more positive view on concealment is found in subsequent paragraphs of the same treatise. Thus, in relation to the question of the Last Day, Abū Rā᾿iṭa defends the idea that God has secrets. The same argument is repeated apologetically on a backdrop of a reported charge in the following way:

> As for what they refer to concerning the Messiah's knowledge, Veneration is for His remembrance! [saying He] was lacking in knowledge of the Hour [of Judgment], and [consequently] they impose the status of a servant on Him, because, according to their suspicion, He is ignorant of this, their ill suspicion can be deterred and they can be turned back to what is correct, if it is not difficult for them to be fair.[12]

The concern of Abū Rā᾿iṭa's opponents is why Christ did not make public his knowledge of the Day of Judgment, insinuating that this fact diminishes Christ's status. Abū Rā᾿iṭa refutes this charge:

> Out of His great beneficence for His servants and His vast benevolence toward them, He keeps knowledge of the Hour [of Judgment] from them, because He, glory be to Him! takes care of them and He knows of the great importance of warning them, and the intensity of the harm that pervades the world [resulting from the anticipation] of losses [when] these are announced, on account of the harm of the announcement of all that is not known if it is announced, and of keeping secret what has been disclosed if it is kept secret. Because God does not

10 *On the Incarnation*, par. 31.

11 *On the Incarnation*, par. 31-32.

12 *On the Incarnation*, par. 63.

> reveal (*muẓhir*) a matter nor keep it hidden (*ḥāǧib*) from His servants, except for the purpose of their benefits and the cause of their usefulness.
>
> For when the disciples asked Him for knowledge about the Hour [of Judgment] so they could be certain of it, He, may he be praised! declined this, because of what we have described of His compassion for them, and His care for them.[13]

In short, the reason why Christ did not share his information about the Day of Judgment is not that God/Christ lacked knowledge, but that he kept this as a secret in order to spare Man. Hence, concealment is valued positively. Not in a general sense, but in the concrete example, where it is taken as a sign of God's compassion.

Based on these two explicit discussions of secrecy in relation to God's knowledge, it is safe to say that Abū Rāʾiṭa's evaluation of secrecy is flexible. Secrecy is perceived positively and negatively, depending on the specific issue in question. Moreover, secret knowledge does not appear to be a major concern for Abū Rāʾiṭa. He only relates to the issue when pressed, and the theme is only treated in connection with other more pressing issues.

The flexible approach to secrecy and concealment is clearly expressed in *The Proof*:

> And this [occurred] because the staff [of Moses] bore the greatest *mysterion* (*sirr*) of the staff which was to come in the Cross, through which the people of the world would be delivered. For this is the customary practice of God, from the first to the last [peoples], in the establishment of His religion and erecting His banner and affirming His proof for His creation: Correction through signs and clarification through miracles, which are not comprehended by creaturely understanding and are not located in the memory of a created heart, [it is] not in the many opinions, nor eloquent speech, nor the strength and courage [of human beings as], as I have described.[14]

A more straightforward translation of the Arabic word '*sirr*', which Keating translates in this passage as '*mysterion*', is, as we have seen above, 'secret'. In this context, it is a rather paradoxical kind of secret. First, Abū Rāʾiṭa makes clear that what links Moses and Christ is the greatest secret, which is contained in both the staff and the cross; second, it is a secret that delivers 'the people of the world'; third, it is, in return, a secret that is only understood by the few.

Revelation

Whereas Abū Rāʾiṭa treats concealment in a flexible way, he is far more consistent in his attitude to revelation. In the passage considered above, he emphasises that God intervenes in the world in order to correct, an act that takes place by the use of 'signs and clarification through miracles'. This emphasis on signs and miracles as clear proofs is a

13 *On the Incarnation*, par. 64-65.

14 *The Proof*, par. 14.

reoccurring theme in his Arabic apologetic writings. Thus, in *The Proof*, he concludes a long line of arguments for the truthfulness of Christianity by stating:

> Since it has been shown that the Christian law differs from [these] six kinds [of false reasons to belong to a religion], it remains that the characteristic of it, the inherent property belonging to it, is that it is evident and demonstrated to be above every religion by the confirmation of the Lord of the Worlds, Who confirmed with it those who proclaimed [the Christian law] through signs and miracles and clear proofs (*āyāt al-muʿǧizāt wa-l-barāhīn al-wāḍiḥāt*) which led all of the peoples to accept it willingly.[15]

In Abū Rāʾiṭa's explanation of why Christianity initially gained acceptance, he emphasises that this happened because those who proclaimed Christianity, did so by providing 'signs and miracles and clear proofs'. Below in the treatise he gives concrete examples of these clear proofs. He explains that Christ's followers:

> [...] gave life to the death in His name, they opened [the eyes] of the blind by His permission and healed the lepers by His strength, and [performed] other wonders by His power, and visible and perceptible marvels (*aʿāǧib al-mubṣirāt aẓ-ẓāhirāt*) that no one is able to reject, be he king or servant, high-born or low-born, educated or ignorant, wise or foolish.[16]

Again, the focus is on the fact that Christianity spread because people of all kinds personally witnessed visible and perceptible marvels and believed. Hence, 'the visible and perceptible marvels' constitute a focal argument for the truthfulness of Christianity.

Moreover, below, he reassures his readers that Christian doctrines, in the case of the incarnation, are from God and thus that they are not doctrines simply developed by Christians:

> There are other statements besides these in all of the prophets which, if we were to give a citation of them, would make the pages longer and many. [Our opponents] should know that our teaching of [the Incarnation] is from the Books sent down by God (*kutub Allāh munazzala*) or those who transmitted them, and this is not fabrication by us or an innovation.[17]

Christian teachings rest on revelation, in the form of books 'sent down by God'. This indicates that Abū Rāʾiṭa is eager to show non-Christians that Christian teachings, in fact, are derived from books, known to all who believe in God, and do not stem exclusively from Christian circles.

---

15 *The Proof*, par. 9.

16 *The Proof*, par. 10.

17 *The Proof*, par. 37.

To sum up, Abū Rā'iṭa defends Christianity not by focusing on secret knowledge in the sense of concealed knowledge, but as knowledge understood as something that is hard to perceive. Moreover, he only admits that God acts secretly in rare cases, and defends the practice by referring to God's compassion. Instead, he is far more eager to use revelation as support for Christianity, and he stresses how visible and clear the proofs are for the trustworthiness of Christianity.

Why, then, this attitude to revelation and concealment? Does it tell us something, specifically, about Christians living in the early Islamic period?

Early Islam[18]

The Challenge from Islamic Prophetology

In a passage quoted above,[19] we encountered the idea of revelation as books that are 'sent down' (*munazzala*) by God.[20] This is a widespread way of referring to revelation in the *Qur'ān*.[21] However, the resemblance between Abū Rā'iṭa's notion of revelation and the *Qur'ān*'s goes even further.

An inevitable part of the *Qur'ānic* notion of revelation is prophethology.[22] The basic feature of *Qur'ānic* prophetology is that, throughout history, God has sent out prophets, determined *nabī* and *rasūl*, in a sequential pattern, each to his own people. Each prophet is sent out with the message of God to warn the people about the last day and lead them back to God's religion. However, instead of welcoming the prophet, the people encounter the prophet with hostility, after which God punishes the people. In *On the Incarnation*, Abū Rā'iṭa alludes to this constellation of ideas in the following passage:

> To be sure, He sent [to the people] some, such as Noah, Abraham, Moses, and other prophets (*anbiyā'*) and messengers (*rusul*), but each one of them was a warner to his people in his own time. But all of [the people] did not follow [the

18 'Early Islam' should not be taken too rigidly as referring to a single coherent belief system. However, this is not the place to go into detail regarding the differentiations within the early Islamic community.

19 From *The Proof*, par. 37.

20 The same terminology is used in *The Proof*, par. 12: 'The proof of this is the statement of God, may He be praised! to his intimate friend, Moses, when he begged Him to save the Sons of Israel from the hand of Pharaoh and from the error of his people, from his enslavement and oppression of them with every painful torment, and to reveal to them His religion and send down (*'inzāl*) to them His book with His practices and His law by His [own] hand in mercy to them here [on this earth]'.

21 The Arabic root is *N-Z-L*, which in form II and IV means 'send down' or simply 'reveal'. In the *Qur'ān*, the formulation 'send down', used about a book, books or the *Qur'ān* is widespread. See e.g. the following verses: 2.176, 3.3, 4.136, 4.140, 4.153, 7.196, 16.89, 17.93, 39.23.

22 The following description of *Qur'ānic* prophetology is based on Rubin 2004 and Zwettler 1990.

prophet], they only followed him a little for a short time, then they returned to what they were before, being overpowered by error.[23]

The close resemblance between Abū Rāʾiṭas prophetology and that of the *Qurʾān* suggests that Abū Rāʾiṭa had either direct or indirect knowledge of the *Qurʾān*.

Based on this comparison, it seems appropriate to suggest that Abū Rāʾiṭa's notions of prophetology and revelation were informed and shaped by Islamic notions. Moreover, his treatment of revelation is probably not a mere reinforcement of Christian prophetology from pre-Islamic times. The very fact that Abū Rāʾiṭa deals substantively with prophetology is remarkable. Thus, as S. Stroumsa has shown, Christian interest in prophetology was low in pre-Islamic times.[24] The fact that it becomes a topic of great concern to Christians living under early Islamic rule, is remarkable, and calls for an explanation.

S. Stroumsa's main explanation goes as follows:

> With the rise of Islam the scene changed drastically. Since Muhammad had claimed to be a prophet, and since this claim had been rejected by both Jews and Christians, the traits that distinguish a true prophet from a false one at once became a key issue.[25]

According to S. Stroumsa, Islamic occupation with establishing Muḥammad as the genuine prophet prompted Christians to come up with a reliable 'proof of prophecy'.[26] Along with S. Stroumsa's explanation, I would argue that Islamic emphasis on the *Qurʾān* as the ultimate revelation, God's actual words to Man, might have prompted Christians to accentuate their notion of revelation at the expense of concealment. The *Qurʾān*, being a strong and visible argument for Islam, made Christians like Abū Rāʾiṭa reshape their notion of revelation and prophetology, emphasising that revelation takes the form of books that are sent down by God. Moreover, the focus is on the performance of wonders and miracles, the visual expression of God's work in the world.

In this regard, it is noteworthy that Abū Rāʾiṭa is not alone in focusing on the visibility of signs and wonders as criterion for the trustworthiness of one's religion in the early 9th century. To give two examples, we find this idea in the apologetic works of the Chalcedonian ('Melkite') theologian Theodore Abū Qurra (mid-8th century – after AD 816), and the Islamic theologian ʿAlī ṭ-Ṭabarī (c. AD 780-c. 860), who was a convert from Christianity.

The latter devotes an entire chapter of his *The Book of Religion and Empire* (*Kitāb ad-*

---

23 *On the Incarnation*, par. 24.

24 Stroumsa 1985, 105.

25 Stroumsa 1985, 105.

26 Stroumsa 1985, 109.

dīn wa-d-dawla)[27] to the miracles of the true prophet, in which the author has gathered various stories which all contain evidence of miraculous deeds committed by Muḥammad together with evidence of how the miracles have been testified. In a concluding remark, he states:

> What can a man say against these miracles, while the Ḳur'ān mentions them and the Muslim community bears witness to their veracity, and all its members subscribe to their authenticity, and men and women converse about them? If, while they are contained in the Ḳur'ān, it is allowed to consider them as false and revile them, we will not believe the adversaries who say that the Torah and the Gospel do not contain falsehood to which the eyewitnesses of events had deliberately shut their eyes. If then this cannot be said about the Torah and the Gospel and their contemporaries, it is not allowed with regard to the Ḳur'ān and its holders.[28]

It is remarkable that ʿAlī ṭ-Ṭabarī attempts to prove the miracles of the *Qurʾān* by implying that if people accept the miracles described in the Torah and Gospel on account of 'the eyewitnesses of the events', the descriptions of miracles found in the *Qurʾān* are equally reliable. The implication appears to be that to ʿAlī ṭ-Ṭabarī and his non-Islamic counterparts visual perception of miracles was considered an important element in the verification of truth claims.

Abū Qurra also stresses that persuasion of people via the performance of wonders is an important criterion for the verification of a prophet. In *Against the Jews*[29] he compares Jesus and Moses:

> The Jews were less justified in accepting Moses than were the Gentiles in accepting Christ … The Gentiles were content with wonders they saw Christ's disciples

27 As for this text, I rely entirely on the translation of the text by A. Mingana (1922). Unfortunately, I have not had access to the manuscript on which A. Mingana bases his translation. On the manuscript, see Mingana 1922, xvi-xxi.

28 *The Book of Religion and Empire* (Mingana 1922, 38).

29 This text is the first part of a lengthy treatise, named *Treatise on the confirmation of the holy law of Moses and the prophets who prophesied about Christ and the holy Gospel which was transmitted to the nations by the disciples of Christ, born of the pure Mary, and on the confirmation of the orthodoxy that people attribute to Chalcedonianism and the refutation of every religious community that lays claim to Christianity other than this community* (*Maymar fī taḥqīq nāmūs Mūsā l-muqaddas wa-l-anbiyāʾ allaḏina tanabbaʾū ʿalā al-Masīḥ wa-l-Inǧīl aṭ-ṭāhir allaḏī naqalahu ilā l-umam talāmīḏ al-Masīḥ al-mawlūd min Miryam al-ʿaḏrāʾ wa-taḥqīq al-urṯūḏuksīya llatī yansubuhā n-nās ilā l-Ḫalkīdūnīya wa-ibṭāl kull milla tattaḫiḏu n-Naṣrānīya siwā hāḏī l-milla*). As J.C. Lamoreaux has pointed out (2005, xxxii-i), the text's two parts were probably two independent texts, which have been joined in transmission. Following J.C. Lamoreaux, I treat the first part as an independent text using the English title given by J.C. Lamoreaux (2005), *Against the Jews*. I quote from J.C. Lamoreaux's translation (2008, 27-39) and refer to Quṣtanṭīn Bāšā's edition (B) of the Arabic text (Bāšā 1905, 7-16). Page numbers refer to Lamoreaux and Bāšā, respectively.

> performing in his name. This was enough to summon them to accept Christ and have faith in everything that he himself said and that his disciples said about him. … The situation is analogous to what happened when Moses came to the children of Israel: They believed him and accepted what he related to them from God, solely because of the wonders he performed among them.[30]

Abū Qurra's argument for why the Gentiles were more justified in accepting Jesus than the Jews were in accepting Moses is that the former both performed wonders (or had people performing wonders in his name) and was prophesied, whereas Moses only performed wonders.[31] However, along the way he reassures his readers that the performance of wonders is an adequate proof:

> So too, the Gentiles would be permitted to believe and trust Christ on account of the innumerable wonders that he himself performed and his disciples performed in his name – even if Moses and the prophets had not prophesied him.[32]

The wonders performed by Jesus and his disciples, and the subsequent acceptance of the Gentiles, make Christianity reliable.

This comparison of these three authors shows that the performance of wonders together with the visual perception of wonders was an important *topos* in apologetic literature in the early Islamic period. This suggests that the ability to provide 'visual' proofs was crucial if you wanted to be taken seriously in interreligious dialogues. This is likely to explain why Christians stressed revelation rather than concealment in the early Islamic period. The challenge that lay in front of them was that there was no time for secrets, when all that counted was clear and visible proof.

From Majority to Minority

A further explanation is that during the 9th century people in the Near East converted to Islam in large numbers to a point where Islam, within a few generations, went from being a minority religion to being the majority religion. Christians, in return, went from being the majority in the pre-Islamic period and way into the early Islamic period to becoming a minority.[33] In this situation, Christian apologists would most likely face

30 *Against the Jews*, 30/B9-10.

31 *Against the Jews*, 31/B10.

32 *Against the Jews*, 30/B10.

33 Needless to say, it is difficult to get precise statistics indicating the relative size of different religious communities in the early Islamic period. R.W. Bulliet, on whose study I base my assessment of the development, bases his estimate on the change in naming reflected in biographical material (Bulliet 1979). In referring to the Near East in this context, I lump together R.W. Bulliet's analysis of the situation in Iraq and Syria (see Bulliet 1979, 78-91, 104-13). The methodology is not without weaknesses. As R.W. Bulliet has pointed out in a later article, one of the problems inherent in basing conversion estimates on name-giving is that both Christians and Jews may have had Arabic names without having converted to Islam, and that not all Muslims necessarily

Muslims who had been Christians or who knew fellow Muslims who had been Christians. In such a situation it would hardly be convincing to focus on the secret nature of Christianity in order to attract new followers or lead lost members back into the flock, as they would know about these 'secrets' already. Instead, it was far more reasonable to enter into a discussion about revelation. Either to remind former Christians about why Christians had the right idea about God and his message, or because this was a question that appealed to Muslims because they showed substantial interest in the matter.

Concluding Remarks

Having taken Abū Rāʾiṭa as a representative of general trends in the early Islamic period, it has become clear that Christian attitudes to secrecy *vis-à-vis* Islamic teachings had a certain accentuation. Christians were far more concerned with the knowledge of God as revealed than concealed. Concealment as *topos* and strategy seems to have been unattractive to Christians in the early Islamic period.

As for possible explanations of why the emphasis was put on revelation at the expense of concealment, we have arrived at two conclusions. Either it was the challenge that the Islamic notion of Muḥammad's prophethood posed to the Christians that made them focus on revelation and prophetology; or it was because a strategy of concealment made no sense in a context where Christians, when defending Christianity, often would face former Christians or someone who knew former Christians. These explanations are not mutually exclusive, and work in concordance with one another. Thus, we should not forget that the *Qurʾān* and Islamic prophetology made sense to Christians to some extent because they referred to many figures and narratives which, in slightly different forms, were known from pre-Islamic, Christian traditions. This shared cultural setting of the 8th and 9th centuries AD was no place to be hiding behind secret knowledge. Whether Christians were facing Muslims who had been Christians or Muslims who had not, they would, to some degree, share knowledge of one another's religious ideas. What was needed in this situation was an ability to clearly prove that one had the right notion of that shared knowledge.

Consequently, this study indicates that the ability to defend one's religion in the right way was an equally important aspect of Christian-Islamic disputes of the 8th and 9th centuries AD, besides the topics in question. Not only were religious rivals fighting about the right definition of God and other related matters. The very criteria by which people disputed were being defined and negotiated.

---

bore Arabic names (Bulliet 1990, 128). In addition, M.G. Morony (1990) has shown that R.W. Bulliet's calculations of conversion patterns, in some regions of the Islamic Empire, are partly falsified when tested upon source material different from R.W. Bulliet's biographical material, for instance literary sources. (For a similar approach, see Haddad 1990). Nevertheless, R.W. Bulliet's book still offers a valuable, tentative picture of conversions to Islam in the Middle Ages, and remains a useful 'heuristic devise' (see Morony 1990, 140-7) for asserting patterns of conversion to Islam in the Middle Ages.

Finally, the study suggests that the notion of secrecy has a supple nature. Whether it is beneficial for a (religious) community to stress either revelation or concealment is dependent on the specific historical context. In the early Islamic period, Christians remained a majority religion, quantitatively speaking, but only for a while. As a result, Christians had an impetus to articulate their teachings lucidly if they wanted to maintain the position they were about to lose.

BETWEEN PUBLIC AND PRIVATE

SIGNE KRAG

The Secrets of the Funerary Buildings in Palmyra during the Roman Period

When approaching the ancient city of Palmyra, one is immediately met with large, scattered heaps of stones and partially preserved structures. These merely give a slight impression of the spectacular funerary buildings that once occupied the surroundings of Palmyra. The buildings housed the bodies, grave goods and funerary portraits of deceased inhabitants from the city. Inscriptions have been recorded which refer to the funerary buildings as 'the house of eternity' – the eternal house for the deceased. But who had access to these eternal resting places other than the deceased? In this article the questions of the funerary sphere and secrecy will be explored through space, architecture, portraits and rituals.

The seminar on secrecy was an outstanding opportunity to explore how the funerary buildings in the Roman world should be understood in terms of space and secrecy, in this case in Palmyra. Even more significant: what secrets did they keep in their own time of use, and to a lesser degree what secrets do they hold in the present time? The aim of this paper is to explore the secrets concealed and revealed by the funerary buildings and their respective owners – as far as this is possible. This will be evaluated through notions of space and visibility.

Palmyra and Its Funerary Buildings

Palmyra is located in modern Syria with the Mediterranean Sea located to the west and the Euphrates River to the east. The city expanded drastically during the Roman period – especially in the 1st and 2nd century AD, when it became a large agricultural and administrative city, although it was primarily a large trading city. The city was plundered, burned and destroyed in AD 273 by the legions of Emperor Aurelian following the dramatic events in the reign of Queen Zenobia who expanded the Palmyrene territory into the Roman.

The funerary buildings in Palmyra were generally located along the main thoroughfares running to and from the city at its northern, western and southern borders (Fig. 1). This can especially be seen in the Valley of the Tombs situated west of Palmyra, where

Fig. 1. *Funerary buildings in Palmyra (copyright: Rubina Raja).*

the highest frequency of funerary buildings is found. The buildings are composed of towers, *hypogea*, temples and houses, where the earliest dated is the tower of Atenatan from 9 BC located in the Valley of the Tombs.[1] Within the buildings there was an elaborate display of funerary portraits of males and females as well as children. Both sarcophagi, banquet reliefs, *loculi* reliefs, *stelae*, statues and wall paintings held portraits. The different media were frequently derived from Greek and Roman types and through an exchange of knowledge and ideas the inhabitants of Palmyra had come to include these in their funerals. However, I would argue that the traditions of portraits and the iconographic elements were either developed locally or included following local interpretations which incorporated local logic, taste, needs and identities.[2] As a result, the portraits give a valuable insight into how Palmyrenes perceived themselves formulated in the funerary space.

Secrecy

'All relationships of people to each other rest, as a matter of course, upon the precondition that they will know something about each other'.[3] This sentence in an article by G. Simmel captures the essence of secrecy: secrecy can only exist if there is a relationship (something known, knowledge) between two or more individuals. The parties involved in any relationship reveal themselves to each other by their words and their mere existence.[4] This also applies to the materialisation of a society, where something can be intentionally or unintentionally hidden which is then intentionally or unintentionally known and respected.[5] However, the whole concept of secrets lies in the act of revealing

1 See Will 1951; Gawlikowski 1970, 45; Henning 2013, 14.

2 Previous research has often approached the portraits as strongly and directly derived from either Western or Eastern traditions, see e.g. Ingholt 1954; Franz 1987; Schmidt-Colinet 1997.

3 Simmel 1906, 441.

4 Simmel 1950, 307.

5 Simmel 1950, 330.

the possession of a secret without revealing the secret itself.[6] Following this, the secret itself might not always be the most significant element. Instead, knowledge and the right to participate in and subsequently to reveal such secrets may be more important.[7] Moreover, secrecy is also a product of various elements which together create the secrets, hence there are multiple layers to a secret, multiple layers to revealing and concealing.[8]

Within archaeology the discussion of secrecy has often focused on space as well as spatial and visual restrictions.[9] Secrecy is socially and culturally constructed and should therefore be considered in the context through which it arose. Within archaeology this can be studied through the materiality of a space that is available to us today, which can be further supported by literary sources. In this paper, space is used to emphasise and reveal aspects of secrecy, but also to examine how secrecy came to play a role in the funerary space created by the implications of this space and the reverse.[10] Through the monumentality of the funerary buildings and also through the portraits a visual scheme of secrecy in terms of, for example, concealment and containment together with strong proclamations of ownership of secrets can be observed.[11] When approaching secrecy through space, the spectra of private and public become interesting and these are aspects which will be considered in the following section. Especially interesting are the aspects of privacy and secrecy in relation to each other, and how these at certain points could reinforce each other, overlap and eventually be mutually initiating.[12] However, private aspects need not be secret, and secrecy need not be private. In this paper, the concept of secrecy is therefore used in relation to public and private spaces to reveal the dynamics between these, and how the different elements and performances within the spaces could ultimately generate knowledge kept from others.

The Landscape: Public and Private Spaces

More recent research on the funerary contexts in the Roman world has focused on the buildings as elaborate displays of status, but also as expressions and affections of beliefs about the afterlife, memory, and personal grief and emotions concerning the deceased, relatives and patrons.[13] The Palmyrene funerary portraits were essentially located inside funerary buildings behind large, dense walls or even in the underground *hypogea*, and could be positioned very high within the buildings. These locations as well as the rituals

6 Bellman 1981, 139-44; Nooter 1993, 24; Blakely 2012, 50.

7 Nooter 1993, 23; Piot 1993, 357.

8 On the concept of secrecy, see Bowden and Wright in this volume.

9 See e.g. Cummings 2003, 25-44; Hastorf 2007, 97-9.

10 See Blakely 2012, 49.

11 See Nooter 1993, 24-5.

12 See e.g. Bok 1982, 10-3.

13 See e.g. Hope 2003, 113-37; Cummings 2003, 32-9; Carroll 2006, 30-1, 279; 2011, 65-9; Fejfer 2008, 106; Birk 2013, 9.

and the emotional displays in the portraits reveal that the function of the space, both internal and external, might not be as simple and approachable as is frequently assumed.

H. Lefebvre reconsidered the question of space and wrote that a social space is: 'the outcome of a sequence and sets of operations, and this cannot be reduced to the rank of a simple object'.[14] Thus, a social space is not related to one object alone, but it holds all of the elements and situations within it, and become the result of various social processes. Following the triad of space, this is composed of a material aspect, a mental aspect and a social aspect; the conceived, the perceived and the lived.[15] As argued by various scholars, places and landscapes generated human experiences and emotions and for us to comprehend and reconstruct certain aspects of these we need to understand the multiple and ambiguous implications of a specific space.[16] There already exists a rather large amount of publications on space within Roman scholarship through the studies of private and public spaces, for example, in Ostia and Pompeii, and here especially with a focus on the domestic space and movement.[17] The aspects of space determine how elements located within a specific space are to be interpreted and conceived in a given society at different points in time.[18] Here the separate spheres of private and public are rather useful analytic tools. Public and private aspects are very different, and the agenda and understanding of, for example, buildings and portraits also vary in these spaces – created by different social and cultural implications.

However, as argued by A. Wallace-Hadrill the aspects of private and public are not simply black and white, but rather a spectrum ranging from public to private in relation to the surrounding landscape and the elements within a specific space.[19] In a private space there are rules affecting the accessibility, rules created by the people in 'control' of the space, and also the space itself can generate privacy. Moreover, one could argue that these rules produced and contained secrets bound to a private space, because not everyone could enter and be a part of it. It is, however, not only a question of physically entering or accessing a space, but also entering or accessing other individuals' memory, emotions and so forth which were stored within a particular space or objects contained by this space. It is exactly here that the concept of secrecy is useful. The variations created by public and private spaces in Palmyra can, for instance, be documented in the portrait sculpture, where females are much more frequent and elaborate in the funerary space. The same thing does not apply in the civic and religious spaces. So the method of dividing the world into public and private in terms of objects and relations appear

14 Lefebvre [1974] 1991, 73.

15 Although H. Lefebvre's definitions are somewhat overlapping they do reveal how a space is both spatial and representational, but thereto a space also holds a lived dimension further nuanced by e.g. L. Pugalis (Lefebvre [1974] 1991; Pugalis 2009, 80).

16 See e.g. Thomas 1996, 83-91; Cummings 2003, 29; Brück 2005, 45-72; Tilley 2010, 25-31.

17 See e.g. Wallace-Hadrill 1994; Laurence & Wallace-Hadrill 1997; Laurence & Newsome 2011.

18 See e.g. Attfield 2000, 179.

19 Wallace-Hadrill 1994, 17-37.

Internal banquet relief, Ny Carlsberg Glyptotek IN 1159 and IN. 1160 (copyright: Palmyra Portrait Project. Courtesy of Ny Carlsberg Glyptotek). **Fig. 2.**

to be very advantageous in Palmyra in order to explain differences between the various spaces in the city landscape.

The Funerary Buildings

The funerary buildings were most frequently located along the main thoroughfares outside the city and as Palmyra was a large trading city, traffic on those thoroughfares must have been frequent with people slowly passing the large buildings either walking or sitting on the backs of camels. The buildings were then unavoidably part of a public visual display because people had unlimited visible access to them as they travelled to and from the city, but they were still separated from the city of the living.

Function and Visual Appearance

The external surface of the buildings – the ones visible above ground – including funerary towers, temples, houses and part of the entrances to *hypogea*, could occasionally display reliefs which portrayed the founder of a building accompanied by their relatives (Fig. 2).

These were banquet reliefs, and the founder was portrayed reclining on a *klinē* with his family standing in the background, as can be seen in a relief dating to AD 40 from the tower of Kitôt.[20] Here the founder is portrayed reclining together with his son, where his wife, another son and a servant are standing in the background. In addition, foundation inscriptions were often located on the outside of the funerary buildings.[21] They identified the founder or founders of the funerary buildings, the date when they were founded, and frequently they held a dedication of the buildings to relatives and descendants. This also included cession texts recording the sale and transfer of entire buildings, or more often sections of the buildings.[22] The foundation inscriptions were frequently located next to or below possible founder reliefs, on door-lintels or door jambs. They give the most detailed picture of different families in Palmyra, often recording many generations of ancestors and thereby underlining the importance of their function in producing a memory of and highlighting specific families and their family burial shrines.[23] Cession texts, on the contrary, were often small and could be located beneath the foundation inscriptions, on door-lintels, on door jambs, or on limestone plaques set into the walls of the graves. However, they could be situated both external and internal, and therefore they were not as consistent a part of the external display as the foundation inscriptions.[24] Through the architecture, foundation inscriptions, banquet reliefs and cession texts, but also through the funerary buildings' chosen locations in the landscape, the founder or founders proclaimed their legitimacy and ability to afford elaborate funerary buildings for themselves and their families. At the same time they expressed a concern for the afterlife of their relatives as well as an interest in establishing an everlasting memory: a continuation of their familial relationship.[25] This is especially evident in the display of families in banquet reliefs, and through the recording of 'for his sons and the sons of his sons forever' in many of the foundation inscriptions.[26]

During the 3rd century AD a striking re-interpretation of the funerary sphere can be traced in Palmyra, when some funerary buildings were erected inside the city walls. Funerary temples, such as no. 86 and 173d, were erected within the urban area of Palmyra, as opposed to the norm of erecting them outside the city walls.[27] The buildings were situated on the colonnaded streets; funerary temple no. 86 was, for instance, located at the intersection of the Large Colonnade Street and the Transverse Colonnade Street. Thus, it appears that space was re-evaluated during this period, and these funerary buildings were strategically situated in a public display within the urban centre, emphasising

20 Will 1951, 70-100; Colledge 1976, 64.

21 For a more comprehensive work and transcription of the foundation inscriptions, see Hillers & Cussini 1996.

22 See Hillers & Cussini 1996.

23 Piersimoni, 1995, 256.

24 Cussini 1995, 235-6.

25 See e.g. Cummings 2003, 32-9; Carroll 2006, 30-1, 279; 2011, 65-9; Fejfer 2008, 106; Birk 2013, 9.

26 See Hillers & Cussini 1996.

27 Yon 2001, 179.

the strength of their functions as mediators of legitimacy, status and memory. They furthermore decreased the physical distance between the spaces of the living and dead, bringing the sphere of death into the city. Certainly, the funerary buildings were part of a visual public space with quite clear agendas, but only on the outside.

Accessing the Funerary Buildings

The foundation inscriptions and cession texts legally and physically located the buildings within the ownership of specific families and lineages. This is a strong indication of the fact that access to the funerary buildings was controlled by ownership and lineage regarding permission to be buried there. Inscriptions recording entire lineages on the funerary portraits located within the buildings also attest to this fact.[28] This demonstrates that funerary buildings could sometimes be occupied by one family alone. However, from the 2nd century AD sections of the buildings were more frequently sold to other families, with the result that several families shared the funerary space – something which is found recorded in the cession texts.[29]

These different families had access to the buildings where they would bury and visit their own lineages, but it can also be documented that the interior of the buildings, including the portraits, were exposed to a larger audience – at least when they were used by multiple families at the same time. Nevertheless, this could be interpreted in relation to, for example, the implications of absence and personal intentions, which has been exemplified in a study by T.F. Sørensen concerning modern Danish burial grounds.[30] Here it is clear that many aspects of a specific burial place will stay private, because although people have access to the burial places of others, both physically and visually, those burial places are private to the relatives and only they have full insight into the story, memory and emotions stored in and conveyed by them.[31] Thereby several aspects will be private and stay concealed in the meeting between a person and the burial place of an unfamiliar person, thus, making it quite clear that privacy is not only generated by physical aspects such as walls.[32]

Doors and Keys

The funerary buildings were sealed by doors. Many of these have been discovered, but only few have been discovered *in situ*.[33] Some have even been found with preserved locking mechanisms which indicate that their function was to seal off and lock the funerary buildings.[34] These doors were elaborately decorated, especially from the middle

28 See e.g. Sadurska & Bounni 1994; Yon 2002.

29 See Cussini 1995; 2005b.

30 Sørensen 2010.

31 See also Bok 1982, 11-2.

32 On the subject of personal intentions stored in grave markers, see Bargfeldt in this volume.

33 Ingholt 1935, 58-9; 1938, 93, 103, 106, 119; 1974, 37-8; Amy & Seyrig 1936, 258; Henning 2013, 31-2; Saito 2005, 158; Higuchi & Saito 2001, 16-8.

34 See e.g. Amy & Seyrig 1936, 231 pl. XXIX, 1-2; Ingholt 1938, 93, 119; Henning 2013, 31-2.

Fig. 3. *Possibly a female servant holding keys with the inscription* bt 'lm', *Ny Carlsberg Glyptotek IN 1065 (copyright: Palmyra Portrait Project. Courtesy of Ny Carlsberg Glyptotek).*

of the 1st century AD, and this decoration could only be displayed fully when the doors were closed.[35] The doors physically and symbolically separated the public and private aspects of the graves, concealing the inside from public display and accumulating secret denotations. This gave the inside a more private character because it could be – and perhaps always was – sealed off from the public and only accessible to the holders of the keys, the owners and their relatives. Thereto the inside and outside were separated by external lightness and internal darkness, aspects which were strengthened by the doors, with strong connotations to secrecy, as light illuminates and reveals whereas darkness conceals.

In relation to doors, the keys displayed in some funerary portraits are very interesting. The keys were held by females or attached to brooches worn by females (Fig. 3). A few of these keys carry inscriptions which sometimes record 'the house of eternity'

35 Henning 2013, 32.

(*bt ʿlm*ʾ), and this might reveal one of their symbolic aspects.[36] The funerary buildings are also called 'the house of eternity' in some foundation inscriptions and this has been connected with the similar inscriptions on some of the keys.[37] If 'the house of eternity' in both key inscriptions and foundation inscriptions refers to the same, it could, visually and symbolically, connect the funerary buildings and their doors with the keys and underline that access was reserved for people who had the opportunity to be buried there, their living relatives visiting the graves, and those to whom the ownership of the buildings was passed on – 'their son and the sons of sons'. Thereby the relationships and memories within the families could be reinforced eternally. The right to be buried in the buildings and have access to them were portrayed through images of women holding the keys, but the keys could also symbolise the access to the next world, the afterlife. The key as a mechanism for opening and closing doors has further ties to the whole concept of secrecy through its control of revealing and concealing. Other scholars have argued that the keys do not always hold the same meaning and that, for example, smaller keys were for jewellery boxes and were carried by females to symbolise domestic values and wealth instead of being connected with the ownership of property.[38] However, the keys with the inscription 'the house of eternity' should clearly be connected with the buildings.

Funerary Rituals

Within some of the buildings, semi-circular water basins composed of soil covered with plaster and bases of vessels have been discovered, located in front of one relief or large groupings of reliefs.[39] The *hypogea* sometimes had a well placed on the right side of their inner entrance, most likely supplying the internal basins with water.[40] In buildings with wells and water basins it can be inferred that libation, or even purification rituals, took place.[41] Furthermore, many lamps were deposited within the funerary buildings in front of specific graves, although they were probably not used continuously because their wicks were often only partially covered with soot.[42] They were only used in a specific ritual, which was very likely connected to a specific ancestor due to their placement. In addition, incense burners positioned in front of some of the sarcophagi have been

36 See e.g. Hvidberg-Hansen & Ploug 1993, 135, IN 1065.

37 See e.g. Ingholt 1935, 60, 75, 109, 115; 1938, 120-121; Böhme & Schottroff 1979, 28; Henning 2013, 85-6.

38 See e.g. Parlasca 1988, 216-20; Balty 1996, 438.

39 Higuchi & Saito 2001, 23, 27, 43.

40 Higuchi & Saito 2001, 20-1; Saito 2005, 158.

41 The research on funerary contexts and rituals is rather comprehensive including works such as Bell 1992; Parker Pearson 1999; Tarlow 1999; Hope 2003, 116-7; Levy 2006a, 12-3; Kyriakidis 2007. Since the 1970s and 1980s, it has been argued that burials are not direct or passive reflections of deceased individuals, but aspects of the society could be negotiated as well as relationships between the relatives and/or the ancestors (See e.g. Hodder 1985, 2; Parker Pearson 1999, 84; Gillespie 2001, 77-8).

42 Higuchi & Saito 2001, 40, 43-4; Saito 2005, 158.

discovered, connecting their usage with specific portraits, and therefore possibly with specific ancestors as well.[43] The evidence implies that burial customs took place in which the descendants would commemorate and mourn their deceased through rites of libation as well as fire and incense burning and that these were repeated and ritualised throughout time. Descendants could return to visit the resting places of their dead ancestors. These resting places also served as places in which the family physically, visually and mentally could gather across different generations. Here they could actively remember and continue their relationships, but in a sphere of privacy.[44] The people who accessed the funerary buildings were strongly motivated by the agenda of commemorating their deceased ancestors and, thus, their own lineage.[45] I presume that the rituals, emotions and experiences were shared between the closest descendants in each case, and these experiences and emotions were connected to and stored within the buildings, although we do not have any direct evidence supporting this.

Emotions[46] have been a focus of study within archaeology in the recent decades, especially within funerary contexts.[47] L. Nilsson Stutz argues that the emotions gave the ritual actions meaning, force and memorability, and movement within the space was an aspect of this.[48] But emotions were also mediated by the body visible in the funerary portraits, which I shall return to, and by the frequently recorded grief expression 'alas' (*ḥbl*) in the funerary inscriptions, which was a cultural and collective written response to death.[49] The rituals performed in each specific case, and the experiences and emotions shared by the specific family members became entangled in secrecy. As with funerals in general, families shared an experience: an emotional time of mourning and commemoration which was private to them.[50] The experiences and emotions were only shared between the closest relatives and their ancestors, who were close at hand through the portraits – underlining one of the functions of portraits as creating relationships as well as enhancing and continuing them.[51] It was essentially only meaningful to them and

43 Gawlikowski 1970, 179; Saito 2005, 33, 123-4.

44 See also Hope 2003, 116-7; Baker 2012, 24-5.

45 Kaizer 2010, 25.

46 Emotions are difficult to define and have been defined as both biological restricted and shared across various cultures and as following a constructivist definition in which emotions are culturally constructed and constituted, see Hope 2007, 173; Tarlow 2012, 170. I would argue, however, that emotions are a combination of the two with different nuances in different societies, needing contextual explanation, as also argued by various scholars, see e.g. Tarlow 1999; Kus 1992, 171-2.

47 See e.g.Thomas 2002, 37; Hope 2007, 172; Carroll 2006, 281. R. Rosaldo is claimed to truly have made archaeologists and anthropologists aware of the different emotional responses to funerary situations, not only including the emotion of grief (Rosaldo 1993, 2-21).

48 Nilsson Stutz 2007, 61.

49 See Derderian 2001, 3-14.

50 It has to be stressed that everyone participating cannot be assumed to have shared the same emotions and perhaps someone could even hold emotions such as relief or happiness which we would not generally connect with loss, see e.g. Tarlow 2012, 176.

51 See e.g. Tanner 2000, 18; Heyn 2010, 639.

not intended to be shared by society. As G. Cubitt has also argued, this experience or memory could not be repeated or re-experienced, and although it could be remembered and narrated, it could not be shared and was lost in translation.[52]

Portraits

As with all other aspects concerning the funerary buildings, the funerary portraits contained several layers generated by aspects of memory, emotions, sacredness and privacy.[53] It was all of these aspects that shaped the space and the visual expression of the portraits, and sometimes vice versa. The portraits became an everlasting image of individuals in their following afterlife and for their descendants in this world who preserved this memory with great care:[54] a memory of their existence and a memory reserved for the descendants as a family tree or shrine containing emotions and legitimacy. As previously noted, the funerary buildings in ancient Palmyra could be seen along the main thoroughfares, but the portraits were most frequently located inside the funerary buildings during the Roman period, hidden away behind the dense walls and large doors. *Necropoleis* composed of inhumation burials with portraits on freestanding *stelae* have been discovered in Palmyra, but they are rare, and, as previously argued, their location in an open space made them visible, but in several aspects not less private.[55]

An emotional display is visible in many of the portraits and their iconographies. For example, mothers, and rarely fathers, may accompany their adolescent or adult children, and either the child or the parent holds their arm around the other person. Sometimes really strong visual indicators of emotions through mourning can be seen with mothers accompanying their adolescent or adult children (Fig. 4). The mothers hold their arm around the person they accompany and can both accompany males and females.[56] The mothers have exposed chests or breasts and can have scratches on the arm and upper body. Emotions were in these scenes intensely mediated through the body – holding the other person and exposing the chest as well as one or both breasts – and through the recorded grief expression 'alas' (*ḥbl*) in the funerary inscriptions. Through the mourning gesture grief concerning the loss and pain caused by death were revealed, and by exposing the upper body, here connected to grief and frustration, a physical pain could also be portrayed through the scratches. It is certainly an aspect of the private funerary space and a display which was not meant to be seen in any other space. This truly reveals aspects of the portraits and the space: the emotions tied to death and loss whether they were grief, anger, fear, frustration or even physical pain inflicted on themselves to feel relief from the pain of grief or in an act of anger and frustration due to loss. In Palmyra

---

52 Cubitt 2007, 66.

53 On funerary portraits and their use as well as portraits in general, see e.g. Zanker & Ewald 2004, 179-201; Fejfer 2008, 105- 37; Birk 2013, 21, 39-44.

54 Carroll 2006, 30; Fejfer 2008, 105-37; Birk 2013, 9, 14-5.

55 Ingholt 1966, 460; Gawlikowski 1970, 34-40; Colledge 1976, 58.

56 See e.g. Ingholt 1928, 145, PS 468, 119, PS 252; 1934, 40-2, pl. X.1; Hvidberg-Hansen & Ploug 1993, 76, no. 31, IN 1084 and 132, no. 86, IN 1025; Heyn 2010, 646, app. 2, cat. 6.

Fig. 4. *Mourning mother with her daughter, Ny Carlsberg Glyptotek IN 1025 (copyright: Palmyra Portrait Project. Courtesy of Ny Carlsberg Glyptotek).*

the mourning gesture is only directed towards the child by its mother, and the hair of the mothers is most often only partly exposed: it is neither pulled by the females nor cut short.[57] The shoulder locks are common in the early portraits but disappear during the 2nd century AD. However, this is not the case with the mourning females: here the shoulder locks were kept in use. They were exposed to generate a further element to the mourning gesture, but the exposed hair was not used actively in the mourning performance – at least not in the portraits.

Moreover, a more religious aspect can be seen in portraits with a *dorsalium*, which is rendered as a piece of fabric most commonly pinned behind the deceased, thought to symbolise the separation of this world from the afterlife with strong allusions to

57 In several other locations, such as Rome, Athens and Egypt, the hair is usually a strong and active part in the mourning rituals performed by females, where it could be torn, cut or elsewise be included in the mourning to express emotions.

Fig. 5

Male with a dorsalium*, Ny Carlsberg Glyptotek IN 1052 (copyright: Palmyra Portrait Project. Courtesy of Ny Carlsberg Glyptotek).*

secrecy (Fig. 5).[58] These types of display are certainly only seen in the funerary space and are only appropriate within it. The portraits were not meant to be part of a public display, but were in themselves private – holding their own secrets, and suitable only for a closed off funerary space.

Civic and Religious Display

Finally, compared to the funerary space where females are portrayed in close to half of the portraits and mentioned in accompanying inscriptions, females are not very well represented through portraits and epigraphy in the civic and religious displays. Females' access to negotiating their identity was on the other hand much more restricted in the public display. They could rarely be the dedicators or beneficiaries of honorary sculptures and buildings, or have honorary sculptures dedicated to them.[59] In the funerary space, females were apparently deemed fitting to represent various values of a more personal and private character which were perhaps not needed in or appropriate for a public display. Females were portrayed in the funerary sphere with elaborate headgear, various attributes, decorated clothing and jewellery, something which rarely occurred in the

58 See e.g. Starcky 1952, 112; Gawlikowski 1970, 37-9; Böhme & Schottriff 1979, 28.

59 See e.g. Hillers & Cussini 1996, PAT 0293, 0300, 0315, 1933, 1429, 0280, 1495, 1506, 2748.

public display and never equally elaborate. This shows that the funerary portraits were located within a space where this sort of display was accepted, allowed and even needed. It should be noted that the display of females was much more elaborate in Palmyrene funerary contexts than can be observed in many areas of the Roman world, and this reflects the very unique implications of the funerary space and society in Palmyra.

Conclusion

The points discussed in this paper make it clear that the social and cultural implications of the funerary space shaped its secretive sphere and internal elements. The external appearance of the funerary buildings was meant for a visual public display, but the inside was a private space with restricted accessibility in both physical and physiological terms. It was not only the walls that had implications for the privacy and secrecy of the funerary buildings: it was very much also the memory, sacredness and emotions connected to this space. The inside held several aspects, such as commemoration and emotions, with ancestors being mourned and remembered within the family, and relationships continued. The display was only appropriate inside the funerary space and was never meant to be shared openly. The rituals, portraits and the space itself generated emotions and a variety of experiences. These emotions and experiences were secret to the families buried within as well as to those visiting the funerary buildings and belonging to their lineage. The secrets could not be retold – they were products of experiences that could not be shared with other groups in Palmyra because they existed in a sphere which was not shared by society: a sphere consisting of the privacy and secrecy of death and loss.

NIELS BARGFELDT

Lucius Iulius Optatus: A Salacious Doctor Revealed?

Even though Roman grave markers offer us valuable glimpses into the society in which they were created they also effectively conceal the actual character traits of the people behind the monuments because of their lauding habitual phrases. This concealment is strengthened by the very nature of intimacy between the deceased and the bereaved that the monuments themselves are an expression of, which is an inherent aspect of funerary culture in general. This article examines the grave marker of a frontier doctor that seemingly breaks the tradition of idealising the deceased and instead reveals a character trait that seems out of place in the funerary context.

In the Roman funerary context, we often find explicit references to the family and status of the deceased on the grave. This serves to position the deceased as well as the bereaved and the family within the community.[1] As such, grave markers are an important resource in understanding the social context of any given Roman site. However, it is important to realise that grave markers are products of a conscious and subconscious manipulation of actual circumstances designed to present an ideal or even aggrandised version of the deceased's life. It is not always easy to establish the extent to which the deceased's life has been idealised and unflattering character traits left out and hidden. To use a modern-day example, it is not possible to judge a person's character on the basis of his or her curriculum vitae alone; it is only with personal interaction that the person's character emerges and any 'inaccuracies' on his or her curriculum vitae is revealed. With an individual that died almost two thousand years ago, it is near impossible that we discover the reality of the person's character and, therefore, we have to trust the positive and idealised words of the grave marker saying that he or she was absolutely splendid. Because of this, it could be argued that grave markers and their epigraphy conceal and is in stark contrast to the notion of exposure and the act of revealing. On the other hand, is it really appropriate to consider epitaphs as deliberate concealment and thereby secrecy?

On funerary monuments, by choosing the right adjectives to go along with the (chosen) facts and by augmenting the whole monument with the appropriate imagery and setting, the desired effect of conveying social standing and family *concordia* can be

1 Carroll 2006, 30-2; Zanker 2010, 170-4; Birk 2013, 189.

achieved. Therefore, there can be little doubt that epitaphs (in general) deliberately leave out unflattering characteristics in favour of an idealised or 'best version' presentation of the deceased. This effectively means that information is withheld.[2] As argued elsewhere in this volume, we should be wary of an oversimplistic view on secrecy, where secrecy as a concept is reserved only for major news revelations.[3]

Furthermore, and just as important for the present article, even though gravestones (generally speaking) can seem plain and immediate, especially when what might seem like valuable elaboration on the given information is left out, they serve to affirm the intimate relationship between the deceased and the bereaved.[4] In effect, for the involved, they encompass the stories of a life lived and shared that are hidden to the random onlooker wandering by and reading the plain facts – such as name, age, occupation and family ties.

This means that grave monuments do involve both a conscious and subconscious concealment and that secrecy, therefore, can be a valuable consideration when dealing with such monuments, even though a grave (at least in the long run) seemingly ends the circle of concealing and revealing, sometimes seen as an inherent trait of secrecy.[5]

In this article, I present a monument that adopts an unusual approach to writing an epitaph (idealised, as they usually are) because, at first glance, the protagonist, Lucius Iulius Optatus, seems to be horribly exposed, yet, I will argue that there is more to this than meets the eye.

A Gravestone from the Banks of the Danube

The monument in question was discovered in 1961 in Petronell-Carnuntum, approximately 30 km east of Vienna in Austria. The piece is categorised as a grave marker of the altar or basis type. It is approximately one meter high and most likely had a base consisting of a few steps (Fig. 1).[6]

Like almost all gravestones from Carnuntum and the surrounding region, it is made of limestone. Owing to its irregular shape at the back, the stone does not form a regular square; instead, from above, it looks like an irregular hexagon. Considering the base and the top, this shape was the intended finished form of the monument. On its upper surface, there is a hole and a groove for a lead fastener that would have held a top part in place, and, on the back, there is an asymmetrical cavity about 20 cm wide. Along with the irregular shape, this cavity could suggest that the stone was placed in a recess in a retaining wall or larger monument.[7] The inscription on the front and the gravestone

2 See Bowden in this volume; Scheppele 1988, 12.

3 See Bowden in this volume.

4 Sørensen 2010, 127-8.

5 See Wright in this volume.

6 Betz 1963, 84.

7 Betz 1963, 84.

The gravestone of L. Iulius Optatus (photos by author. Copyright: State of Lower Austria – Archaeological Park Carnuntum, Bad Deutsch-Altenburg). **Fig. 1.**

type places it very broadly within the 2nd century AD.[8] The letters of the inscription are well-preserved and the inscription is easily legible. At first glance the writing may seem crude, but considering other epitaphs from Carnuntum it does not stand out and is neither particularly bad nor wonderful.[9] It reads as follows:

L IULIUS OP
TATUS MEDICUS
H I S E FUTUTOR
L IULIUS FAU
STUS DE SUO
FECI

Grave altars come in various shapes and sizes and are not always as imposing as the well-known versions located along the road towards Herculaneum outside the gates of Pompeii.[10] Most grave altars in the Danube region are considerably more modest.

8 Betz 1963, 86; Vorbeck 1980, 25; Genser 2005, 75.

9 For a gravestone for a veteran, see e.g. Lupa 225; *CIL* 3.11223. For a soldier, see e.g. Lupa 102; Genser 2005, 34. For a freedman doctor, see.e.g. Lupa 1783; Vorbeck 1980, no. 106.

10 Carroll 2006, 91-2.

The element that would have been attached to the top could have been a *pulvinus*, an elongated pyramid with a pinecone top, a relief or even a statue/statuette. It is therefore questionable whether the gravestone should be categorised as a grave altar. The odd hexagonal shape makes reconstruction of the missing upper element conjectural and whether or not it originally was intended as an altar or (statue) base must remain open.[11]

Currently the grave marker is housed in Hainburg Kulturfabrik in the storage facilities of the Carnuntum Museum, though it is listed in a fairly recent publication and in databases as being in the Kurpark in front of the Museum Carnuntinum in Bad Deutsch-Altenburg.[12]

A Provincial Capital and Legionary Garrison

In antiquity, Carnuntum was a major centre on the Roman Danube frontier, and at the beginning of the 2nd century AD, the site was made the capital of the newly established province of Pannonia Superior.[13] As such, Carnuntum housed the *praetorium* (headquarters) of the provincial governor and, during the reign of Hadrian, the town was elevated to the status of *municipium*. However, just as it had begun its Roman history as a military stronghold, above all, Carnuntum was a legionary garrison site. Notably, Carnuntum served as the headquarters for Marcus Aurelius during the Marcomannic Wars and, while serving as governor, Septimius Severus was hailed as Emperor at the site.[14]

Just like most legionary garrison sites on the northern frontier, the community at Carnuntum consisted of the actual legionary fortress as well as two geographically separated settlement areas. One settlement, termed *canabae legionis* or just *canabae*, developed outside the fortress walls, while a second settlement could be found approximately two kilometres away. The inhabitants of the settlements were a mixture of camp followers or sutlers – sometimes called *lixae*.[15] These could be merchants, soldier families, prostitutes, or anyone who wanted to, needed to or were forced to live in the vicinity of 6000 men with a regular salary. As well as these inhabitants, there would also have been members of the local peregrine population in the settlements. Over time, as the sites developed into important towns (and not simply military garrisons), a leading municipal class – present to a greater or lesser extent in other Roman cities – emerged.[16]

Despite the civilian urbanisation process, the legion had profound influence on its surroundings, for instance through veterans, family relationships between soldiers and civilians and daily trade between individuals from both spheres.[17] This close relationship between the military and civilian spheres combined with cultural encounters between

11 From now on it is simply called grave marker.

12 Genser 2005, 75; Lupa 1770.

13 Genser 2006, 78-9.

14 M. Aur. *Med.* 2.17; SHA *Sev.* 5.1; Kandler, Humer & Zabehlicky 2004, 18; Mócsy 1974, 139, 218.

15 Petrikovits 1991; Vishnia 2002.

16 Bargfeldt (forthcoming).

17 Franzen 2009.

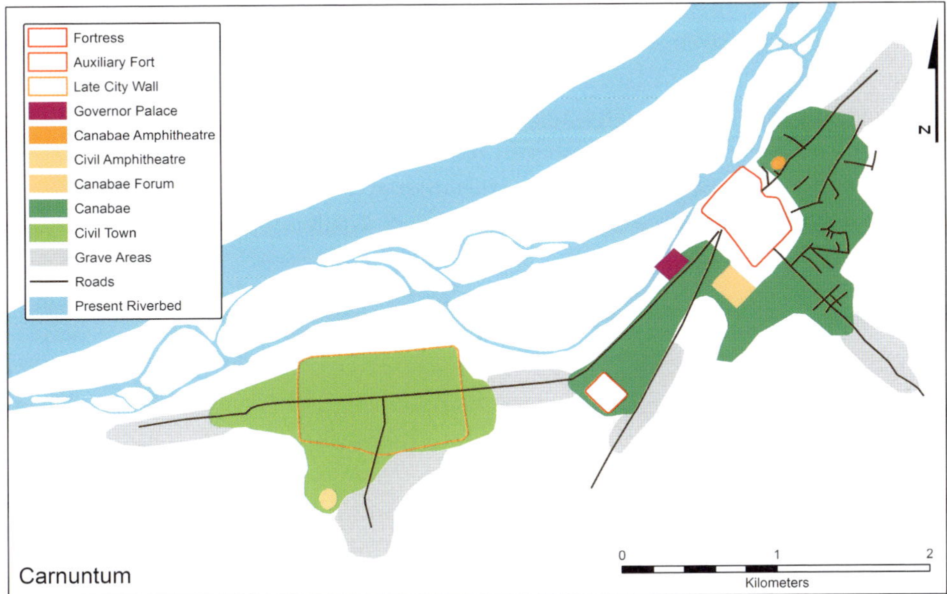

Plan of Carnuntum (plan by author). **Fig. 2.**

individuals from different parts of the Empire made the garrison communities places where existing norms and traditions were challenged and adapted.[18]

Just as at other towns, residents of the garrison communities were buried along the streets leaving the town limits. Yet, the often rapidly expanding settlements easily came to encroach on earlier grave sites and throughout antiquity graves were built over and gravestones reused. The grave marker in question was found together with a number of other graves situated along the so-called Gräberstraße running east-southeast from the canabae. At this point, the Gräberstraße ran south of an auxiliary fort placed between the canabae and the civil town to the west (Fig. 2).[19]

The fort was manned by different supporting units at different times. The grave marker itself was not discovered in its original setting but lay on its front against a wall running parallel to the street.[20] This repositioning had taken place already in antiquity.

A Gravestone for a Frontier Doctor

Let us now examine the abbreviated Latin inscription on the stone. This inscription can be confidently transcribed as: *L(ucius) Iulius Optatus medicus h(ic) i(ntus) s(itus) e(st) fututor L(ucius) Iulius Faustus de suo feci(t)*, which can be translated into English

18 Bargfeldt 2015.

19 Doneus, Gugl & Doneus 2013, 118, fig. 73, no. 1079.

20 Weiler 1963, 67.

as: Lucius Iulius Optatus – the doctor – is buried here – the fucker – Lucius Iulius Faustus – made this at his own expense.

Doctors were not rare at legionary garrison sites. Another example of an epitaph to a doctor from Carnuntum is an inscription plaque dedicated to a slave named Eucratus, who was a *medicus*.[21] Eucrates' master, L. Iulius Euthemus, was himself a *medicus* and took care of burying his deceased 25-year-old slave. The traditional view of Roman doctors has been that they were slaves, freedmen or Greeks, or all of the above.[22] Yet, as this last example illustrates, a *medicus* could also be a *dominus*. And having said this, the *dominus* in this case sports a full Roman *tria nomina*, which could signify that he was a full Roman citizen. However, at the edge of the Empire, name giving is a complex matter that does not necessarily render a clear-cut answer.[23]

One thing that does seem certain is that L. Iulius Optatus was not part of the legion per se, since military doctors in legions were usually styled as such in their inscriptions.[24] As a general rule, non-combatants enrolled in the legion were referred to as pertaining to the legion – *legionis*. This is the case irrespective of occupation, so it would apply to *medici* and, for instance, organ players.[25] In yet another inscription from Carnuntum, the beloved wife of a *pequarius legionis* is commemorated by her bereaved husband and her mother.[26] In this case, the title refers to her husband's duties as a caretaker of the animals of the legion, probably in the capacity as a kind of veterinarian.[27] However, those people not directly on the legion's payroll would have occasionally served under private contracts or sold services to the legion. At the same time, the individual soldiers may have sought the services of civilians in the surrounding settlements. Therefore, L. Iulius Optatus would most likely have treated both civilians and legionnaires.[28]

A Naughty Word

Though the word *fututor* is easily translated, its exact meaning and intent in the epitaph is not entirely clear. One of the main issues is which of the two men in the text can be considered to be 'the fucker'. Of course, the textbook example of an epitaph would often have the deceased in the dative case and the bereaved (who commissioned the stone) in the nominative case.[29] On the present stone, both men (as well as *fututor*) are in the nominative case. Therefore, the identity of 'the fucker' has to be determined in another way.

---

21 Lupa 1783; Breitwieser 1998, 60.

22 Jackson 1993.

23 Birley 1979, 15-8.

24 See e.g.: Lupa 3255; *CIL* 3.4279 (Brigetio). Lupa 10435 (Aquincum). Lupa 2841; *CIL* 3.14347 (Aquincum); Breitwieser 1998, 42-7.

25 An example of a legionary organ player can be found in Aquincum, Lupa 3025; *CIL* 3.10501.

26 Lupa 221.

27 Genser 2005, 17.

28 Breitwieser 1998, 59-60.

29 Keppie 1991, 106-7.

It might be logical to assume that *fututor* would be positioned closest to the person it describes and, therefore, that it describes Faustus, the bereaved – especially as *hic intus situs est* (is buried here) is placed between *medicus* and *fututor*. However, such logic cannot be applied directly to Roman funerary epigraphy. Yet, it is highly probable that both the deceased and the bereaved would be described in some way, since grave monuments served to position both within the social framework of the community. Descriptions usually consist of professions or social positions and formalistic remarks on personal qualities.[30] In the last case, this would usually be accompanied by a reference to the relationship between the deceased and the bereaved – for instance *filiae carissimae* (for the dearest daughter).[31] As an extension of this, the bereaved could describe their own unhappy circumstances, for instance with a phrase such as *pater infelix* (the unfortunate father).[32] Certain social groups appear in Roman epigraphy more often than others; in the frontier garrison communities, these groups are often the soldiers and veterans but also the frequently occurring *liberti* (freedmen).[33] As mentioned, Optatus occupied the position of *medicus* as a profession within the community, but it is unclear how *fututor* fits with this. For the sake of argument, it could be suggested that it is a profession or social standing, but it seems much more likely that 'the fucker' describes either the qualities of one of the men or something about the relationship between the two.

In the initial publication of the gravestone, A. Betz marvelled at the presence of the word 'fucker' and the wonder of being surprised yet again by the content of ancient epigraphy. In his translation, *fututor* became the German 'Beischläfer', implying that Faustus erected the stone for his homosexual partner Optatus. In addition to this, A. Betz speculated that 'Faustus der libertus des Optatus gewesen ist und diesem schon als Sklave zu Zwecken gedient hat, die das Appellativum fututor rechtfertigen'.[34] Although rather exceptional, this seems a neat and tidy reading of the text, and it was presented again in the 1980 and 2005 publications of (a selection of) inscribed stones from Carnuntum.[35] With this reading, *fututor* describes the relationship between the two men, so the general meaning remains largely the same regardless of whether it refers to Optatus or Faustus. However, this reading is not unproblematic and, in an article and a short exposé from 2006, *fututor* was translated literally as 'der Ficker' as a description of Optatus.[36]

In order to better understand the motivation for this, we first need to examine the known use of *fututor* in more detail. The word *fututor* comes from the verb *futuere*, and, although this can be translated simply as 'fuck', it carries a host of connotations and meanings. A translation closer to the actual meaning would be 'the male act of

30 Cooley 2012, 128-9.

31 See e.g. Lupa 3283; *CIL* 3.3666

32 See e.g. Lupa 3481; *CIL* 3.11045.

33 McMullen 1982, 238-9; Cooley 2012, 53-4

34 Betz 1963, 85-6. See also Selinger 2006a, 518.

35 Vorbeck 1980, no. 84; Genser 2005, 75.

36 Selinger 2006a; 2006b, 43.

sexual intercourse with a woman' and hence *fututor* would be the one performing the act of *futuere* – 'one who vaginally penetrates'.[37] In literature and graffiti, it is almost exclusively, though by no means entirely, used in a heterosexual context with the male playing the active role.[38] Otherwise, as J.N. Adams points out, the choice of word would likely be different.[39] This is illustrated by an obscene epigram by Martial. In this epigram, Augustus utters the following verse or jest:

> ... *quod futuit Glaphyran Antonius, hanc mihi poenam Fulvia constituit, se quoque uti futuam. Fulviam ego ut futuam? Quid si me Manius oret pedicem? Faciam? Non puto si sapiam.*
>
> ... Because Antony fucks (*futuit*) Glaphyra, Fulvia is determined to punish me by making me fuck (*futuam*) her in turn. I fuck (*futuam*) Fulvia? What if Manius begged me to sodomize (*pedicem*) him, would I do it? I think not, if I were in my right mind.[40]

As seen here, *pedico* is used instead of *futuo* when Augustus mentions intercourse with Manius.

The word *futuo* often appears in graffiti, which is perhaps our best source for examining it.[41] An example of this is 'I fucked the barmaid', which was inscribed on a wall in Pompeii.[42] Such literature would have undoubtedly been found on walls throughout the Roman Empire in places where people had the meekest of literary experience. In many of the known examples (including the epigram by Martial), the boast is quite obvious. At the same time, there can be no doubt that *futuo* is an obscene word and is used as such. In the context of brothels, the word might have been used as a technical term by the buyers and sellers of sexual favours.[43] In some of the known examples an enlisted soldier plays the active part, and it seems more than reasonable to suppose that if the walls (and plaster) of the settlements of Carnuntum had been preserved like those in Pompeii quite many similar graffiti catch phrases would have been known to us. Such slang would have been part of everyday language and would have taken on different connotations depending on the context. How and whether it was used behind closed doors by sexual partners or even lovers is difficult to specify.

It has been ventured that graffiti with words as for instance *futuo* and accompanying phallic representations should in fact be understood in the context of apotropaic

37 Williams 1999, 167.

38 Adams 1982, 118-22.

39 Adams 1982, 123.

40 Mart. *Ep.* 11.20, translation by D.R. Shackleton Baily, Loeb Classical Library.

41 Selinger 2006a, 521.

42 *CIL* 4.8442.

43 Adams 1982, 120; Lund 2006, 35.

symbols.[44] In the suggestion an emphasis is put on anthropological distinctions between popular and learned culture, and that the aim is 'to look for the apotropaic implications of ordinary scribbles'.[45] No doubt, graffiti is a form of communication that for the 'artist' has both conscious and subconscious connotations related to the framework of a given society and as such taps into religious, political and other trends. Therefore, it makes sense to suggest that elements in graffiti hinting at virility is a potent reference to the mechanisms of seeking well-being and good luck likewise found in, for instance, the religious sphere.[46] Boosting male virility through the use of language and imagery does fortify position and can perhaps as such be considered to serve as wards against bad luck. On the other hand, it seems over-zealous of the 'learned culture' to imbue every obscene scribble done by teenage boys on lavatory walls or by soldiers on brothel walls with a religious connotation. Placing all focus on the possible apotropaic functions of such scribbles is a neat explanation, but it is a 'learned culture' evaluation that serves to simplify their place in the cityscape to an extent that they become detached from their authors. Quite simply, it also robs the inhabitants of the Empire of the ability to curse, swear and use foul language. At least in the quoted epigram above, the use of *futuere* does not seem to have been chosen for its apotropaic value. However, the use of *futuere* is enigmatic in some contexts where it does seem misplaced, such as in the present context of the grave marker or with the words *veni futu(u)e* found on a 2nd-3rd-century AD copper alloy ring from Essex.[47]

Despite its lewd character, the word *futuo* in antiquity does not seem to have incorporated the modern-day, negative meaning of the word 'fucker' as a despised or abhorrent person. On the contrary, in antiquity, the word is used as either a boast or a neutral description of the male act of penetration. However, because of the nature of the word, we cannot conclude unequivocally that it was only used in relation to male vaginal penetration.[48]

Although *futuo* is a common word that appears frequently in written evidence from antiquity, it still seems grossly inappropriate for a grave marker – even at a military garrison. So what exactly is going on here?

A Couple of Possible Comparisons

Although inscriptions bordering on the obscene are rare in a Roman funerary context, they are not unheard of. A fairly famous epitaph (and accompanying portrait of a reclining man) from a necropolis beneath the Vatican offers an example of a grave marker that advocates unrestrained pleasure-seeking (though perhaps not actual lewdness). The depiction of the deceased shows a mature man reclining on a coach and leaning on his

44 Funari 1995.

45 Funari 1995, 11.

46 Funari 1995, 15.

47 *PAS* ESS-887174.

48 Adams 1982, 121-2; Lund 2006, 186.

left arm. He has a beard, is partly bald and is dressed only in a mantle thrown around his lower body and his left shoulder. While his right hand is busy crowning himself or adjusting a wreath on his head, the left hand supports a drinking vessel. The portrayal of the reclining man, now in the Indianapolis Museum of Art,[49] is all that is left of the monument. The base of the monument originally contained a commemorative epitaph to the man himself, Flavius Agricola, and his wife, Flavia Primitiva, as well as a verse that called for licentious living and merriment. It advised the reader to take pleasure in drinking and the company of beautiful women before death caught up with him.[50] When the stone monument was discovered upon building the baldacchino in St. Peter's church in the first half of the 17th century, the inscription (presumably doubly so because of this particular context) enraged the Pope to such an extent that he had it destroyed and forbade any mention of it.[51] However, despite the frivolous nature of Flavius Agricola's monument, it is by no means comparable to the candour required to use *fututor* as a description of either Optatus or Faustus.

A much lewder sexual reference is found in another epitaph that L. Calidius Eroticus commissioned for himself and his wife, Fannia Voluptas, while he was still alive.[52] The gravestone was discovered in Aesernia (Isernia, Italy) and, apart from the obvious connotations of the individuals' names, it presents a half-sordid joke accompanied by a small relief. The relief shows a man in a hooded traveling cloak holding on to the reins of his mule, while handing something to another figure. The joke reads:

> *Copo computemus habes vini I(sextarium) I pani(s) / a(sse) I pulmentar(ium) a(ssibus) II convenit, puell(a) / a(ssibus) VIII et hoc convenit faenum / mulo a(ssibus) II iste mulus me ad factum / dabit.*
>
> Barkeeper, let us settle the bill. You had a *sextarius* of wine, the cost of one *as*. Bread, one *as*. Relish, two *asses*. That's correct. You had the girl, the cost of eight *asses*. That is also correct. And hay for the mule, at the price of two *asses*. That mule will be my end![53]

Even though this epitaph seems more sordid than the example with Flavius Agricola above, it is still no parallel for Optatus' gravestone. We might expect to find more gravestones with references to lewd behaviour, but, in fact, they are rare. As far as I can establish, the *fututor* example is unique in grave epigraphy[54] – though a Greek parallel might be found in an epitaph from Aizanoi in Phrygia, where the word βείνησον ap-

49 Indianapolis Museum of Art, Inv.no. 72.148.

50 Dunbabin 2003, 103.

51 Dunbabin 2003, 103-4.

52 HD000649.

53 HD000649, translation by author.

54 If the reader is aware of other examples, I would welcome the information.

pears.[55] Here it also stands out as a 'gross expression' among the epitaphs celebrating the pleasures that are to be found while still alive.[56] So, what were Optatus and Faustus trying to say? Are they revealing anything at all aside from the fact that Optatus is a doctor?

A Lewd Secret Revealed?

Firstly, if *fututor* is a reference to Optatus and Faustus' homosexual relationship, it is without a doubt a strange way to advertise it. Not because homosexuality was particularly strange to the Roman world, but because *futuo* does not generally carry such connotations. Another choice of words could convey this meaning much better.[57] This does not exclude the possibility that the two men found sexual pleasure in each other's company, but, even if they did, this would not be effectively conveyed by *fututor* on the stone.[58]

Secondly, *fututor* does not carry the modern-day meaning of 'the despised person'. Therefore, it cannot be viewed as Faustus' attempt to take revenge on Optatus for being an abhorrent person throughout his life.

Perhaps it is more useful to concentrate on *fututor* as a boastful word that celebrates male sexual prowess and relegates the woman (or women) to the passive role of the unidentified other, as in the case of *hic ego puellas multas futui* ('here I fucked a lot of girls').[59] At the same time, groups of men are found celebrating intercourse without naming the prostitutes involved.[60] In light of this, we could view *fututor* on the gravestone as a boastful reference to a character trait – almost an actual nickname,[61] either in the case of Optatus or Faustus. As Optatus is the main character, I consider it most likely that he is the *fututor*. However, for Faustus to include this information on the stone, the two men must have shared the same attitude. It could therefore be argued that *fututor* is a celebration of their mutual knowledge of exploits they shared and the debauchery in which they submerged themselves. Nevertheless, in general terms writing *fututor* on a grave marker would have been outrageous considering the sacred nature of a Roman necropolis – *locus religiosus*.[62] At the same time, as illustrated by the joke on the grave marker from Aesernia, it was not beyond some individuals to stand out by applying vulgar humour to their epitaph. Even though acknowledging intended humour is a tricky matter in archaeological contexts,[63] the Aesernia epitaph seems to be a clear-cut example of where we can actually say with certainty that it was intended as a joke –

55 *CIG* 38461.
56 Kajanto 1969, 360.
57 Selinger 2006a, 519-22.
58 For the complexity of (not) defining heterosexuality and homosexuality in the Roman world, see Williams 1999, 4-8.
59 *CIL* 4.2175.
60 *CIL* 4.2192. See Adams 1982, 121.
61 Selinger 2006a, 523.
62 Carroll 2006, 9, 79.
63 Croxford 2008.

even though the 'barriers' between now and then means that some of the more subtle points are lost on us.[64] It does seem reasonable to also find some humour in giving an individual a sexually laden descriptive 'nickname'. Optatus' epitaph, whether or not it is a grave altar or basis, could be viewed as coarse humour or to stretch it even further as a sardonic mockery of the sanctity of Roman funerary customs; perhaps not merely of funerary customs, but of death itself. In this way, the gravestone becomes a response to the brevity and frailty of life. This last stance on death finds some resonance in Flavius Agricola's epitaph, but there is a marked difference between the poetic merriment of Agricola and the blunt coarseness used to characterise Optatus. Thus, the euphemistic revelation of lovemaking (albeit plenty of it) is replaced by the copulating sexual act. Just how obscene, lewd or salacious we can consider it to be is of course another matter, just as some of the joke is lost on us, but it is undoubtedly more direct and obscene.

At the same time, because it is such a unique occurrence, there is a disclosure literally hewn in stone for all eternity to witness, even if the nickname (character trait) of Optatus was not a secret to people who knew him in his own time. Spelling out this character trait in graffiti on a wall would as such not have been a revelation, but spelling it out in a context where such phrases do not occur does constitute a break with the idealised curriculum vitae – revealing is thus very much context specific.

The unique character of the text separates it as a revelation among the myriads of stones that describe the best, the sweetest and the dearest. Here, something new is finally revealed. With the word *fututor*, sordid details are for once laid bare for the world to see, and the endless cycle of congeniality that conceals the individual's character is broken. Having said this, owing to the peculiarity of the context, the precise implications and string of events that the word refers to remain unclear, and we lack the adequate tools to decipher the 'joke' that Optatus and Faustus share. But then again this mechanism of concealment is in fact an inherent part of the relationship between deceased and bereaved found on grave markers in general.[65] It confirms the intimacy between them, and in turn grants an afterlife for the deceased in the mind of the bereaved, while at the same time consoling that same distraught mind. As such, Optatus and Faustus are little different than others. By nature such intimacy is hidden, even when outspoken in epitaphs, as we the onlookers took no part in the events shared or how they were internalised by shared remembrance. There is little difference in this mechanism whether the onlooker is a casual wanderer unknown to them passing by the grave marker a few days after the internment or scholars reading the words 2000 years later. Obviously the ancient passer-by could be better equipped to know the context, but they did not share in the intimacy between the involved, just as we do not today. By default the mutual knowledge and stories are hidden from us. In the case of Optatus and Faustus, it is like somebody saying to us, "we know a dirty story, but, to you, it is a secret!"

---

64 Croxford 2008, 159.

65 For more deliberate control of access and space in relation to graves, see Krag in this volume.

MARIA MUNKHOLT CHRISTENSEN

"The Lord has Bidden Us to Pray in Secret": Reconciling Personal and Collective Identity through 'Secret Prayer' in 3rd-Century Christianity

This article focuses on what appears to be a contradiction in three 3rd-century treatises on prayer written by the Christian authors Tertullian, Origen and Cyprian. In each of these texts, Christians are admonished to pray in secret, i.e. alone and secluded (in accordance with the New Testament teachings, Matthew 6.6) while also being taught that prayer is especially effective if a congregation of Christians pray together. Both settings for prayer are thus presented as beneficial. By employing the modern term 'identity' as an analytical tool, the social and historical implications of the combination of secret and collective prayer are investigated.

Around AD 250,[1] while the Decian persecution was raging against the Christians,[2] bishop Cyprian of Carthage composed a treatise on prayer, in which he wrote: 'The Lord has bidden us to pray in secret'.[3] With these words Cyprian referred to the Gospel of Matthew 6.6, where Jesus admonishes his followers on prayer by saying: "But you, when you pray, go into your inner room, close your door and pray to your Father who is in secret, and your Father who sees what is done in secret will reward you".[4] This Matthean verse belongs in a passage where Jesus also admonishes his followers not to be like those who make their charity known in order to 'have glory from men', and who pray and fast to impress other people.[5] Such behaviour is hypocritical, and Jesus warns against it: "When you pray, you are not to be like the hypocrites; for they love to stand and pray in the synagogues and on the street corners so that they may be seen by men".[6] Instead

1 All dates given in this article are AD.
2 For a treatment of the persecution and the motives behind, see Engberg 2007.
3 Cypr. *De Dominica oratione* 4.
4 Matth. 6.6. All English translations of quotes from the Bible come from *The New American Standard Bible* (*NASB*).
5 Matth. 6.1-18, it is a part of the Sermon on the Mount (Matth. 5-7).
6 Matth. 6.5.

Fig. 1. *A 3rd century fresco of 'The Veiled Woman' from the Catacomb of Priscilla in Rome. The Christian woman stands with her arms outstretched in prayer and her eyes gazing upwards. She is posing in an* orans *position, a presentation that signified piety in Late Antiquity, both in Christian and Pagan milieus (courtesy of Catacombe di Priscilla).*

of such ostentatious behaviour, Jesus stresses that charitable deeds and prayers should be conducted 'in secret': secrecy will annul the possibility of erroneous motives such as the intention of gaining praise and fame. When illustrating this admonition, Jesus goes as far as saying that when doing charitable deeds, the right hand should not even know what the left hand is doing.[7] With such a hyperbole Jesus calls for an extreme level of concealment in charity and prayer.[8] What follows in the biblical passage is that Jesus teaches his followers The Lord's Prayer, which is also called Our Father, and which had already by the 3rd century become the Christian prayer par excellence.[9]

7 Matth. 6.3.

8 Keener 2009, 208. C.S. Keener mentions how also others used such exaggerations, e.g. Marcus Aurelius (M. Aur. *Med.* 8.9).

9 The high reverence for The Lord's Prayer in the early church is manifest for instance in the treatises under investigation. In his treatise, Tertullian admiringly defines The Lord's Prayer as a summary of the entire Gospel, '*breviarium totius evangelii*' (*De Oratione* 2). Furthermore, M.-B. von Stritzky writes: 'Ein Überblick über die frühchristliche Literatur zeigt, daß sich das Vaterunser sowohl in der östlichen wie in der westlichen Kirche zum vorrangigen Gebet der Christen entwickelt, das besonders in der Liturgie der Taufe und der Eucharistie eine hervorragende Stellung einnimmt. … Ist die Bezeugung des gesamten Vaterunsertextes durch die uns erhaltene christliche Literatur

Because Jesus himself was quoted in the Gospel as saying that prayer should be performed 'in secret', the first Christian theologians writing on prayer had to deal with this admonition. The theologians therefore faced something of a challenge, since Christian worship was a profoundly congregational and communal matter centred on the Eucharistic celebration.[10] However, the authors themselves did not verbalise this ambiguity, but dauntlessly admonished their congregations to pray three to five times a day – and at best, all the time.[11]

With the aim of examining how the relation between individual and communal Christian prayer was balanced in the early church, the leading questions in this article are: What did the Christians in the 3rd century understand by 'secret prayer'? What might the Christian community have gained from the concept of secret prayer? And are there indications to substantiate the hypothesis that the combination of secret prayer and communal prayer in the early church might have contributed to the establishment of a more congruent Christian identity? The answers will be sought in 3rd-century sources on prayer.

3rd-Century Sources on Christian Prayer

Three Christian treatises on The Lord's Prayer have been preserved from the first half of the 3rd century: Tertullian's *On Prayer* (c. 200),[12] Origen's *On Prayer* (c. 233),[13] and Cyprian's *On the Lord's Prayer* (c. 253).[14] These treatises are the earliest of their sort, consisting partly of commentaries on The Lord's Prayer, and partly of general reflections and instructions on prayer. The geographical provenances of the texts are Carthage in the Roman province of Africa Proconsularis where Tertullian and later Cyprian wrote their treatises on prayer, and probably Caesarea in Palestine where Origen wrote his, shortly after he had left Alexandria in the Roman province of Egypt. Tertullian and

---

des 1. und 2. Jh.s auch als spärlich zu bezeichnen, so läßt sich an den vergleichsweise häufigen Anspielungen auf dieses Gebet und den Zitaten der einzelnen Bitten ablesen, daß das Vaterunser bereits in frühester Zeit zum Grundbestand christlichen Betens gehörte' (Stritzky 1989, 7).

10 The importance of collective worship is expressed by several early theologians, for instance in relation to Matthew 18.20 where Jesus says: "For where two or three gather in my name, there am I with them". Both Tertullian and Cyprian connect this saying with the existence of the church (Tert. *De paenitentia* 10; Cypr. *De unitate ecclesiae* 12).

11 Tert. *De Oratione* 24-5; Orig. *De Oratione* 12, 31; Cypr. *De Dominica oratione* 34-6.

12 Tert. *De Oratione* (Schleyer 2006). There is no indication in *De Oratione* about its time of origin. It shows no sign of Montanism, and it is therefore possible that it belongs to Tertullian's premontanist phase, i.e. before 203 (Dunn 2004, 5).

13 Orig. *De Oratione*, from Greek: Περὶ Εὐχῆς (Koetschau 1899). 'The general consensus is that *On Prayer* was composed after Origen moved to Caesarea, but before the beginning of the persecution of Maximinus, probably in 233 or 234' (Heine 1993, 14-5). See also Koetschau 1899, LXXV-LXXVII.

14 Cypr. *De Dominica oratione* (Réveillaud 1964). Cyprian's treatise bears resemblance to his writing *De unitate ecclesiae* from 251 because of the recurrent themes of unity, brotherhood and unanimity. *De Dominica oratione* is therefore dated to 253 (Bindley 1914, 14).

Cyprian are Latin authors, whereas Origen wrote in Greek and belonged to another theological sphere. Some differences naturally exist between the treatises, but with respect to content they have a lot in common and are all examples of 'prayer discourse' that attempt to communicate a certain standard idea of Christian prayer. Since the texts were probably used to teach lay people, it is reasonable to assume that the treatises give a historical glimpse of how Christians in a congregational context were instructed regarding prayer.[15]

Analysing 'Prayer Discourse'

What is Secret Prayer?

In all three treatises the authors either directly quote or strongly allude to Matthew 6.6, where Jesus recommends secret prayer, and as a result they all recommend that Christians should pray 'in secret'.[16]

In the treatment of the sources, I will move from east to west and thus from Origen to Tertullian and Cyprian. In his treatise, Origen quotes the text from Matthew directly and introduces the quotation with the authoritative formula: 'our Saviour says on this matter'.[17] When explaining where one ought to pray, Origen writes that: 'every place is rendered fit for prayer by one who prays aright … But to arrange the performance of prayer in quiet, and without distraction, each person should select, if possible, what one might term the appropriate place in his house'.[18] At first, Origen thus says that the admonition to pray in secret should be taken quite concretely. However, it soon becomes evident that what is most important to him is not so much the place of prayer but rather the level of attention reached when praying. After all, according to Origen, a Christian can pray anywhere without any outward indication that he is doing so.[19] The

15 M.-B. von Stritzky presents Tertullian's treatise as a catechetical text with emphasis on ethical and practical issues. She specifies that Origen's treatise was a text for the philosophically learned among the Christians, and she reckons that both Tertullian's and Origen's treatise had the objective of edifying the congregation (Stritzky 1989, 49). H. Buchinger does not draw conclusions about the exact *Sitz im Leben* of the treatises, but he acknowledges that all three texts might have belonged in a catechetical setting (Buchinger 2003, 317-8, n. 47). A. Stewart-Sykes finds it 'entirely reasonable to see these discourses reflecting the instruction that was given to catechumens' (Stewart-Sykes 2004, 22-6).

16 In the Greek New Testament (Nestle-Aland) 'in secret' is rendered as ἐν τῷ κρυπτῷ, which bears the connotation of something 'hidden', 'covered' or 'concealed' (*LSJ*). Hence, prayer is to be performed secluded and alone. In the 3rd century, when commenting on the biblical passage, Origen stays true to the biblical source and uses its phrase for secret: ἐν τῷ κρυπτῷ, while the Latin authors express 'in secret' with *secrete*, an adverb from *secerno*, which refers to what is set apart (Lewis & Short 1879).

17 Orig. *De Oratione* 19.1. All translations of Origen, Tertullian and Cyprian are by A. Stewart-Sykes (2004).

18 Orig. *De Oratione* 31.4.

19 Orig. *De Oratione* 31.2.

crucial thing is that prayer takes place in a location where it is possible to concentrate on God. Origen therefore presents the ideal Christian worshipper as someone who prays in 'his own room', which for Origen means someone who is able to withdraw from the surrounding world and find God present within:

> He does not recognize the outside world, he pays no attention to anything outside, but shuts up every door of the senses, so that the world of the senses should not distract, nor his mind receive any impression from sense-perception, praying to the Father who neither shuns nor deserts such a secret place but dwells there together with his only-begotten one.[20]

It thus becomes clear that for Origen, secret prayer in its finest form is something purely internal that has to do with paying complete attention to God.[21] Prayer therefore earns its own merit, because God is present with those who pray. According to Origen, secret prayer is to some degree like modern meditation *mutatis mutandis*: it is a way for the believer to experience God's presence via an act of introverted concentration. 'A person exalts God when he has dedicated to him a dwelling place within himself'.[22]

Moving westward to the Latin authors, the comments on secret prayer are to a significant extent like Origen's, although less intimate and mystical[23] in nature. The Latin authors also allude to Matthew 6.6 in their treatises on prayer. At the beginning of a passage on Jesus' teaching, Tertullian writes: 'Therefore let us consider, blessed ones, his heavenly wisdom, firstly regarding his instruction to pray in secret'.[24] Half a century later, Cyprian, who might depend on Tertullian's work,[25] remarks: '… the Lord in his pronouncements commands each of us to pray in secret, in hidden and private places, in our hidden rooms'.[26] As in Origen's text, both Tertullian's and Cyprian's opening idea of 'secret prayer' is quite concrete: they think that one should pray in a hidden chamber. However, they quickly emphasise that what matters is not so much the place of prayer itself as the confidence in the fact that God can hear even a secret prayer and penetrate even a hidden chamber. Cyprian states that 'the plenitude of his [God's] majesty penetrates into secluded and hidden places'.[27] It is important for the Latin authors to point to the fact that God is very close to the person praying wherever he

---

20 Orig. *De Oratione* 20.2.

21 This is at least one way in which Origen thinks of prayer; he also defines prayer broadly as life itself, e.g. Orig. *De Oratione* 12.2, 22.5 (McGuckin 2004, 176).

22 Orig. *De Oratione* 24.4.

23 'Mysticism' is a debated concept. Here I use it as defined by A. Louth: '… it can be characterized as a search for and experience of immediacy with God. The mystic is not content to know *about* God, he longs for union with God' (Louth 1981, xiii-xiv).

24 Tert. *De Oratione* 1.

25 For a discussion of Cyprian's possible dependence on Tertullian's treatise, see Stewart-Sykes 2004, 31-3.

26 Cypr. *De Dominica oratione* 4.

27 Cypr. *De Dominica oratione* 4.

or she prays, and they furthermore stress the idea that God looks for motives rather than for words and gestures. Therefore the act of praying does not in itself satisfy God, regardless of where it takes place. On the contrary, the important thing is the underlying motivation for the prayer, as well as the attitude of the one praying. Hence, a wicked person praying for his own worldly good cannot expect his prayers to be answered by God. Tertullian makes this clear by saying that God is a listener 'not to the voice but to the heart',[28] and Cyprian reminds his audience that God is 'an examiner of the kidney and heart'.[29] The Latin authors understand secret prayer to be not only actual prayers kept secret from other human beings, but also prayers whose underlying motives are correct, although these motives are secret to the world. In summary, all three authors share the conviction that God is present with the one praying, and this divine presence is so close and so pervasive that God knows not only the prayer spoken in secret, but also the underlying motives and everyday behaviour of the one who prays. Motivation and behaviour are therefore understood as a part of prayer. This is expressed directly when Origen explains the meaning of Paul's admonition to the Christians to 'pray without ceasing':[30] 'Since works of virtue and the keeping of the commandments have a part in prayer, the person who prays 'ceaselessly' is the one who integrates prayer with good works and noble actions with prayer. For we can only accept the saying 'Pray ceaselessly' as realistic if we can say that the whole life of the saint is one mighty, integrated prayer'.[31]

The Rationale behind Secret Prayer

According to the three authors, the main reason why prayer should be secret is that Christian prayer should not be ostentatious; and in agreement with the above-mentioned Matthean text, Christians should not pray only for the sake of appearing holy. In his treatise, Origen lingers on the term 'appear' (φαίνω). He writes: 'We should pay careful attention to the term "appear", for nothing that is merely apparent is worthy, since it seems to exist but does not actually do so, deceiving sense-perception and not giving a true or accurate representation'.[32] In continuation of this, Origen attacks the Jews and admonishes the Christians that they should not pray only in order to appear holy like the Jews. Origen sarcastically calls the synagogue a 'theatre of the Jews' and writes that in the synagogues, the Jews wear 'masks' that do not coincide with their actual character. The ritual prayer in the synagogue is not in itself an expression of a true religious sentiment, and the dissimilarity between appearance and inner sentiment is deceitful and wrong. For Origen, it is imperative that Christians do not perform their

28 Tert. *De Oratione* 17.

29 Cypr. *De Dominica oratione* 4 (see Apc 2.23; Ps 7.9).

30 1 Thess 5.17.

31 Orig. *De Oratione* 12.2.

32 Orig. *De Oratione* 20.2. Origin is very strict in prohibiting deceptive behavior here. U.H. Eriksen shows that in another context Origen presupposes that the devil deceived himself when taking Christ as ransom. Furthermore, U.H. Eriksen demonstrates how the opinion among later theologians was that God in fact had actively deceived the devil, see Eriksen in this volume.

worship 'as actors'.[33] To him, an actor is a prime example of someone who appears to be something that he is not. The Christians should strive not only to appear, but actually to be righteous and faithful.[34] The Latin authors also agree that prayer should not be performed in order for it to be noticed, and Tertullian ironically asks: 'What more reward will there be gained by those who pray too noisily except of distracting those nearby?'[35] The consensus of the 3rd-century authors is that humility and sincerity should be the attitude among praying Christians.

A second reason to pray in secret is that such a prayer proves the faith of the one praying, since the one who prays in secret shows faith in the ability of God to hear a secret prayer, even a silent prayer. Praying in secret is thus a confession of God's omnipresence, a *credo*. In his treatise, Tertullian ironically asks: 'Do God's ears listen out for a noise?'[36] The answer is of course: No, God does not need a noise to hear a prayer, God is aware of even the unuttered prayers. This belief in God's transcendence of physical location and acoustic range was something that separated 3rd-century Christians from much of the surrounding society where silent prayer was unusual, though not unheard of.[37] In Roman society worship most often took place near an altar or holy place, either privately or publicly.[38]

A third reason to pray in secret is that it makes it possible for the one praying to withdraw from the world and become aware of God's presence. Especially Origen, who has since gone down in history as a great mystical theologian,[39] dwells on this point. This awareness of God's presence also necessitates living a life that is worthy of being constantly scrutinised by a God who knows all unspoken motives and hears all secret prayers.

---

33 Orig. *De Oratione* 20.2. In Greek, there is an etymological coincidence because a 'hypocrite' and an 'actor' are both called ὑποκριτής (*LSJ*). In the New Testament the Jewish scribes and Pharisees were accused of being hypocrites (people who only pretended to be righteous, but in fact were not, e.g. Matth. 23.23). Origen mentions 'actors' as deceitful agents, in contrast to Christians, thus alluding to the Biblical use of the word.

34 However, later on Origen remarks that in the same way as actors have responsibilities towards their audience, the Christians 'are under obligation to the whole world, to all the angels as to the human race' (Orig. *De Oratione* 28.3).

35 Tert. *De Oratione* 17.

36 Tert. *De Oratione* 17.

37 Bitton-Askelony 2012; Horst 1994; Versnel 1981, 29-32; Dover 1974, 258.

38 K.J. Dover writes about this and states that: 'it is doubtful whether anyone was prepared to assert explicitly that there were limits to the range of divine hearing; the point of taking an oath at an altar or in a sanctuary was to enhance its solemnity and leave no room for doubt that the taker was acting deliberately and in full consciousness of what he was doing' (Dover 1974, 257). The materiality of pagan religion is explained by the Neoplatonic philosopher Porphyry as a means of remembering: 'For images of living creatures and temples were built for the sake of remembrance in order that those who frequent those places meditate when they arrive there' (Porph. *Adversus Christianos*, frag. 76, translation by R.M. Berchman (2005)).

39 See e.g. Louth 1981, 72.

Admonitions to Pray Together in the Congregation

Although the authors, as previously shown, stress the rightfulness and benefit of 'secret prayer', they leave no doubt that common prayer is also of great importance and should be performed regularly. One of the most striking recommendations for common prayer is to be found in Cyprian's treatise, when he writes:

> Before all else, the teacher of peace and master of unity desires that we should not make our prayer individually and alone, as whoever prays by himself prays only for himself. We do not say: "My Father who are in the heavens" … Our prayer is common and collective.[40]

Compared to the above-mentioned admonitions to pray in secret, this is a completely different recommendation; but the author himself does nothing to reconcile the two concepts. The same situation is found in Origen's treatise. Origen is equally sure about the benefits of collective prayer; and he even imagines that when Christians pray together, they are not only praying with each other, but also with Christ, with already deceased Christians and with angels. He thus envisions a cosmic gathering that is called forth by Christians praying in a group – a gathering that makes the prayer as efficient as possible. Origen writes:

> A place of prayer that has a particular blessing and benefit is the place where believers gather. It seems probable that angelic powers are in attendance at the assemblies of the faithful, as well as the power of the Lord and Saviour himself, and indeed holy spirits – I think of those who have gone to their rest before us. It is clear that they are around us who continue in life, even if it is difficult to say precisely how.[41]

Moreover, Tertullian recommends responsory prayer, which is collective prayer with one person leading the prayer and the rest answering with a response such as 'hallelujah' or the like.[42] According to Tertullian, such responsory prayer is an excellent practice, and something that is obviously part of communal prayer.

With such encouragements, the authors make it clear that prayer has the greatest benefit when said together with other Christians. Cyprian explains that this is the will of God, who is the father of all and therefore wants his people to pray united. He writes that: 'Our prayer is common and collective, and when we pray we pray not for one, but for all people, because we are all one people together'.[43] A further rationale for common prayer is that the form of prayer then matches the ideal content of prayer – the content of prayer should always be concerned with the common good – which is why the fourth

40 Cypr. *De Dominica oratione* 8.

41 Orig. *De Oratione* 31.5.

42 Tert. *De Oratione* 27.

43 Cypr. *De Dominica oratione* 8.

A 3rd century fresco from the Catacomb of Priscilla in Rome. It depicts 'The Three Men in the Fiery Furnace' from the Book of Daniel (Dan 3.19-100). The men stand in the typical orans *position which shows that they are praying. In* De Dominica oratione *8 Cyprian uses the three men as a good example of collective prayer because their prayer in the furnace was made 'with one voice' (Dan 3.51) (courtesy of Catacombe di Priscilla).* **Fig. 2.**

petition of The Lord's Prayer is not: 'Give *me* today *my* daily bread', but 'Give *us* today *our* daily bread'.[44]

These encouragements for common prayer show the strong ecclesiastical and ecclesiological interest of the authors: they all had an interest in forming and maintaining their particular Christian community in a time of distress and persecution. Therefore it is

44 Cypr. *De Dominica oratione* 8. Translation by A. Stewart-Sykes (2004), italics added by author.

only natural that the 3rd-century authors call for collective prayer in order to strengthen their congregations and to create an idea of coherence and union.

Summing up this text-based analysis, the Christian authors in the 3rd century encouraged both secret prayer and collective prayer, and seem to have expected that it was possible for Christians to do both in their everyday lives at different times. None of the forms of prayer takes priority; each is presented as important and beneficial. Furthermore, it should be noted that secret prayer is presented in the treatises as not mainly a question of physical location, but rather a question of being in the appropriate mental and behavioural state when praying. Therefore there is not necessarily any inconsistency in the emphases on both secret prayer and collective prayer, as secret prayer is to be understood in part as a state of mind dominated by humility and the absence of wrong motives – and such a state of mind is also expected from Christians when they pray as part of a congregation.

Applying a Modern Theory

In this final section of the article, the focus is on modern theories on prayer and identity. These theories are brought into focus in order to investigate whether there is a certain traceable effect of holding collective and individual prayer together like the theologians did in the 3rd century. About a hundred years ago, the French sociologist M. Mauss proposed some theories concerning prayer and wrote a thesis, *On Prayer*, that was never completed. One of the elements to which he wanted to draw attention in his thesis is the idea that prayer has 'a social content – it is a social act'.[45] In other words, prayer has an effect on the social world and is itself affected by it. Thus, no praying man is an island, but receives the impetus to pray in a certain way from his religious community and its way of believing, acting and praying. M. Mauss writes:

> Even when prayer is individual and free, even when the worshippers choose freely the time and mode of expression, what they say always uses hallowed language and deals with hallowed things, that is, ones endorsed by social tradition. Even in mental prayer where, according to the formula, Christians abandon themselves to the Spirit … this spirit which controls them is the spirit of the Church. The ideas that they generate are those of the teaching of their own sect and the sentiments which they speculate on are in accord with the moral doctrine of their denomination. … Prayer is social not only in content but also in form.[46]

Consequently, in M. Mauss' view, even the secret prayer links the praying individual to a social group, because the same idea of God and the same idea of perfection, morality and world are present in the individual's consciousness as well as in the social consciousness. According to M. Mauss, prayer is not only the uttered (or unuttered) words, but

45 Pickering 2003, 12.

46 Pickering 2003, 31.

also the cluster of ideas that lies behind, i.e. the worldview, moral codex and dogma. Agreeing with M. Mauss on this, I argue that the act of praying is an act of acceptance and wrestling with the ideas of the social world. When thought of in this way, it seems likely that the act of praying has an influence on both personal identity and group identity because prayer is a heavily loaded symbol of what the church stands for, and in the act of praying the individual and the church influence each other. The notion that the church constrains the individual in the act of praying has been illustratively expressed by A. Hamman: 'A Christian, even in the midst of his most intimate prayer, existentially carries the Church within himself in the same manner as the turtle carries its shell'.[47]

A Coherent Identity as an Effect of Prayer

Insights from modern identity studies suggest that the self is:

> ... something which has a development: it is not initially there at birth but arises in the process of social experience and activity, that is, develops in the given individual as a result of his relations to that process as a whole and to other individuals within that process.[48]

In social interaction, the individual activates certain aspects of his or her self in accordance with the context, and such representations of the self are what we refer to as identities.[49] Every person has multiple identities and draws on a specific identity in a specific situation. However, the different identities do not have the same importance; some identities are more essential and salient to the individual than others. S. Stryker describes this in the following way: 'Identities are ordered in a salience hierarchy, defined as the likelihood that an identity will be invoked in a variety of situations'.[50] The fact that people have more identities and can switch between them is a characteristic feature of liberal postmodern societies. However, the terminology of 'identity salience' also helps verbalise elements of social life in antiquity. For instance, one can assume that Christian identity had a high salience for converts during the first centuries when being Christian was a choice with possible extreme consequences.[51] According to the prevailing assumption, an individual is, however, not completely in command when it

47 Quoted from Perrone 2003, 264.

48 Mead 1934, 135.

49 Leary 2003, 132.

50 Stryker 2008, 20.

51 For an idealised example of Christian identity being propounded as a salient identity, one can look at Perpetuas' account in *The Martyrdom of Saints Perpetua and Felicitas*: During her arrest, Perpetua's father tries to free her by making her renounce her faith, but even in that situation she says: "... I cannot be called anything other than what I am, a Christian" (see Stouck 2009, 10). In this case, Perpetua is portrayed as holding her Christian identity so salient that she breaks her family ties because of it. Of course an individual maintaining a strict Christian behaviour while nevertheless keeping his or her Christian ties secret in the face of persecution would also be an example of an individual that gives the Christian identity a high salience.

comes to his or her identity, since identity also has to do with the social world in which the individual is embedded. Therefore '[c]ompared to self and self-concept, identity is an even more social conception as it indicates a specific location within some form of social structure'.[52]

Identity has to do with *who you are* and correspondingly with *who you are not*; and at the same time identity is influenced by how other people classify you. As such 'identity formation' has to do with both an including and an excluding categorisation. The positive categorisation has to do with the qualities or attributes that we prescribe to ourselves or to our own group; the negative categorisation has to do with how we perceive other people or groups in contrast to ourselves. In fact, 'one may infer that 'identity' generally has to do with the perception of the 'self' in relation to the 'other'', writes L. Perrone, 'thus implying a dialectic of similarity and difference'.[53] Identity formation is thus a process during which social actors influence the development of one another.[54]

Identity is a slippery term that encapsulates a lot,[55] often a distinction is made between 'social', 'collective' and 'personal' identity.[56] Social and collective identity has to do with the overall categories to which an individual belongs, e.g. religious affiliation, whereas the personal identity is more distinct and has to do with how the individual thinks of himself/herself. However, the social and personal aspects of identity are interdependent. J.B. Rives hints at this insight when he points out that religion has both an individual and a collective form, and religious identity can therefore 'bridge between individual and group'. J.B. Rives claims that this was the reason why religion had 'such an important place in the history of the Roman empire'.[57] In fact, according to J.B. Rives: 'Christianity more than anything else provided the means both to define collective religious identity suitable for an empire and to enforce a very high degree of individual conformity to that collective norm'.[58]

For the early Christians, prayer seems to have played an important role in their life, although due to the scarcity of source material, we cannot know much about how they prayed individually. However, from the treatises on prayer we do know that they were strongly encouraged to pray 'in secret', especially The Lord's Prayer. When praying alone, the individual Christian had a chance to personalise and interiorise the concept of God and the moral obligations that came with it. The individual was of course to some degree bound by tradition in his or her secret conversation with God; nevertheless, at the same time secret prayer allowed the individual to shape the tradition anew as there are no inherent restrictions in an individual's personal relationship with God.

---

52 Reynolds & Herman-Kinney 2003, 368.

53 Perrone 2003, 262. For a treatment of how 'secrecy' as such can play a part in social life and in the formation of social identity, see Wright in this volume.

54 Stachel 2005.

55 Brubaker & Cooper 2000.

56 Rives 1995, 3-4.

57 Rives 1995, 3.

58 Rives 1995, 310.

In other words, individual prayer both shaped the individual and offered the individual an opportunity to shape tradition.

Besides individual prayer, the early church made substantial use of collective prayer. One can imagine that when there was correspondence between the individual's secret prayer and the collective prayer of the group, prayer in both forms was a confirmation of the individual's appropriate place in the group. Prayer thereby created a sense of belonging and a sense of coherence in the world of the individual, because what was done alone and in private was aligned with what was done collectively. The individual's self-understanding and ensuing identity were thereby acknowledged by the group with whom he or she prayed; and from the 3rd-century Christian point of view, acknowledgement from the congregation meant acknowledgement from God.

Conclusion

Among the 3rd-century authors investigated in this article, 'secret prayer' was understood literally as prayer conducted somewhere apart from or hidden from other people. However, secret prayer was interpreted not primarily as a matter of location, but as a matter of a certain mental and moral state that always should prevail when praying.

3rd-century Christians were encouraged to pray both secretly and collectively: secretly, because it was a way to be close to God; and collectively, because God is the father of all Christians, and God ought to be met by a united people. Early on it was thus integral to the Christian understanding of prayer that prayer is something that brings the individual both close to God and close to the Christian community.

Correlating these historical insights with modern theories on prayer and identity, it seems likely that part of the success of Christianity in antiquity could be related to this dual function of prayer as something with both an individual and a collective importance that unites the individual and the community. For the individual the act of praying contributed to the establishment of a coherent identity and a strong sense of belonging to the Christian community.

SECRETS IN THE CULTIC SPHERE

WIEBKE FRIESE

Trick or Treat? Secrecy and Performative Space in the Sanctuary of Glycon Neos Asclepius

Taking Lucian's text Alexander, the False Prophet *as a starting point and confronting the source with the archaeological evidence, this paper aims to trace and reconstruct the ritual background and the architectural setting of the Glycon Neos Asclepius cult in Roman Paphlagonia. By comparing Lucian's description to contemporary architecture, it will be argued that not only its ritual but also its architectural elements were already established in several well-known Roman sanctuaries. The Glycon cult recombined these elements to emphasise a ritual over-stimulation and an atmosphere of secrecy – spiritually as well as physically.*

The emotional experience of the participating, practicing and believing individual, expressed through many different rituals, is one of the key aspects of every religion. As humans are three-dimensional moving beings, they tend to not only shape their environment by their own hands but also to be shaped by it themselves. The material context, especially the architecture, meant as a frame in which these rituals take place, has a significant impact on these experiences.

While the ritual aspect of material culture has constantly been studied within Anthropology and History of Religion, the aspect of the performative space has been surprisingly less discussed.[1] The scholars of the early 20th century ascribed religious architecture a simple material function to create – as the ritual itself – boundaries between the sacred and the profane.[2] In the 1980s, the 'cognitive movement' in the archaeological disciplines also emphasised the aesthetics of the ritual, while its material

1 For the ritual aspect of material culture, see e.g. Kyriakidis 2007 with older literature. See also Bouvrie 2012. The term 'performative space' is described by E. Fischer-Lichte, a professor of Performance Studies, as a space for movement and perception which structures and organises relations between actors and the audience. Fischer-Lichte 2004, 187. J. Maran puts this concept into an archaeological context. Maran 2006.

2 On sacred centres, see Eliade 1959. On liminality, see Gennep 1909; Turner 1969.

culture was used to contextualise their argumentation.[3] Only recently has architecture, as a material and cultural frame for human actions (including rituals), been put back on the map.[4]

Drawing on the material as well as epigraphic and written data, this paper discusses the ritual elements that influenced the architectural appearance of a cult. Did the form indeed follow the function? Or was it the other way around? The Roman Glycon Neos Asclepius cult, introduced in the mid-2nd century AD by the self-appointed prophet Alexander of Abonuteichus, provides a very applicable case study for answering these questions. Unlike most cults and their related architecture, which developed and grew over centuries, there were no dynamic changes in its rituals or any outer influences, which subsequently changed the appearance of the performative space.[5] It was an entirely newly invented cult. Its rituals and architectural visualisation were based on the ideas of a single mind (and his companions) and realised within a comparatively short time. Earlier cult inventions, like the Hellenistic cult of Sarapis, which combined elements from the indigenous Egyptian gods Osiris and Apis, as well as the Greek Zeus and Asclepius, took much longer to establish.[6] But how innovative can a new cult and its sanctuary be?[7]

Alexander's cult was predicated on three main elements: an oracle, a healing ritual and a mystery ritual. In the 2nd century AD these cult types, offering the individual salvation from physical and spiritual suffering, were extremely popular, also because they addressed the people on an individual basis and in a highly emotional way.[8] Secrecy played a fundamental role in their success.[9] This becomes most apparent through the oath of silence – taken not only by the initiates but also kept by most of the contemporary authors writing about these cults. But secrecy also became an important feature for the architecture, which was built for these rituals.[10]

The architectural material related to the cult of Glycon Neos Asclepius is very limited, but the Abonuteichus' *temenos* can be reconstructed by comparing Lucian's description

3 For an introduction to the concept of ritual and material culture, see Renfrew & Zubrow 1994.

4 On the dynamic changes in ritual and its subsequent architectural and structural adjustments, see Mylonopoulos 2006. For a more theoretical approach, see Elsner 2012.

5 For a dynamic change in ritual architecture of much older cult centres like Demeter/Kore at Corinth or Poseidon at Isthmia, see Mylonopoulos 2008.

6 The establishment of the Sarapis cult in Ptolemaic Egypt of course had a totally different intention. On the foundation of the Serapis cult in Hellenistic times, see Bergmann 2010 with a discussion of the older literature.

7 A similar question concerning the ritual elements of the cult is asked by A. Chaniotis (2002).

8 On the use of emotions in Roman cults (also the cult of Abonuteichos), see Chaniotis 2012a.

9 For the aspect of secrecy in Roman mystery cults, see Burkert 1995 with older literature. For secrecy and oracles, see Friese 2013b, 231-5. For secrecy in healing cults, see e.g. Ehrenheim 2011, 119-56.

10 E.g. the cave-like appearance of the delphic *adyton* increased the mystic performances of the Pythia. Friese 2013b, 231; the seclusivness of the incubation rooms in Graeco-Roman Asclepieia deepened the sleep of the incubating worshippers. Ehrenheim, 2011, 78-83; the dark dromos-like meeting rooms of the Mithras devotees intensified their initiation ritual. Nielsen 2014, 152-69.

of its topographical, architectural and performative appearance to contemporary, ritually related cult sites in Asia Minor. Lucian himself connects particular ritual elements to well-known contemporary cults, like Alexander's performance of 'sacred madness' on the agora of Abonuteichus to the Magna Mater cult in Rome and the Glycon mysteries to Athens/Eleusis.[11] As the architecture functioned as a stage for these rituals, it was most likely based on the same predecessors.

The Sacred Topography: Choosing a Place for a Cult

During the 2nd century AD, Rome was overwhelmed by many different cults from across the Empire. Religious competition was a logical consequence. To attract new and preferably wealthy devotees, a former itinerant preacher, Alexander, born in Abonuteichus on the southern Black Sea coast, created a unique new cult. Archaeologically attested by inscriptions, coins and figurines, its rise and fall is most extensively described by Lucian of Samosata in his text *Alexander, the False Prophet* published after AD 180.[12] However, we have to consider that Lucian was not only one of the most famous satirist of his time and an adherent of the Epicurean philosophy; he was also one of Alexander's worst enemies, making it difficult to create an objective impression of the cult. Drawing on that, some scholars deny any historical and ritual background, interpreting the text as a parody of Epicurean exposure of religious charlatanry.[13] On the other hand, it is verified that Lucian visited the cult place in person,[14] and what he describes differs little from what we know of other cults in the 2nd century AD, ritually as well as archaeologically. Lucian obviously had an interest in giving his tale a plausible frame which his audience could associate with a familiar religious landscape. That is why he made references not only to well-known cults but also to historical events, such as the Parthian War of AD 161-6,[15] and that is also why Lucian, who obviously exaggerated concerning the person of Alexander, still must have given an accurate account on the cult praxis, rituals and elements of cult architecture.[16]

According to Lucian, Alexander was trained as a public physician and introduced to Pythagorean or Neopythagorean ideas by his teachers. He travelled around as an itinerant doctor and magician when he met Cocconas, a Byzantine writer of choral songs.[17] Together they drew up a plan to found a prophetic shrine and oracle. As the

11 On Magna Mater, see Luc. *Alex.* 13. On Athens/Eleusis, see Luc. *Alex.* 38.

12 As Lucian is mentioning the emperor Marcus Aurelius as a 'god', the text must be dated after the emperor's deification in AD 180. Luc. *Alex.* 48. Rostad 2011, 208.

13 See e.g. Branham 1989; Gerlach 2005. For the cult's trickery and its exposure, see Elm von der Osten 2006, 141-57. On the historicity of Lucian's text, see Petsalis-Diomidis 2010, 44-60; Rostad 2011, 211-4 with a discussion of the older literature.

14 Flinterman 1997, 280-2.

15 Luc. *Alex.* 27.

16 See Lane Fox 1988, 243-50.

17 Cocconas mysteriously died in Calchedon from a snakebite before ever reaching the newly built sanctuary. Luc. *Alex.* 10.

location of the sanctuary seems to have been one of the most important parameters of this cult foundation, 'they began planning, first about the place, and next, what should be commencement and the character of the venture'.[18] While Cocconas thought Chalcedon, situated at the northern shore of the Sea of Marmara, a suitable place, Alexander preferred his hometown Abonuteichus, arguing that the inhabitants were simple and superstitious enough to believe in every mockery they were exposed to. They finally agreed on Abonuteichus; however, as they did not have the money to build a sanctuary on their own, they invented their first trick. Bronze tablets stating that very soon Asclepius and his father Apollo would move to Pontus to take up residence at Abonuteichus were buried at night in the Apollo Sanctuary of Chalcedon. The following day, they staged a public discovery of the tablets; following the subsequent spread of the oracle to all Bithynia and Pontus, the 'divinely chosen' people of Abonuteichus quickly started to build a temple at their own expense in expectation of the new god.[19]

The transmission of cults from one place to another has a long tradition in antiquity. One of the most documented examples is the import of the Asclepius cult from Epidaurus to Athens in the last quarter of the 5th century BC.[20] After the great plague in 420/19 BC, the Athenian Telemachus founded the sanctuary on the south slope of the Acropolis and brought a statue of the new god, via Piraeus, in a procession to the newly built temple. The Athenian sanctuary incorporated most of the architectural elements, which were already essential for conducting the rituals in Epidaurus: the temple, the incubation rooms and the sacred spring.

Unfortunately, to date all archaeological attempts in Abonuteichus to find the *temenos* of Glycon Neos Asclepius have failed. In 2010, an archaeological team from the University of Zürich, under the direction of C. Marek, surveyed the area around the small coastal town of Inebolu east of Sinope (the name serving as a reminder of the ancient predecessor of the town, Ionopolis, formerly Abonuteichus).[21] However, despite a couple of Roman architectural fragments and a small altar with floral décor found on the Abastepe Hill west of the river and the modern town centre, nothing was reported. With only Lucian's account to rely on in the effort to locate the sanctuary, it is worthwhile considering that the people of Abonuteichus started to build their temple immediately after receiving the oracle from Chalcedon, and therefore it is likely that they chose an undeveloped area outside the town and harbour (Fig. 1). Furthermore, it was predicted

18 Luc. *Alex.* 9. All quotes are translated by A.M. Harmon.

19 Luc. *Alex.* 10.

20 Clinton 1994; Mitchell-Boyask 2008, esp. 105-21; Mylonopoulos 2008, 60-3. Wickkiser 2008. For the Asclepieion of Athens, see Riethmüller 2005, 1, 241-78. A similar transmission of the Asclepius cult was made from Epidaurus to Rome in 293 BC. Livy 10.47. Val. Max. 1.8.2. Ov. *Met.* 15.622-745. For a comparison of Asclepius and Glycon, see Mastrocinque 2008. Another example from early Roman times is the introduction of the Magna Mater cult to Rome during the Second Punic War in 204 BC. After consulting the Sibylline Books, the Senate decided to send a delegation to the Phrygian sanctuary of Cybele in Pessinus to bring back the aniconic cult image of the goddess. Ov. *Fast.* 4.258.

21 Kunnert 2011. For the architectural remains, see also Marek 2003, 117.

Fig. 1. Arial view of the modern town of Inebolu with the Abastepe Hill to the left (photo: http://www.karalahana.com/makaleler/tarih/osmanli-arsivlerinde-inebolu-inebolu-adinin-kokeni.html, accessed November 2014).

to be a sanctuary for the Epidaurean healing god, Asclepius. Most of his cult sites were located in natural, non-urban spaces not too far from a settlement, so that the sanctuary could benefit from urban transport, accommodation and supplies.[22] This was also the case for the Asclepieion of Pergamum, which was probably known to the former itinerant doctor Alexander, as it was not far from Pontus and Bithynia and, moreover, was one of the most popular healing sanctuaries in the 2nd century BC. Therefore, the suburban area of the Abastepe Hill, or a similar place nearby, but not inside the town centre of Abonuteichus, seems an appropriate place to have built a temple for Asclepius/Glycon. Further extensive excavations might reveal better evidence.

The *Temenos*: Housing a God

Lucian further describes that, predicted by several other false oracles, which suddenly turned up on the Black Sea coast, Alexander arrived at Abonuteichus dressed like a priest with long hair and white clothes. He pretended sacred madness by filling his mouth with the foam of soapwort roots.[23] In the morning, he ran out into the market place, naked and with wild hair, climbed a high altar and spoke in tongues, until all of the inhabitants paid attention to him. He then ran to the temple, 'went to the excavations and the previously improvised fountainhead of the oracle, entered the water and sang hymns in honour of Asclepius and Apollo'.[24] At the same place on the previous night, Alexander had buried a goose egg with a recently hatched snake inside next to the 'foundations of the temple, where a pool of water had gathered, which either issued from springs somewhere in the foundation themselves or had fallen from the sky'.[25] If one is to believe Lucian's account, the people from Abonuteichus first built a temple in

22 Riethmüller 2005, 1, 334-59.

23 Luc. *Alex.* 12.

24 Luc. *Alex.* 13.

25 Luc. *Alex.* 13.

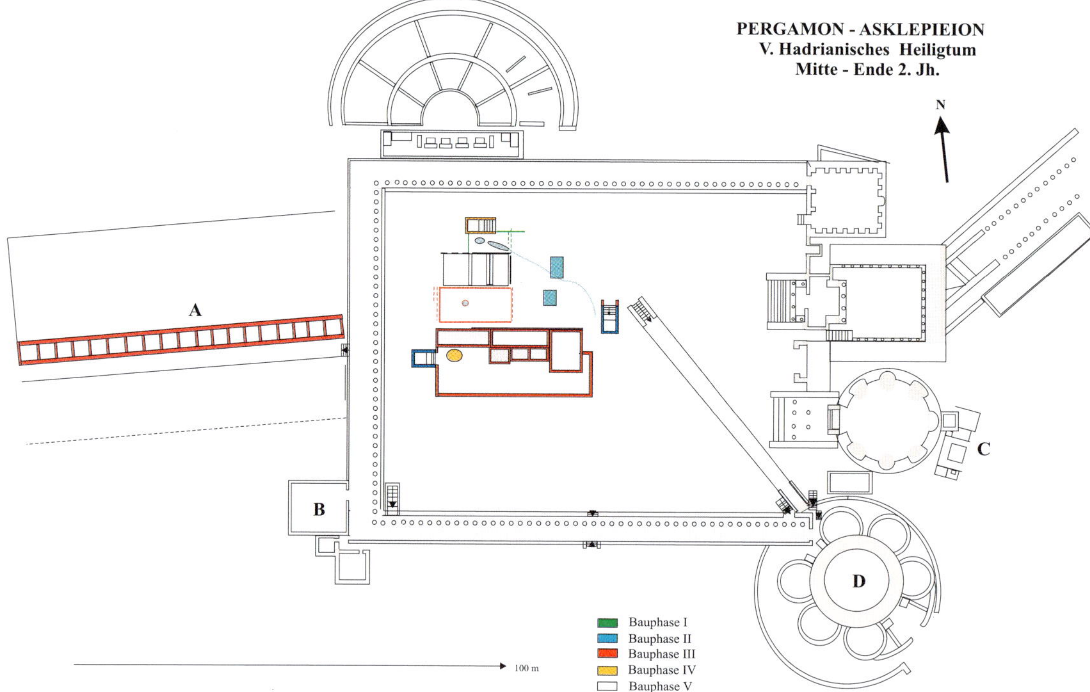

Fig. 2. *Floor plan. Asclepieion of Pergamum (plan by author).*

the vicinity of a fountain or sacred lake. A sacred source of water was essential for many cults, especially for healing gods. Many of these springs were already venerated long before they became incorporated into the healing gods' *temenoi*. In the main sanctuary of Asclepius at Epidaurus, the area around the spring was the oldest part of the cult site. The water of the spring later fed two fountains, one in the portico of the *abaton*, another in the area of building E, where the ritual meals took place. Also in the Asclepieion of Pergamum, the sacred spring next to the 'Felsbarre' was collected into two different fountains, one for bathing and another for drinking the sacred water (Fig. 2). Even in the newly founded Asclepieion at the south slope of the Athenian Acropolis, a sacred spring was essential for choosing the cult location. It is situated close to the temple in a grotto behind the incubation stoa.[26]

Many oracle sanctuaries were built at places with natural springs, especially oracles of Apollo, since the drinking of the sacred water was one of the most common methods

26 The cult of Asclepius in Epidaurus is attested from the 6th century BC. For Asclepius sanctuaries, see Riethmüller 2005, 1, 148-74 (Epidaurus), 344, Abb. 52 (Pergamum), 252, Abb. 35 (Athens). For the use of water in Greek sanctuaries in general, see Cole 1988, 161-5.

to enter into the state of divine trance in his cults.[27] The priestess of Apollo's sanctuary at Didyma as well as the priest in the cellar underneath the Apollo Temple of Clarus, which were the two most successful oracle sanctuaries of Asia Minor at Alexander's time, touched or drank from a sacred fountain before answering the oracle questions.[28] As Lucian mentions a 'fountainhead of the oracle', he implies that the oracle ritual of Glycon Neos Asclepius was meant to incorporate a sacred spring.[29] However, the oracle ritual, which finally took place in the sanctuary, had nothing to do with the drinking or touching of water. Furthermore, it is very unlikely that a water source inside or in the vicinity of a 2nd-century AD town like Abonuteichus would not have already been dedicated to another god. It could be, therefore, as Lucian cynically mentioned, that the pool of water had 'fallen from the sky'.[30]

The Oracle: Staging the Truth

Alexander finally decided on more than one method to get guidance from the new god.[31] The method chosen by a client depended on how much they wanted to spend and how important they were in terms of social status. A very common and probably less expensive answer could be received by writing down a question in a scroll, sealing it with clay, and handing it to Alexander in front of the temple doors.[32] The prophet then entered the inner sanctuary, together with a herald and a priest, and presented the scroll to Glycon. After receiving an answer from the god he gave the scroll back with the unbroken seal and the reply endorsed upon it.[33] This was exactly how the oracle

---

27 For the importance of water in the *temenoi* and cult of oracles, see Friese 2010, 86, 96, 252-65. Apollo oracles with water as a divinatory agent: Delphi, Clarus, Didyma and Ptoion. Friese 2010, 30-4, 128-42, 152-4, 175-9.

28 For Didyma, see Iambl. *Myst.* 3.2. For Clarus, see Tac. *Ann.* 2.54.

29 The connection to the healing god Asclepius, which was predicted in the oracle from Chalcedon, seems to become less important in the active cult which seems to focus on the divination. Although Lucian mentions the sale of medical treatments and remedies by advice of the divine snake (Luc. *Alex.* 22), there is no hint to other typical healing rituals, which usually took place in an Asclepieion. Lucian never mentions incubation or its related architecture, the *abaton*. U. Victor (1997, 4-5) assumes that incubation took place at Abonuteichus; A. Chaniotis (2002, 72) is more critical.

30 Luc. *Alex.* 13.

31 Having different divination methods at one oracle sanctuary was very common in antiquity. Also in Delphi, next to the famous Pythian oracle, which in the beginning was only given once a year, there was also a lot oracle all year round. In Clarus, excavations of a bronze knucklebone refer to an astragal oracle. Friese 2010, 102.

32 Luc. *Alex.* 19.

33 A little later Lucian uncovers the trickery behind it: 'The first, my dear Celsus, was a well-known method; heating a needle, he removed the seal by melting through the wax underneath it, and after reading the contents he warmed the wax once more with the needle, both that which was under the thread and that which contained the seal, and so stuck it together without difficulty. Another method was by using what they call plaster; this is a compound of Bruttian pitch,

Fig. 3. *Marble statue of Glycon from ancient Tomis, 2nd century AD (Friese 2013a, 115 fig. 17).*

ritual at Didyma took place, where most people had to wait for their answers in front of the raised threshold of the temple's entrance.[34] However, the most exclusive ritual at Abonuteichus was the autophone oracle, given by the god himself in his incarnation as a snake with an equine head. Long before Alexander arrived in Abonuteichus, he had bought a snake of uncommon size, beauty and sweet temper in Pella, where they were kept as pets. Sitting on a throne, coiling the snake around his neck and letting the tail stream over his lap and the floor, he kept the snake's head hidden under his arm. Instead, a linen mask was seen, to which windpipes from cranes were attached. A collaborator hid outside and spoke through these tubes, pretending that the snake was speaking.[35] Many coins and cult statues from the 2nd century AD, which were found all over the Black Sea area, Asia Minor and as far away as Athens, give an impression of the deified

asphalt, pulverised gypsum, wax, and gum Arabic. Making his plaster out of all these materials and warming it over the fire, he applied it to the seal, which he had previously wetted with saliva, and took a mould of the impression. Then, since the plaster hardened at once, after easily opening and reading the scrolls, he applied the wax and made an impression upon it precisely like the original, just as one would with a gem. Let me tell you a third method, in addition to these. Putting marble-dust into the glue with which they glue books and making a paste of it, he applied that to the seal while it was still soft, and then, as it grows hard at once, more solid than horn or even iron, he removed it and used it for the impression'. Luc. *Alex.* 21.

34 Only the wealthy clients could get access to the open courtyard of the Didymaen sanctuary, where the priestess sat in a small *naos*, which was built over the sacred spring (Iambl. *Myst.* 3.2). Friese 2010, 167-70.

35 Luc. *Alex.* 15.

snake (Fig. 3).[36] To make the oracle clients believe in this performance, not only the appearance of the god was important, but also the surrounding performative space:

> Now then, please imagine a little room, not very bright and not admitting any too much daylight; also a crowd of heterogeneous humanity, excited, wonder-struck in advance, agog with hopes. When they went in, the thing, of course, seemed to them a miracle ... and before they could look closely, they were forced out, were immediately crowded towards the exit, by those who kept coming in, for another door had been opened on the opposite side as an exit.[37]

To conceal the masquerade of the snake, Alexander used three very common tricks: restricting the space, light and time visitors were allowed to investigate more closely. So, next to a spacious and monumental temple building to worship the god and his prophet in a more public and monumental way, there was also a special oracle chamber or building. It was very likely attached to the temple, as Lucian mentions that visitors had to wait outside the temple doors for the scroll oracle while Alexander went inside to meet Glycon.[38] The room was deliberately kept small, with few or no windows, to create an impression of claustrophobic, cave-like constriction. Of course, this atmosphere not only served to keep the question and identity of the oracle client a secret but also the trickery of the oracle prophet.

The artificial modification of ritual space, as well as its visual separation from the monumental sanctuary architecture, is known from most of the successful operating oracle sites of the Roman period.[39] In Delphi, since the founding of the oracle, the Pythia sat on a tripod above the sacred chasm with mantic vapours. The chamber could not be seen from the outside; visitors had to enter the monumental temple first and then descend into the *adyton*.[40] Once inside, there was no natural light and the Pythia was probably obscured by a curtain or fence, affording only a dim view. The Clarian temple had an underground chamber, which could not even be seen from the outside. The structure was vaulted and probably totally renewed in the 2nd century BC, with access only through a labyrinthic entrance *dromos (*Fig. 4).[41] The oracle priest sat in complete darkness next to the basin with the mantic source. The most sophisticated artificial modification was designed in the sanctuary of the oracle hero Trophonius at Lebadaea in Boeotia. The entrance of a former natural cave, where the hero gave oracles since the 5th century BC, was in the 2nd century AD overbuilt with an oven-like superstructure,

---

36 For the iconography of Glycon Neos Asclepius, see Miron 1996, 155, 173-6; Victor 1997, 1-3; Sfameni Gasparro 1999, 278-81; Petsalis-Diomidis 2010, 14-41.

37 Luc. *Alex.* 16.

38 Luc. *Alex.* 19.

39 Most of the architecture which incorporated the central oracle ritual was deliberately hidden or separated from the places where the 'public' veneration took place. Friese 2011.

40 Plut. *Mor.* 397a, 498c, 438b.

41 Friese 2010, 175-9 (Clarus), 128-35 (Delphi).

Fig. 4. *Vaulted underground chamber, Clarus (photo: Leon Ziemer).*

in which the oracle client had to enter by night with a ladder; on reaching the bottom, he lay down in complete darkness with his feet secured in a narrow hole, before being dragged into a second cave, supposedly to meet Trophonius in a dreamlike state.[42] In obvious contrast to the competitively monumentalised architecture of the temples, treasuries and banqueting rooms of an oracle sanctuary, the artificial structures of these *adytoi* did not suit a representative purpose. Their main designation was to intensify the ritual experience. The invisibility of the performative space was made not only to intensify tension on the waiting client outside but also to increase the privacy of the ritual inside and the aura of secrecy of the whole cult. Particular features, like the narrowing of the entrance of Clarus and Lebadaea, could even have a physical impact on the clients, as they had to squeeze through it. The total darkness and the undetermined proportions of space, intensified by architectural modifications, like the labyrinthic shape of the Clarian corridors, were intended to confuse the clients' perception of space and direction. Alexander of Abonuteichus probably followed the same ideas, constructing his own oracle architecture. On the one hand, oracle clients expected an oracle to 'look like an oracle'; therefore, Alexander associated both ritual practice and performative space to already existing cult centres. Furthermore, oracles had to be 'old' to be reliable. By being 'officially introduced' by the old established oracle of Chalcedon, and by imitating traditional oracle centres like Delphi, Clarus or Didyma in their rituals as well as their architecture, the credibility of the new cult was confirmed. On the other hand, there was strong competition among the cults of the Roman Empire. An innovative element, like the snake-like figure of the new god and the possibility of direct contact with him through an autophone oracle could help to attract potential followers, who were already bored with the traditional cult places. However, Alexander of Abonuteichus did not rely solely on the oracle aspect of his cult invention.

42 Paus. 9.39.4; Plut. *Mor.* 590-592.

The Mysteries: Visualising a Secret

Probably a while after the oracle was well introduced, 'he established a celebration of mysteries, with torchlight ceremonies and priestly offices, which was to be held annually, for three days in succession ... as in Athens'.[43] Adding another component to the new sanctuary was a clever manoeuvre by Alexander. The celebration of secret rites not only attracted more visitors than the oracle alone, but it also kept them inside the sanctuary longer. By asking the surrounding cities of Paphlagonia and Pontus to send choruses of boys for a period of three years to sing hymns and praise the new god,[44] he tightened the connection between his cult and the civic community.[45] Last but not least, by spreading his Neopythagorean doctrines of reincarnation and leading the ceremonies as a high priest, instead of the snake Glycon, he himself became the focus of the worship – Alexander of Abonuteichus was now at the zenith of his career. People from many regions of Asia Minor, the west coast of the Black Sea, Greece and even Rome came to Abonuteichus to consult the oracle and to be initiated in the mysteries.

While Lucian clearly connected the ritual performance of the secret rites to the *Eleusinia* of Athens, he does not say much about the performative architecture in which these spectacles took place.[46] On the first day, there was a proclamation and the first part of a ritual drama about the mythical ancestry of Glycon Neos Asclepius. On the following two days, the drama continued, with its climax in a nightly performance of a *hieros gamos* on the third day, the 'Day of Torches'.[47] The drama appears to have been very sumptuously staged. Alexander wore gilded leather to give the impression that his skin was golden;[48] and, at least technically, the stage architecture appears to have been state-of-the-art: 'While he lay in full view, pretending to be asleep, there came down to him from the roof, as if from heaven, not Selene, but Rutilia, a very pretty women, married to one of the Emperor's stewards'.[49] To make Rutilia fly, the stage construction would at least have needed a hidden *mēchanē* or *deus ex machina*, probably attached to a temporary or permanent stage building or *skēnē*.[50] Furthermore, as the drama lasted for three days, at least the privileged spectators would have needed a seat. It is, therefore, very likely that the *temenos* of Abonuteichus incorporated a small but fully equipped

---

43 Luc. *Alex.* 38. For Alexander's eschatological ideas, see Miron 1996, 164; Victor 1997, 44-8; Chaniotis 2002, 74-8. For a general discussion on mysteries (with the basic literature), see Sfameni Gasparro 2012, 276-324.

44 Luc. *Alex.* 41.

45 For boy singers (phythaists) from Athens sent to Delphi, see *IG* II2 2336. For Clarus, see *SEG* 37.961-80.

46 For the connection, see Jones 1986, 142-4; Miron 1996, 156; Victor 1997, 140-2; Sfameni Gasparro 1999, 299-302; Chaniotis 2002, 78.

47 Luc. *Alex.* 38.

48 Luc. *Alex.* 40.

49 Luc. *Alex.* 38.

50 Stage machinery was already very common in Greek theatres, see e.g. Pl. *Cra.* 425d; *Cli.* 407a. App. *B Civ.* 2.147. For the practical use and dangers of the *mēchanē*, see e.g. Aristoph. *Pax* 146-176; Plut. *Vit. Sul.* 11; Suet. *Ner.* 12.2

Fig. 5. *Theatre in the Asclepieion of Pergamum (photo by author).*

theatre building. In antiquity, theatres were important stages for ritual activity of any kind; since Homeric times, the dramatising of a myth was one of the main parts of an initiation ceremony in many mystery cults.[51] In the earlier sanctuaries, these ritual dramas were performed in an appropriate open space, like the altar courtyard in front of the temple. The spectators would sit or stand on stairs, which often led from the courtyard to a higher building or terrace. During the course of the grand procession of the Eleusinian mysteries, dramatic performances of the myth were presented at fixed locations next to the sacred way leading up to the *telestērion*, where the climax of the festival took place by night, similar to the climax of the three-day festival in Abonuteichus.[52] To give at least the more important of the *mystēs* a better view, an *exedra* was built, right behind the Eleusinian *propylon* next to the Plutonion.[53] A larger *theatron* was cut into the rock at the north side of the southern courtyard, right in front of the side entrances of the *telestērion*. While in pre-Roman times there were only steps leading on to the terrace above, the area was enlarged during the Hadrianic restoration of the sanctuary so that up to 600 spectators could sit watching the rituals in the courtyard. It appears that in Roman times the architectural establishment of ritual performances became more monumental.[54] In the same period, the large reconstruction of the Asclepieion of Pergamum took place. The old centre, with the two temples for Asclepius and Hygea, the spring and the *abaton* were kept untouched, but were surrounded by a

51 For a general work on the ritual use of theatres, see Nielsen 2001. For mystery sanctuaries with a dramatisation of a myth as part of the initiation ritual, see Nielsen 2001, 134-6 (Samothrace), 106-10 (Lycosura), 234-6 (Nemi).

52 The *drōmena* of Eleusis included a representation of Demeter's search for Persephone, the sacred wedding of Zeus and Demeter and probably the birth of a divine child. For the similarities in the Eleusinian and the Abonuteichus mysteries, see Chaniotis 2002, 78-80.

53 Nielsen 2001, 127-8, fig. 56.

54 For a similar development of architecture in the Artemision of Sparta, see Mylonopoulos 2008, 54-6.

large portico. Around the sides, several buildings were attached: an impressive *propylon*, a domed structured temple for Asclepius Soter, a library, a bigger *abaton*, a meeting room, and a *hieron theatron*[55] with a richly decorated *scaenae frons* (Fig. 5). It was used not only to stage the hymns to the god, but also for non-sacred performances and speeches. These modifications made the Asclepieion of Pergamum one of the most modern and successful healing sanctuaries of Roman times. Alexander very likely chose a similarly elaborate theatre for the central ritual of his mysteries, the singing of the hymns and the propagation of his Neopythagorean ideas.

Conclusion

Earlier research has demonstrated that the success of the Glycon cult was based on the exploitation and adaptation of traditional, and therefore familiar, cult practices of Roman society.[56] The same can be assumed for its architectural appearance. By comparing Lucian's description of the topographical, architectural and performative space to contemporary, popular and ritually related cult sites in Asia Minor (Clarus, Didyma, Pergamum), a potential architectural reconstruction of the *temenos* of Abonuteichus is generated. Thus, it had a suburban location with a good connection to the nearby harbour; as with many contemporary Roman sanctuaries, it probably had a courtyard surrounded by porticos, accessible by a monumental *propylon* (Pergamum); inside, a temple of unknown size was erected to worship the new god and his prophet Alexander; a sacred lake or source was situated close to the temple, which relates to the cults of traditional healing and oracle gods (Pergamum, Clarus and Didyma); water was collected in a well construction (fountainhead), though in all likelihood not intended for drinking or bathing, as Lucian does not mention this in connection with the ritual; the oracle took place in a separate building or chamber, attached to or even under the temple and was, due to the needs of the ritual, narrow, dark and fitted with two doorways (Didyma and Clarus); the sanctuary included a theatre for staging the mysteries and for singing the sacred hymns (Pergamum); during their stay, visitors to the sanctuary probably resided in tents outside or in hostels inside the town, or they may have slept in the porticos of the sanctuary.

So how functionalised was Alexander's cult architecture? As J. Elsner recently argued, there 'need be no relation at all between the architectural logic of a building or religious enclosure and the ritual logic of what went on inside or around it'.[57] This might be true for a cult place that developed organically, adapting its shape over centuries and making compromises according to: space, money, taste, political or ideological reasons or external influences like violent interactions, migration or cross-cultural communica-

55 Aristeid. 49.21.

56 See esp. Chaniotis 2002 with older literature. Many earlier scholars have studied the syncretistic orientation, facilitated by the integration of the eastern provinces into the Roman Empire. See Chaniotis 2002, 81, but also Victor 1997, 38; Sfameni Gasparro 1999.

57 Elsner 2012, 18.

tion. In contrast, the sanctuary of Glycon Neos Asclepius was the invention of a single person at a particular time and at a deliberately chosen place, whose only purpose was to attract as many visitors or followers as possible. In this case, it would be most sensible to relate the architectural logic of the buildings (form) to the ritual logic inside (function). According to Lucian, Alexander's intention of his cult foundation was based on the discernment 'that human life is swayed by two great tyrants, hope and fear, and that a man, who could use both of these to advantage would speedily enrich himself'.[58] Playing safe, Alexander provided a package of different rituals that worshippers usually had to seek in separate locations: healing, divination and eschatological ideas. For these rituals he chose an appropriate architectural translation. Most of these elements, ritual as well as architectural, were not at all innovative, but already successfully established in other sanctuaries of Asia Minor, Greece and Rome. In the 2nd century AD, the external visualisation of a ritual was much more evident than in pre-Roman times. At the same time, ritual space was used to create an atmosphere of secrecy – spiritually as well as physically. As Alexander of Abonuteichus did not have to take into consideration the traditions of rituals already in existence or the topography of an already established cult place, he could pick whatever suited him best and whatever made the most effective impression on potential devotees. The architecture of his *temenos* thus followed two main purposes: to trick (oracle *adyton*, mystery stage) and to treat (healing, entertaining) the worshippers in equal measure. Against Lucian's hope that his exposure had 'some usefulness, refuting as it does certain falsehoods and confirming certain truth in the minds of all men of sense',[59] the archaeological evidence shows that the Glycon Neos Asclepius cult outlived both founder and critic by more than a century.[60]

58 Luc. *Alex.* 8.

59 Luc. *Alex.* 61

60 See esp. Miron 1996.

SINE GROVE SAXKJÆR

The Locrian *Pinakes*: Revealing Secrets of Cult Practice?

More than 6000 terracotta pinakes *have been unearthed in the Mannella sanctuary in Locri Epizephiri, South Italy. The unparalleled iconography provides us with an invaluable insight into Greek religion and ritual practice in the 5th century BC; however, there is much scholarly debate regarding the interpretation of the* pinakes. *In this article, I will evaluate the main interpretations, which connect the iconography to the themes of marriage or death, as well as attempt to use the iconography to reveal the possible secrets of cult practice in the Mannella sanctuary.*[1]

Ever since the first Locrian *pinakes* became known at the end of the 19th century, scholars have been fascinated by the fragments and their intriguing low-relief iconography. At the present moment, there are records of over 6000 individual plaques.[2] One particular point of interest is that the iconography seems to reflect a form of female ritual, which is rarely illustrated in the ancient world.[3] The *pinakes* show scenes from the myths surrounding Persephone as well as rituals performed in relation to her worship. Scholars have found the *pinakes* invaluable for developing an understanding of Greek religion, belief systems, society and rituals. The question remains, however, as to what kind of rituals and religious practice the *pinakes* depict. Since the 1970s, scholars have suggested that the *pinakes* pertain to women's rituals, namely, *rites de passage* – in this case, the female transition from maiden to matron. Meanwhile, others have suggested that the scenes depicted on the *pinakes* extend beyond marriage, even beyond life itself. Moreover, several studies have related the *pinakes* and the worship of Persephone to the Orphic gold tablets found in burials in South Italy.

This article will focus on these two predominant lines of thought – marriage or death – in relation to the *pinakes*. Furthermore, I will explore the common feature of these two 'pivotal moment' interpretations, that is, the rite of passage and the implied initiation.[4] In relation to the Locrian *pinakes* both lines of interpretation are connected

1 I am most grateful to Anna Collar for the useful comments as well as the proofreading of this article. I should note that any remaining errors are my own.

2 Cardosa, Grillo & Schenal Pileggi 1999, 25.

3 Redfield 2003, 353.

4 Gennep [1908] 1960, 65.

to female transitions from one stage in life to another. Although rituals of initiation do not necessarily entail a secret collective or society, it can be argued that the ritual markings of 'life-transitions', the *rites de passage,* which includes both marriage and death,[5] can be compared to initiation rites into secret societies or cults. Such comparisons have long been made: in 1908, H. Webster stated that 'The tribe becomes, in fact, a secret association, divided into grades or classes out of which as a later development arise the "degrees" of the secret societies. The passage from one class to another immediately higher usually attended with various ceremonies of a secret and initiatory character'.[6] Entering a new stage of life entailed a ritual admission into a certain group in society that only encompassed initiates, who shared a certain knowledge and solidarity. An additional element, which further allows for the comparison with secret societies, is the strict gender segregation within these *rites de passage* practices.[7]

It has been suggested that the *pinakes* were dedicated in the Mannella sanctuary by women in relation to so-called 'pivotal moments' or 'life-transitions' such as marriage, childbirth or death;[8] can we go further, however, and see on the *pinakes* rites of initiation that go beyond *rites de passage*? Could the *pinakes* and their imagery bear witness to an initiation into a cult? Could the worship of Persephone at the Mannella sanctuary be connected to some sort of mysteries reserved only for women? And if so, could the *pinakes* reveal secrets of the cult practice? Or does the iconography of the *pinakes* merely provide us with vague indications of secret knowledge, only known to the initiated and thereby lost to the modern interpreter?

In order to approach the *pinakes* within the framework of initiation and secrecy, I will first provide a short introduction to the material, its historical and archaeological context, as well as outline the history of archaeological research related to the *pinakes.* This will be followed by an outline of the two main lines of interpretation of the *pinakes*' iconography. Based on this, finally I will reconsider the *pinakes* and their potential revelations of cult practice in the Mannella sanctuary.

The *Pinakes* from the Mannella Sanctuary in Locri Epizephiri

The Greek colony of Locri Epizephiri was situated on the Ionian coast on the far southern end of the Italian peninsula. The history of the city is partly known from literary sources.[9] Part of the literary tradition surrounding Locri Epizephiri is the foundation myth, of which one version closely resembles the foundation myth of the Greek colony of Taras. The myth, originally known from Aristotle, was debunked by the historian Timaeus, only for Polybius to later support Aristotle's version and paraphrase it in his attack on

5 Gennep [1908] 1960, 3.

6 Webster 1908, 20.

7 La Fontaine 1985, 38.

8 Sourvinou-Inwood 1973, 14; Price 1978, 172; Gluckman 1962, 2.

9 Niutta 1977.

Timaeus.[10] Briefly summarised, the myth is as follows: during the (most likely First) Messenian War, when the Locrian men were at battle as allies of Sparta, the Locrian women had liaisons with their slaves. Before the Locrian men returned from war, the women and the slaves fled to Italy, where they founded Locri Epizephiri.[11] Polybius further describes how the mixed linage meant that the ancestry of the inhabitants of Locri Epizephiri was traced down the female side.[12] According to the chronological fixed points given by Pausanias, the First Messenian War ended in 724 BC;[13] however, looking at the archaeological material from Locri Epizephiri, the earliest Greek objects unearthed are Corinthian *aryballoi*, dating to the first quarter of the 7th century BC.[14] Although the Greek material does not necessarily equal a Greek presence, it is assumed that the foundation of the city should be placed within the early 7th century BC.[15]

P. Orsi led the first archaeological investigations of Locri Epizephiri in 1890, and he subsequently ran a further eight campaigns at the site. P. Orsi's work focused on the necropoleis and the sanctuaries.[16] In addition to excavating approximately 1600 burials, P. Orsi identified various important religious areas in Locri including the Marasà temple, the Casa Marafioti temple, a small temple to Athena and the Mannella sanctuary, which is the source of the majority of *pinakes* (Fig. 1).[17]

The Mannella sanctuary was founded in the late 7th century BC, and it was situated on a long narrow terrace at the edge of the Mannella hill.[18] From an inscription, it is known that the sanctuary was dedicated to Persephone,[19] and the wealth of the sanctuary is further attested by Livy.[20] Aside from the remains of a temenos wall, no monumental temple structures have been identified, however, based on the finds of architectural terracottas it seems likely that smaller buildings existed inside the temenos enclosure in the archaic period.[21] According to the literature, the lack of a monumental temple is consistent with the chthonic nature of the goddess Persephone.[22] During excavation campaigns in 1908 and 1909, P. Orsi unearthed a large votive deposit near the temenos wall. Parts of the deposit had already been subjected to illegal excavations, from which a

---

10 Plb. 12.5.
11 Sourvinou-Inwood 1974, 188.
12 Plb. 12.5.
13 Paus. 4.13.7.
14 Redfield 2003, 210.
15 Osanna 1992, 205.
16 Unfortunately, P. Orsi never published the extensive material from his excavations apart from preliminary reports.
17 Redfield 2003, 207-8.
18 Mertens Horn 2006, 8.
19 Sabbione 1996, 32.
20 Liv. *Hist.* 29.18.3-18.
21 Grillo 1996, 44.
22 Sabbione 1996, 32.

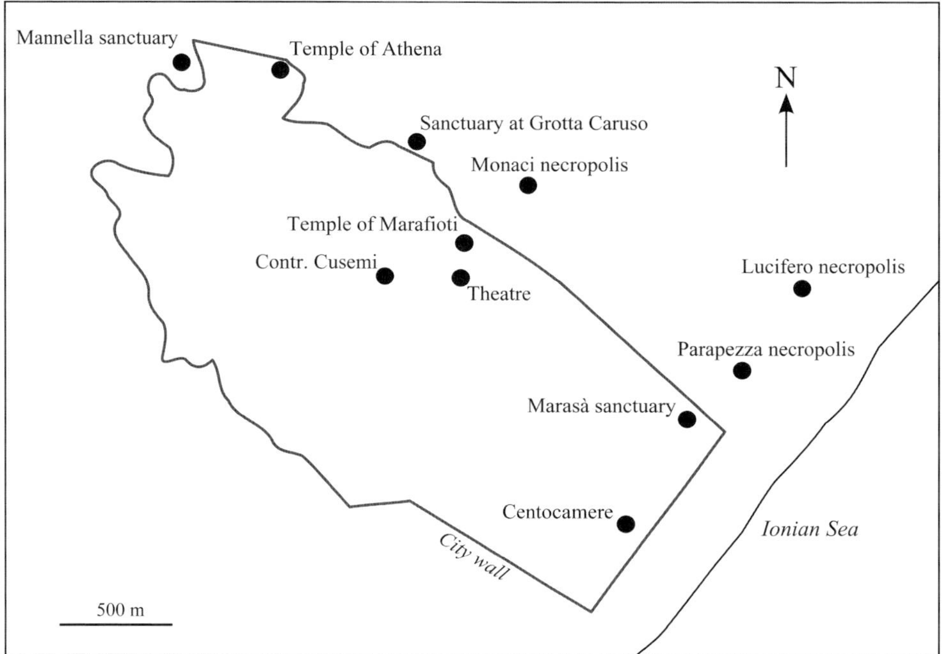

Fig. 1. *Map of Locri Epizephiri (map by author).*

quantity of artefacts had been sold on the art market.[23] Based on the material from the deposit, it is evident that the sanctuary was cleared in the mid-5th century BC, and that the accumulated votive objects were buried in the deposit – all intentionally broken like similar items found in other deposits from sanctuaries.[24] The majority of the Locrian *pinakes* derive from this deposit in the Mannella sanctuary, in which all of the material was deposited in layers arranged by type – the layer of fragmentary *pinakes* was found above a layer of figurines and pottery.[25]

The *pinakes* are rectangular terracotta plaques with low-relief decorations. They differ in size as the individual *pinax* is adjusted in width and height according to the iconographical representation, although the size rarely exceeds more than 30 cm. The thickness varies from 0.5 to 2.0 cm.[26] Pigments of paint are still preserved on some fragments, which suggests that the *pinakes* were once vibrantly coloured. It also seems that multiple copies of the *pinakes* were produced using moulds, and the design included

23 A large quantity of the illegally excavated material was identified in the private collection of Cav. Domenico Candida. The collection was bought and transferred to Museo Nazionale di Taranto in 1907. Q. Quagliati published the recovered *pinakes* the following year, see Quagliati 1908.

24 Mertens Horn 2006, 9.

25 Redfield 2003, 208.

26 Redfield 2003, 346.

suspension holes for hanging the plaque, perhaps on walls of buildings or in trees in the sacred precinct of the goddess.[27] The majority of the *pinakes* can be dated to the second quarter of the 5th century BC.[28]

P. Orsi originally entrusted the publication of the Locrian *pinakes* to the Italian archaeologist D. Zancani. However, when D. Zancani passed away before he could carry out the work, P. Orsi passed on the task to P. Zancani Montuoro, D. Zancani's widow, in 1933.[29] P. Zancani Montuoro published the first of her papers on the subject in 1935,[30] and although she never published the *pinakes* collectively, she did establish a classification system of the various known types, recognising ten different categories of scene, each with their own variations.[31] In the 1960s, the German archaeologist H. Prückner based his doctoral dissertation on the fragments of Locrian *pinakes* held at the Archaeological Institute at Heidelberg University,[32] which, after the collections at Reggio and Locri, holds the largest quantity of *pinakes* from Locri.[33] H. Prückner published his book on the *pinakes* in 1968,[34] which includes an extensive interpretation of the iconography. His results, which centre on the role of Aphrodite, were not very well received,[35] yet despite the controversy surrounding his interpretations, H. Prückner's book should be recognised as the first comprehensive study of the *pinakes*.

The *pinakes* have recently (1999 – 2007) been collectively published along with illustrations, photographs, descriptions and additional information on technique as well as on the various interpretations. A team of archaeologists engaged by the Società Magna Grecia carried out the project, and their work was published in the periodical *Atti e Memorie della Società Magna Grecia*.[36] The new publication is divided into three parts, of which the first comprises four volumes; the second comprises five volumes, while the third and final part consists of six volumes. P. Zancani Montuoro's classification system for the Locrian *pinakes* is still used in the recent publication, which divides the *pinakes* into ten iconographic groups:[37]

1) *Animali sacri alla dea, mobili e arredi del culto, senza personaggi* (i.e. scenes depicting sacred animals of the goddess, utensils and furniture related to the cult, but no human characters)

27 Zancani Montuoro [1961] 1995, 153.
28 Mertens Horn 2005, 49.
29 Borelli 1995, 145.
30 Zancani Montuoro [1935] 1995.
31 Mertens Horn 2005, 50.
32 Prückner 1968, xi.
33 Redfield 2003, 248, n. 7.
34 Prückner 1968.
35 MacLachlan 2012, 344; Redfield 2003, 349; Boardman 1971, 145.
36 I will use the abbreviation Pi.LE for *I pinakes di Locri Epizefiri*, when referring to illustrations in the publication.
37 Rubinich 1999, 14.

2) *Il ratto di Kore ad opera di Plutone o, più spesso, d'un delegato, probabilmente un Dioscuro* (i.e. scenes depicting the abduction of Kore by Hades or by a representative of Hades)
3) *Scene di sacrificio e allestimento del rito* (i.e. scenes depicting sacrifice and preparation of rituals)
4) *Raccolta delle frutta per la sposa ed altre scene con alberi e piante* (i.e. scenes depicting women collecting fruit, scenes with trees and plants)
5) *Preparazione, trasporto e consegna alla dea del peplo nuziale insieme con la corona e le frutta; ed altre processioni* (i.e. scenes depicting the preparation, transportation and delivery of the matrimonial peplos to the goddess along with a wreath and fruits, scenes depicting processions)
6) *Vestizione ed acconciatura della dea (kosmesis)* (i.e. scenes depicting adornment of the goddess)
7) *Preparazione del letto, corteo nuziale e porta del talamo* (i.e. scenes depicting the preparation of the bed, wedding processions and the door to the *thalamus*)
8) *Persefone sola o con Plutone riceve altre divinità o semi-dei, recanti dono (anakalyptèria)* (i.e. scenes depicting Persephone, alone or together with Hades, receiving gods or demi-gods bearing gifts)
9) *Persefone apre la cista, che contiene un bimbo o una bambina* (i.e. scenes depicting Persephone opening a chest containing a baby or a child)
10) *Rappresentazioni varie o dubbie e frammenti incerti* (i.e. unidentified scenes)[38]

The new editorial team did not strictly follow these categorisations, since their interpretations differ from that of P. Zancani Montuoro,[39] and in addition, types unknown to P. Zancani Montuoro are included in the new publication, so it has been necessary to expand the number of types within a category.[40]

In light of this recent and comprehensive work on the *pinakes*, this article will not attempt to make any all-encompassing analyses of the iconographic presentations or even of the full range of iconographic categories. Instead, I will explore the *pinakes*' potential revelations of cult practice through selected examples.

Interpretations of Iconography

The iconography of the Locrian *pinakes* refers to the female realm: we see scenes with women adorning themselves, bathing, picking fruits and handling fabric. The scenes include elegant furniture and ornaments as well as fruits and flowers, basketry and chests.[41] At first sight, the *pinakes* seem to be a window into a largely unknown female world, an invitation to a hidden domain of female behaviour and activities. J. Redfield

38 Zancani Montuoro [1961] 1995, 156.

39 Mertens Horn 2006, 12.

40 Rubinich 1999, 18.

41 Redfield 2003, 353.

suggests that 'The life of Locrian women, presumably like other Greek women secluded, took place in an enclosure within an enclosure; it is part of the fascination of the *pinakes* that they seem to take us right into this hidden world'.[42]

Although the vast majority of *pinakes* seem to depict this female sphere, there are some differences between the settings shown in the scenes. M. Mertens Horn has suggested that the *pinakes* can be divided into two overall groups: scenes that take place in the sanctuary of Persephone and scenes that relate to the myths surrounding Persephone.[43] Among the scenes taking place in the sanctuary are those on *pinakes* in Group 3, e.g. Type 3/6,[44] which depict a couple standing in front of a temple with two cult statues visible inside. Despite the fact that some of the scenes like this one may relate to 'earthly' matters while others reference the 'mythic', the representations are often very similar: the composition, clothing, behaviour, animals and objects are more or less the same.[45] This means that some scenes are very hard to classify, for instance: is it Persephone or a mortal girl who adorns herself (e.g. Type 6/8)?[46] Is the preparation of the bridal peplos for the wedding of Persephone and Hades or is it a peplophoric ritual taking place in the Mannella sanctuary (e.g. Type 5/5)?[47] The blurred lines between the 'mythic' and the 'earthly' representations are far from unique for the Locrian *pinakes*; on the contrary, it is a persistent element within ancient Greek imagery. In Greek vase-painting, for example, it is often hard to distinguish scenes from everyday-life and mythical images, as non-mythical figures can be combined with mythical ones.[48] In the same way, it can be almost impossible to identify whether e.g. the iconography on sanctuary pottery is depicting a mythical scene, a general reproduction of a ritual (which is perhaps derived from a myth) or a specific ritual action, which took place within the sanctuary.[49] It follows that a clear distinction between 'mythic' and 'earthly' scenes often proves to be illusionary – perhaps because this clear-cut division is most of all a modern construction.[50] Instead, the blurred lines between scenes from myths and from everyday life underline the close connections between the two spheres in antiquity.

The Transition from Maiden to Matron

The most common scene among the *pinakes* is the abduction scene (Group 2). There are fragments from over 400 individual *pinakes* with this type of iconography, made from at least 81 different moulds.[51] The motif varies, but the consistent components are the abductor, the girl and the chariot, with which she is being taken away. Most

42 Redfield 2003, 353.
43 Mertens Horn 2005, 49.
44 Zancani Montuoro [1940] 1995, pl. LXVII, 1; Pi.LE II (5), fig. 6, tav. XVII.
45 Mertens Horn 2005, 49.
46 Mertens Horn 2006, Abb. 12.
47 Mertens Horn 2006, Abb. 16; Pi.LE II (5), fig. 23, tav. LII.
48 Junker 2012, 52.
49 Saxkjær 2013, 189-90.
50 Junker 2012, 50-9.
51 Mertens Horn 2006, 50.

Fig. 2. *Type 2/30. Abduction scene with the additional figure of Hades (Pi.LE I (4), fig. 32a. Courtesy of Società Magna Grecia).*

often, the abductor is naked except for a cloak. He appears on the *pinakes* both as an older bearded man as well as a young man without beard. The abducted girl is always dressed in a simple peplos or chiton and himation, apart from two exceptions, which are found on Type 2/22[52] and Type 2/30.[53] The abductor lifts the girl onto a chariot harnessed to horses, sometimes depicted with wings, e.g. Type 2/10.[54] It is agreed that scenes with the bearded abductor should be identified as Hades capturing Kore, whereas the interpretation and identity of the young abductor is much debated.

One possibility, as suggested originally by P. Orsi, is that the young abductor is simply another iconographical type of Hades, a youthful Hades.[55] However, this idea has never gained much support – partly due to the *pinakes* of Type 2/30, where the young abductor and Hades are depicted side by side (Fig. 2). Another possibility was proposed by P. Zancani Montuoro, who interpreted the young abductor as a middleman, who is abducting Kore on behalf of Hades. She believes the middleman to be either a Dioscurus[56] or Thanatus.[57] H. Prückner, on the other hand, has put forward another interpretation: he believes that the young man is a pre-Greek hero abductor, who was associated with the myth of Hades and Persephone due to the similarity in the legends, but continued to be worshipped independently alongside Hades and Persephone.[58] The latter interpretation was never widely accepted, as no other indication of such a pre-Greek hero abductor is known from Locri Epizephiri.

Common to the interpretations listed above is the close relationship to the myth of

52 Prückner 1968, pl. 12; Pi.LE I (4), tav. CCXV-CCXXVII.
53 Mertens Horn 2006, Abb. 43-4; Pi.LE I (4), fig.32a, tav. CCXLI-CCXLII.
54 Prückner 1968, pl. 14; Pi.LE I (4), tav. CLIa.
55 Sournivou-Inwood 1973, 13.
56 Zancani Montuoro [1954] 1995, 201.
57 Zancani Montuoro [1954] 1995, 198.
58 Prückner 1968, 73-4.

Hades abducting Kore, carrying her off to the Underworld and making her his bride and queen. C. Sourvinou-Inwood follows this line of interpretation, although she takes the interpretation one step further as she moves the scene of the young abductor away from a mythical sphere; '… the Young Abductor scenes are not mythological, but represent a different type of subject, the representational expression of which was modelled upon the iconographical pattern of Persephone's abduction'.[59] The combination of the young abductor and the (occasional) willingness of the abducted girl led C. Sourvinou-Inwood to interpret the scenes as belonging to a marriage theme. Furthermore, she suggests that *pinakes* with this motif were dedicated to Persephone by girls as part of a prenuptial ritual.[60] J. Redfield supports C. Sourvinou-Inwood in her interpretation and underlines the close connection between myth and ritual, where the mythology seems to be evoked in as well as be evocative of a ritual context.[61] The blurred line between ritual and myth would also explain the presence of the winged horses in some of the scenes.[62] Moreover, C. Sourvinou-Inwood states that the scenes should be seen as idealised depictions of a bride and bridegroom.[63] She proposes that the scenes could depict a 'mock' ritual, a Locrian marriage rite, but that it could likewise just be a rite that felt somehow related to that of abduction,[64] i.e. the marriage rite and the transition to the husband's household, the transition from maiden to matron.

The idea that the abduction scenes are somehow related to the rite of marriage fits well with a range of interpretations of other scenes depicted on the *pinakes*. For instance, the scenes classified as Group 7, i.e. the *pinakes* with scenes depicting the preparation of the bed, wedding processions or the door to the *thalamus*.[65] The meaning of *thalamus* is inner or secret chamber – more precisely, a secret chamber for women[66] (e.g. Type 7/4).[67] Although the interpretation of these scenes is altered in the recent publication, where the scenes are no longer connected to the sacred marriage (*theogamia*), but understood as real-life nuptial-related scenes,[68] their relation to marriage is maintained. Another example is found in the recent publication, where Type 2/24[69] and 2/25,[70] which were originally classified as abduction scenes, have been reinterpreted as depictions of a bridal procession (Fig. 3). As clarified by R. Schenal Pileggi, the scenes show the bridal couple of Hades and Kore 'raffigurati

59 Sourvinou-Inwood 1973, 14.
60 Sourvinou-Inwood 1973, 14.
61 Redfield 2003, 249.
62 Redfield 2003, 363.
63 Sourvinou-Inwood 1973, 14.
64 Sourvinou-Inwood 1973, 18.
65 Zancani Montuoro [1961] 1995, 156.
66 Oxford English Dictionary, cf. Müller, Welcker & Leitch 1852, §48.
67 Pi.LE II (5), fig. 52, tav. CXXXIV.
68 Schenal Pileggi 2003, 734.
69 Pi.LE I (4), fig. 26, tav. CCXXIX-CCXXX.
70 Pi.LE I (4), fig. 27, tav. CCXXXI.

Fig. 3. *Type 2/24. Bridal procession (Pi. LE I (4), fig. 26. Courtesy of Società Magna Grecia).*

non più come rapitore e rapita ma come coppia di sposi in procinto di mettersi in viaggio verso la futura dimora'.[71]

Lastly, the various scenes of Group 5, the so-called peplos scenes, have also been related to rites of marriage, although in the recent publication M. Rubinich understands the peplos scenes as the preparation and dedication of a peplos to the cult statue in the Mannella sanctuary.[72] M. Mertens Horn interprets the various peplos scenes as scenes of a narration, which depict a peplophoric ritual related to womanhood and, most likely, marriage. The climax of the narrative is, according to M. Mertens Horn, the scene with the presentation of the peplos to the goddess (Type 5/15),[73] which would be followed by the scene on Type 5/2 (Fig. 4),[74] where Persephone deposits the folded peplos into a chest. M. Mertens Horn connects the peplophoric narrative to the ritual of dedicating a peplos or a cloth at times of 'life-transition' for women; 'Anche in altri santuari, come quello attico di Artemis Brauronia, le giovani donne dedicavano alla dea le stoffe più belle fatte con le loro mani, prima del matrimonio o dopo il parto'.[75] C. Sourvinou-Inwood also draws a parallel between Artemis Brauronia and the Locrian Persephone.[76]

The nature of Persephone in the Mannella sanctuary clearly differs from the nature of Persephone known from the sanctuary of Eleusis, where the connection between mother and daughter is the central feature.[77] In the Mannella sanctuary, Demeter was

71 Schenal Pileggi 1999, 815.

72 Rubinich 2003, 247.

73 Mertens Horn 2005, fig. 2; Pi.LE II (5), tav. LXXIV-LXXX.

74 Mertens Horn 2005, fig. 5; Pi.LE II (5), tav. XL-XLI.

75 Mertens Horn 2005, 56.

76 Sourvinou-Inwood 1978, 105.

77 On the worship of Demeter and Persephone in relation to the Eleusinian Mysteries, see Bowden in this volume.

Fig. 4. *Type 5/2. Persephone deposits a folded peplos into a chest (Pi.LE II (5), fig. 20. Courtesy of Società Magna Grecia).*

almost completely absent, although she was worshipped in an extramural sanctuary situated just outside the city walls of Locri in the Parapezza district, where the worship was connected to the rites of *thesmophoria*.[78] In contrast, it seems that the central theme of the Mannella cult was the goddess' transition from Kore to Persephone and her role as the wife of Hades. In line with this, C. Sourvinou-Inwood considers the Locrian Persephone to be a protectress of marriage and weddings. She has further argued that the worship of Persephone also had a kourotrophic nature, where she was worshipped as the nurturer and protectress of children.[79] T. Price offers a similar view with her characterisation of Persephone as both maiden and matron, and a *kourotrophos*. The idea of Persephone as a nursing deity originates from the *pinakes* in Group 9, where a woman (interpreted as Persephone) opens a chest with a child or baby inside, e.g. Type 9/1 (Fig. 5). The child could be a depiction of a newly-born or unborn mortal child, who was put under the protection of Persephone.[80] Another possibility is that it is a representation of a stillborn child or a child which died in early infancy, and which accordingly was transferred to the Underworld and to the care of the goddess. In both cases it is conceivable that mothers dedicated the *pinakes* with these representations to Persephone.

78 Mertens Horn 2005, 51.

79 Sourvinou-Inwood 1978, 105.

80 Price 1978, 172.

Fig. 5. *Type 9/1. Persephone opens a chest with a child inside (courtesy of Società Magna Grecia).*

The Transition to the Underworld

Some scholars have questioned the interpretation of the *pinakes*' proposed relation to marriage and the transition from maiden to matron. For instance, M. Mertens Horn does not agree that the abduction scenes are metaphors for marriage.[81] She even questions whether the scenes should be connected to the myth of Hades and Persephone, as only one type of *pinakes* (Type 2/22)[82] securely depicts the divine abduction as it is described in the *Homeric Hymn to Demeter*. Instead of linking the abduction scenes to the myth of Persephone, M. Mertens Horn suggests that the scenes could be connected to the founding myth of Locri, which, as described above, includes the 'abduction' of women.[83] Another possible explanation is found in the famous *votum* of 477/6 BC. In the *votum* or oath, the inhabitants of Locri Epizephiri vowed their virgin daughters to sacred prostitution at the festival of Aphrodite in return for a granted victory over the tyrant Leophron of Rhegion, who was attacking the city.[84] C. Sourvinou-Inwood has proposed a possible connection between the nature of the *votum* and the founda-

81 Mertens Horn 2006, 52.

82 Mertens Horn 2006, Abb. 41; Pi.LE I (4), tav. CCXV-CCXXVII.

83 Mertens Horn 2006, 56.

84 Justin 21.3.2-5.

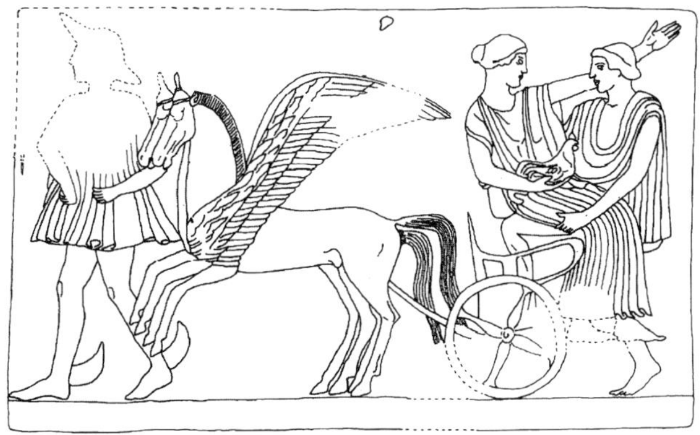

Fig. 6. *Type 2/28. Abduction scene with the additional figure of Hermes (Pi.LE I (4), fig. 30. Courtesy of Società Magna Grecia).*

tion myth of Locri Epizephiri.[85] Moreover, M. Mertens Horn has pointed out that the *pinakes* with the abduction scenes were produced in the same period as the *votum*; a time when the abduction of young girls must have been fresh in the minds of the Locrians. According to M. Mertens Horn, this is hardly a coincidence.[86]

However, some types of *pinakes* cannot be explained by the *votum* of 477/6 and the foundation myth of Locri Epizephiri. This is the case for Type 2/28[87] (Fig. 6) and the previously mentioned Type 2/30[88] (Fig. 2). The imagery on Type 2/28 depicts Hermes (Psychopompus?) alongside the abductor and the maiden, whereas the imagery on Type 2/30 shows Hades together with the abductor and the maiden.[89] These iconographical representations lead to the other prevailing line of interpretation of the Locrian *pinakes* and the possible connection to an Orphic sphere.

Some of the earliest studies of the iconography of the *pinakes* proposed links to eschatology and death. As early as 1908, Q. Quagliati proposed a connection between the imagery of the Locrian *pinakes* and contemporary conceptions of the afterlife. He related the various iconographical elements to an eschatological sphere, where the scenes from the myth of Persephone were inseparable from the imagery of deceased maidens' transitions to the Underworld.[90] For instance, Q. Quagliati suggested that the *pinakes* belonging to Group 8, where Persephone (alone or with Hades) is seated on a throne and receives gifts, could be related to the worship of a deceased. Q. Quagliati interpreted the seated woman, i.e. Persephone, as possibly being a heroised woman, whose worship could be paralleled to that taking place in a *hērōon*.[91] Moreover, the rooster, which is a recurring element throughout the various types of *pinakes* (see e.g. figs. 2, 3 and 6),

85 Sourvinou-Inwood 1974.

86 Mertens Horn 2006, 58.

87 Pi.LE I (4), fig. 30, tav. CCXXXIII-CCXXXIV.

88 Pi.LE I (4), fig. 32a-32b, tav. CCXLI-CCXLII.

89 Mertens Horn 2006, 60.

90 Quagliati 1908, 145.

91 Quagliati 1908, 142.

was firmly identified by Q. Quagliati as a chthonic symbol, since the rooster stands by the entrance to the Underworld and facilitates the journey to Hades.[92] In addition, Q. Quagliati interpreted the abduction scenes as images of death and the transition to the Underworld. In this view, the abducted maiden should be seen as a deceased woman, who was carried to the Underworld by Hades or – as in the case of Type 2/28 and 2/30 – by one of his messengers, Thanatus or Hermes Psychopompus. In relation to the latter, Q. Quagliati refers to Book 24 of the *Odyssey*, which he considers to be an Orphic interpolation in the Homeric epic poem.[93] With this reference, Q. Quagliati does not directly connect the *pinakes* to an Orphic cult, although he clearly interprets the iconography of the Locrian *pinakes* as being related to the mysticism surrounding the Greek concepts of death and the state of the soul in the afterlife.[94]

Following a similar line of interpretation, the *pinakes* have also been connected to Orphism by G. Giannelli,[95] among others, who believed that the imagery on the Locrian *pinakes* reflects Orphic beliefs and doctrines. Moreover, although G. Giannelli admitted that the iconography was reminiscent of the Eleusinian mysteries, he found Demeter's absence from the Mannella sanctuary to be another proof of the Orphic nature of the cult.[96] The Locrian *pinakes* have further been seen in relation to the Orphic gold tablets found in burials in Thurii, Petelia and Hipponion.[97] All three places are situated in southern Italy, and Hipponion was founded as a colony of Locri Epizephiri. It is believed that the gold tablets belonged to those who had been initiated into the mysteries of Dionysus[98] and into the Orphic cult. The gold tablets were adorned with words from the mythic character of Orpheus, who was a poet and prophet in the mysteries.[99] In Greek mythology, the Underworld was a sad and dark place, which could be avoided by no one. However, a mystery cult like the Orphic cult represented an alternative to this miserable fate – as stated by A. Bernabé; 'They [i.e. mystery cults] present an underworld in which the believer can reach different states, better or worse, by performing certain acts during his lifetime'.[100] To become a member of such a cult, one had to go through rites of initiation, where secret information was given to the initiated. The Orphic gold tablets have been interpreted as belonging to an initiatory context, as they provide instructions to the deceased in the afterlife. In other words, they reveal the existence of a secret knowledge, which could result in a better afterlife in the Underworld. The largest group of the gold tablets present Persephone as the queen of the Underworld.[101]

---

92 Quagliati 1908, 152.
93 Quagliati 1908, 153.
94 Quagliati 1908, 142.
95 Giannelli 1924, 226-7.
96 Giannelli 1924, 227.
97 Giannelli 1924, 230; Mertens Horn 2006, 36.
98 Graf 2013, 140.
99 Graf & Johnston 2013a.
100 Bernabé 2009, 95.
101 Mertens Horn 2005, 50.

If ascribing the Locrian *pinakes* to this Orphic sphere, it is clear that the central feature in their imagery would no longer be Persephone's transition from maiden to matron, but her transition from the world of the living to that of the deceased as well as her reign in the Underworld. However, in the various works that relate the *pinakes* to an Orphic context, the exact function of the *pinakes* remains unclear. Evidently, the *pinakes* were not inscribed with a secret knowledge as the Orphic gold tablets were, just as they were never placed in burials along the initiates, but are found specifically within the Mannella sanctuary. The *pinakes* were equipped with suspension holes and were most likely hung on display in the sanctuary prior to their final deposition in the votive deposit. Moreover, they were vibrantly coloured and must have been highly visible to the people frequenting the sanctuary. As mentioned above, the common feature of the two dominant lines of interpretation is the ritual of transition and initiation. In this context it is worth considering if the imagery on the *pinakes* could be portraying an initiation ritual, which might have taken place within the Mannella sanctuary.

In relation to the *pinakes*' potential depiction of an initiation ritual, M. Mertens Horn has proposed an alternative interpretation of Type 2/30 (Fig. 2) within the Orphic sphere. First and foremost, she understands the scene as being a synoptic narrative: it depicts the abduction of a girl to the Underworld and – at the same time – a Dionysian ritual. M. Mertens Horn identifies the Dionysian ritual from the heavy dress of the girl, which she recognises as a cult robe, similar to that worn by girls in initiation rites performed in Athens in the same period.[102] Furthermore, she interprets the wreath worn by the young man as symbolising Hades (who is likewise adorned with a wreath) and therefore supportive of her theory; the presence of Hades is a symbol of the transition into the spiritual realm of Persephone. The girl is being initiated; she is not Persephone, as she is depicted in smaller scale than Hades, and the divine couple is otherwise always equal in size.[103] M. Mertens Horn connects the scene with the rite of ritual death, which she finds to be the most important act of initiation within the Orphic context. M. Mertens Horn further interprets the rooster as support for the scene depicting the rite of ritual death because of its symbolism, which she links to a chthonic sphere as well as to rebirth.[104] The connection of the ritual to Dionysus is grounded in the Orphic myths, where Dionysus is a central figure, as he is likewise a symbol of rebirth. In the Orphic myth, Dionysus was the child of Zeus and Persephone, and he was killed by the Titans. After his death, his heart was placed in the womb of a mortal woman, Semele, by whom he was reborn.[105] The figure of Dionysus does occur from time to time in the Locrian imagery, and the same is true for the grapevines and the *kantharos*, both part of Dionysian symbolism. Dionysus is depicted in front of a seated Persephone and Hades on Type 8/20,[106] and the *kantharos* is seen in the background of

102 Mertens Horn 2006, 62.

103 Mertens Horn 2006, 62.

104 Mertens Horn 2006, 17, 63.

105 Johnston 2013, 66-93.

106 Prückner 1968, pl. 25.

Type 5/2 (Fig. 4). Returning to Group 9, which was previously mentioned in relation to the possible kourotrophic nature of Persephone (Fig. 5), M. Mertens Horn suggests that the child in the chest is Dionysus, who was given to Persephone by Zeus.[107]

Revealing Secrets of Cult Practice?

The common elements of the two lines of interpretation are that of transition and the element of initiation. The structure of the myth of Persephone follows the basic three steps established by the early anthropologist A. van Gennep for the *rites de passage*. The steps are separation, liminality and reintegration.[108] Kore is abducted and thereby separated from her mother, she is disoriented on the threshold between maiden and matron, unsure of her new position, and then, finally, she is reintegrated, as she enters her role as the wife and queen of Hades. As illustrated by the exposition of the prevailing interpretations of the *pinakes* in the above, this narrative can be related to both marriage and death, to both the transition to adulthood and to the afterlife. Moreover, in relation to the Locrian *pinakes*, it does not only prove difficult to separate the different meanings of the myth of Persephone, it is further difficult to establish whether the narrative depicted on the *pinakes* should be connected with the rites of passage or to an initiation into a secret collective or cult, as these two types of rituals are likewise closely connected. On one hand, it seems plausible that the iconography as well as the *pinakes* themselves could indeed have been connected to female rites of passage and the initiation into a new stage of female life. Several scholars have suggested that the *pinakes* were dedicated as a prenuptial offering, and M. Mertens Horn even connects the peplos-related iconography to rituals that could have taken place in the Mannella sanctuary, in which women dedicated a peplos or a cloth in response to particular 'pivotal moments',[109] such as birth, marriage, childbirth and death.[110] It seems plausible that the actual *pinakes* were likewise dedicated in the Mannella sanctuary in connection to a woman's transition and initiation into a new life stage, a new level of knowledge, and that at this time the *pinakes* may have been suspended from the trees in the sanctuary. As death is also characterised as a transition in life and as a so-called 'life-crises', the connection to rites of passage could be valid in relation to the other prevailing line of interpretation, i.e. that of a possible relation to a chthonic sphere.

Initiation rituals into a secret society or cult are very similar to rites of passage. Among the studies relating the iconography of the *pinakes* to initiation, the prevailing interpretation links the *pinakes* to the Orphic sphere. However, this link is extremely difficult to establish with any certainty. In general, the evidence for Orphic cult practice in the archaeological record is very sparse, apart from the actual gold tablets.[111] In this

107 Mertens Horn 2006, 46.

108 Lincoln 1979, 234; Kimbali 1960, vii; Gennep [1908] 1960.

109 Mertens Horn 2005, 56.

110 Gluckman 1962, 2.

111 Petersen 2011, 168.

case, there are considerable differences in the material record. As mentioned above, the golden tablets were placed in burials with straightforward Orphic instructions to the deceased, whereas the *pinakes* were displayed in a sanctuary and only potentially have a link to the Orphic sphere through the iconography. Nevertheless, the *pinakes* could be connected to a cult practice that included Orphic elements, even if it was mainly women who worshipped in the Mannella sanctuary. We know that women took part in mystery cults, e.g. in the rites of *thesmophoria* that related to the worship of Persephone and Demeter, and which excluded men.[112] Furthermore, it is evident that women could be initiated into the Orphic cult, since some of the Orphic gold tablets were found in female burials, e.g. in Hipponion.[113]

I argue that there is more to the Locrian *pinakes* than 'just' being votive offerings given in relation to rites of passage. With their unparalleled imagery, their large number and their apparent visibility in the sanctuary, the *pinakes* must have played a central role in the cult practice in the first half of the 5th century BC. Based on this, I believe that we are dealing with the imagery of a strong female religious sphere – highly probable, in the form of a mystery cult. Although I am not convinced that the cult should be related to Orphism, I agree that there must have been a strong focus on the afterlife, as is generally the case in mystery cults.[114] However, I do not agree that this should exclude rites connected to the transition from maiden to matron, as the cult could potentially encompass various stages and transitions of the female life and include rituals entwined with rites of passage. Moreover, I support the interpretation of the iconography of the *pinakes* as reflecting various rites within the cult practice, such as peplophoric rituals as well as the initiation rites.

However, while the *pinakes* probably reveal the existence of a mystery cult as well as offering indications of the rites performed within this cult, there is still a level of knowledge, secret to the uninitiated and the modern viewer, which is not depicted. For instance, we do not see exactly how the women were initiated. If M. Mertens Horn is correct in her assumptions, we might see the initiation garment, but not the ritual itself. If the cult did include rites related to the various stages of the female life cycle, several elements remain hidden. For instance, B. Lincoln refers to the *Homeric Hymn to Demeter*, where Kore's defloration changes her utterly, and she even takes a new name, Persephone. He describes the scene as if Kore has 'been initiated by rape'.[115] If this is the case in marriage, we do not see it depicted, although the *pinakes* of Group 7 (which depict the preparation of the bed, wedding processions or the door of the inner chamber) might indicate the sexual part of transition from maiden to matron. In the same manner, we do not see childbirth – we simply see a baby in a chest. We see the journey and transition to the Underworld, but – as in the case of the Orphic gold tablets – we are not informed of the secret knowledge within the cult that should

112 Stehle 2007, 165.

113 Graf & Johnston 2013b, 4.

114 Bernabé 2009, 95.

115 Lincoln 1979, 228.

make this final transition bearable. Moreover, the way that myth and ritual mirror each other, and, at times, seem to completely fuse in the iconography of the *pinakes*, helps thicken the veil of secrecy surrounding the cult activities.

I believe the Locrian *pinakes* continue to hold secrets; some waiting to be revealed, others lost for ever and concealed for eternity. However, I hope that the present article has helped to broaden the understanding of the *pinakes* and their intriguing iconography in relation to the worship of Persephone in the Mannella cult.

Bibliography

Concealing and Revealing in Ancient Greek Religion and Beyond

Beerden, K. 2013. *Worlds Full of Signs: Ancient Greek Divination in Context*. Leiden: Brill.

Bok, S. 1983. *Secrets: On the Ethics of Concealment and Revelation*. New York: Vintage.

Bowden, H. 2004. "Xenophon and the Scientific Study of Religion", in: Tuplin 2004, 229-46.

Bowden, H. 2005. *Classical Athens and the Delphic Oracle: Divination and Democracy*. Cambridge: Cambridge University Press.

Bowden, H. 2010. *Mystery Cults in the Ancient World*. London: Thames & Hudson.

Boyer, P. 1994. *The Naturalness of Religious Ideas: A Cognitive Theory of Religion*. Berkeley: University of California Press.

Bremmer, J.N. 1995. "Religious Secrets and Secrecy in Classical Greece", in: Kippenberg, Stroumsa 1995, 61-78.

Burkert, W. 1987. *Ancient Mystery Cults*. Cambridge: Harvard University Press.

Burkert, W. 1995. "Der geheime Reiz des Verborgenen: Antike Mysterienkulte", in: Kippenberg, Stroumsa 1995, 79-100.

Calinescu, M. 1994. "Secrecy in Fiction: Textual and Intertextual Secrets in Hawthorne and Updike". *Poetics Today* 15 (3), 443-65.

Clinton, K. 1993. "The sanctuary of Demeter and Kore at Eleusis", in: Marinatos, Hägg 1993, 110-24.

Flower, M.A. 2008. *The Seer in Ancient Greece*. Berkeley: University of California Press.

Geertz, A.W. (ed.) 2013. *Origins of Religion, Cognition and Culture*. Durham: Acumen.

Gordon, R.L. (ed.) 1981. *Myth, Religion & Society: Structuralist Essays*. Cambridge: Cambridge University Press.

Gray, V.J. 1996. "Herodotus and Images of Tyranny: The Tyrants of Corinth". *American Journal of Philology* 117, 361-89.

Harding, L. 2014. *The Snowden Files: The Inside Story of the World's Most Wanted Man*. London: Faber.

Hazelrigg, L.E. 1969. "A Reexamination of Simmel's 'The Secret and the Secret Society': Nine Propositions". *Social Forces* 47, 323-30.

Kermode, F. 1979. *The Genesis of Secrecy: On the Interpretation of Narrative*. Cambridge: Harvard University Press.

Kippenberg, H.G. & Stroumsa, G.G. (eds.) 1995. *Secrecy and Concealment: Studies in the History of Mediterranean & Near Eastern Religions* (*Studies in the History of Religions* 65). Leiden/New York/Köln: Brill.

Kwapisz, J., Petrain, D. & Szymanski, M. (eds.) 2012. *The Muse at Play: Riddles and Wordplay in Greek and Latin Poetry*. Berlin: de Gruyter.

Lardinois, A. & McClure, L. (eds.) 2001. *Making Silence Speak: Women's Voices in Greek Literature and Society*. Princeton: Princeton University Press.

Leigh, D. & Harding, L. 2011. *Wikileaks: Inside Julian Assange's War on Secrecy*. London: Guardian Books.

Marinatos, N. & Hägg, R. (eds.) 1993. *Greek Sanctuaries*. London: Routledge.

Martin, L.H. 1995. "Secrecy in Hellenistic Religious Communities", in: Kippenberg, Stroumsa 1995, 101-21.

Maurizio, L. 2001. "The Voice at the Centre of the World: The Pythias' Ambiguity and Authority", in: Lardinois, McClure 2001, 38-54.

Naerebout, F.G. & Beerden, K. 2012. "'Gods Cannot Tell Lies': Riddling and Ancient Greek Divination", in: Kwapisz, Petrain, Szymanski 2012, 121-47.

Nedelmann, B. 1995. "Geheimhaltung, Verheimlichung, Geheimnis – einige soziologische Vorüberlegungen", in: Kippenberg, Stroumsa 1995, 1-16.

Parker, R. 1991. "The 'Hymn to Demeter' and the 'Homeric Hymns'". *Greece & Rome* 38, 1-17.

Piot, C.D. 1993. "Secrecy, Ambiguity, and the Everyday in Kabre Culture". *American Anthropologist* 95, 353-70.

Scheppele, K.L. 1988. *Legal Secrets: Equality and Efficiency in the Common Law*. Chicago: Chicago University Press.

Seaford, R. 1996. *Euripides Bacchae*. London: Aris & Philips.

Segal, C. 1997. *Dionysiac Poetics and Euripides' Bacchae*. Princeton: Princeton University Press.
Simmel, G. 1906. "The Sociology of Secrecy and of Secret Societies". *American Journal of Sociology* 11 (4), 441-98.
Tuplin, C. (ed.) 2004. *Xenophon and his World: Papers from a Conference held in Liverpool in July 1999*. Stuttgart: Steiner.
Vernant, J.-P. 1981. "The Myth of Prometheus in Hesiod", in: Gordon 1981, 43-56.
Wood, M. 2004. *The Road to Delphi: The Life and Afterlife of Oracles.* London: Chatto.

Simmel, the Cycle of Secrecy, and the Socio-Spatial Dimension of Concealing and Revealing in the Gospel of Mark

Best, E. 1986. *Disciples and Discipleship: Studies in the Gospel According to Mark.* Edinburgh: T. & T. Clark.
Bok, S. 1982. *Secrets: On the Ethics of Concealment and Revelation.* New York: Pantheon Books.
Collins, A.Y. 2007. *Mark: A Commentary.* Minneapolis: Fortress Press.
De Jong, A. 1995. "Secrecy I: Antiquity", in: Hanegraaff 1995, 1050-4.
Durkheim, E. "Sociology and its Scientific Field", in: Wolff 1964, 354-75.
Foerster, W. 1964-76. "ὄρος", in: Kittel, Friedrich 1964-76, 475-87.
Frisby, D. 2002. *George Simmel*, revised ed. London/New York: Routledge.
Hanegraaff, W.J. 1995. *Dictionary of Gnosis and Western Esotericism* 2. Leiden/ Boston: Brill.
Hock, R.F., Chance, J.B. & Perkins, J. (eds.) 1998. *Ancient Fiction and Early Christian Narrative.* Atlanta: Scholars Press.
Hultgren, A.J. 1979. *Jesus and His Adversaries: The Form and Function of the Conflict Stories in the Synoptic Tradition.* Minneapolis: Augsburg.
Hurtado, L.W. 1986. "Following Jesus in the Gospel of Mark – and Beyond", in: Longenecker 1986, 9-29.
Jenks, C. (ed.) 1998. *Core Sociological Dichotomies.* London/Thousand Oaks/New Delhi: Sage.
Kermode, F. 1979. *The Genesis of Secrecy: On the Interpretation of Narrative.* Cambridge: Harvard University Press.
Kippenberg, H.G. & Stroumsa, G.G. (eds.) 1995. *Secrecy and Concealment: Studies in the History of Mediterranean & Near Eastern Religions* (*Studies in the History of Religions* 65). Leiden/New York/Köln: Brill.
Kittel, G. & Friedrich, G. (eds.) 1964-76. *Theological Dictionary of the New Testament* 5, trans. G.W. Bromiley et al. Grand Rapids: Eerdmans.
Longenecker, R.N. (ed.) 1986. *Patterns of Discipleship in the New Testament.* Grand Rapids/Cambridge: Eerdmans.
MacDonald, D.R. 1998. "Secrecy and Recognitions in the *Odyssey* and Mark: Where Wrede Went Wrong", in: Hock, Chance, Perkins 1998, 139-53.
Malbon, E.S. 1983. "Fallible Followers: Women and Men in the Gospel of Mark". *Semeia* 28, 29-48.
Malbon, E.S. 1986. *Narrative Space and Mythic Meaning in Mark.* San Francisco: Harper & Row.
Malina, B.J. 2001. *The New Testament World: Insights from Cultural Anthropology*, 3rd ed. Louisville: Westminster John Knox.
Marshall, C.D. 1989. *Faith as a Theme in Mark's Narrative* (*SNSTMS* 64). Cambridge/New York: Cambridge University Press.
Nedelmann, B. 1995. "Geheimhaltung, Verheimlichung, Geheimnis – einige soziologische Vorüberlegungen", in: Kippenberg, Stroumsa 1995, 1-16.
Pilch, J.J. 1994. "Secrecy in the Mediterranean World: An Anthropological Perspective". *Biblical Theology Bulletin* 24, 151-7.
Seitz, O.J.F. 1949. "Criteria for the Esoteric Logia in Mark". *Anglican Theological Review* 31 (4), 218-24.
Simmel, G. 1906. "The Sociology of Secrecy and of Secret Societies". *American Journal of Sociology* 11 (4), 441-98.
Slater, D. 1998. "Public/Private", in: Jenks 1998.
Stroumsa, G.G. 1996. *Hidden Wisdom: Esoteric Traditions and the Roots of Christian Mysticism* (*Studies in the History of Religions* 70). Leiden: Brill.
Theissen, G. 1995. "Die pragmatische Bedeutung der Geheimnismotive im Markusevangelium", in: Kippenberg, Stroumsa 1995, 225-45.
Tolbert, M.A. 1989. *Sowing the Gospel: Mark's World in Literary-Historical Perspective.* Minneapolis: Fortress Press.
Warren, C. & Laslett, B. 1977. "Privacy and Secrecy: A Conceptual Comparison". *Journal of Social Issues* 33 (3), 43-51.
Watson, D.F. 2010. *Honor among Christians: The Cultural Key to the Messianic Secret.* Minneapolis: Fortress Press.
Wrede, W. 1901. *The Messianic Secret*, trans. J.C.G. Greig 1971. London/Cambridge: James Clarke.
Wolff, K.H. (ed.) 1964. *Essays on Sociology and Philosophy by Emile Durkheim et al.* New York: Harper & Row.

Hooked on Concealing: The Descent to Hell in Doctrine and Drama

Alfeyev, H. 2009. *Christ the Conqueror of Hell: The Descent into Hades from an Orthodox Perspective*. New York: St Vladimir's Seminary Press.

Bauckham, R. 1992. "Descent to the Underworld", in: Freedman 1992, 145-59.

Bernstein, A.E. 1993. *The Formation of Hell: Death and Retribution in the Ancient and Early Christian Worlds*. London: UCL Press.

Brock, S. 1983. *The Harp of the Spirit: Eighteen Poems of Saint Ephrem* (*Studies Supplementary to Sobornost* 4), 2nd enlarged ed. London: Fellowship of St. Alban and St. Sergius.

Carpenter, M. 1970. *Kontakia of Romanos: Byzantine Melodist* I. Columbia: University of Missouri Press.

Constas, N.P. 2004. "The Last Temptation of Satan: Divine Deception in Greek Patristic Interpretations of the Passion Narrative". *Harvard Theological Review* 97 (2), 139-63.

Daly, R.J. 2009. *Apocalyptic Thought in Early Christianity*. Grand Rapids: Baker Academic.

Daniélou, J. 1955. *Origen*. New York: Sheed and Ward.

Elliot, J.K. 1993. *The Apocryphal New Testament: A Collection of Apocryphal Christian Literature in an English Translation*. Oxford: Clarendon Press.

Eriksen, U.H. 2013. *Drama in the Kontakia of Romanos the Melodist: A Narratological Analysis of Four Kontakia*. PhD Dissertation, Aarhus University.

Easterling, P. & Hall, P. 2002. *Greek and Roman Actors: Aspects of an Ancient Profession*. Cambridge: Cambridge University Press.

Frank, G. 2009. "Christ's Descent to the Underworld in Ancient Ritual and Legend", in: Daly 2009, 211-26.

Freedman, D.N. (ed.) 1992. *The Anchor Bible Dictionary*. New York: Doubleday.

Grosdidier de Matons, J. 1967. *Romanos le Mélode. Hymnes* (*Sources Chrétiennes* 128). Paris: Les éditions du cerf.

Harvey, S.A. & Hunter, D.G. 2008. *The Oxford Handbook of Early Christian Studies*. Oxford/New York: Oxford University Press.

Kelly, J.N.D. 1960. *Early Christian Creeds*, 2nd ed. London: Longmans.

Larsen, K.B. 2008. *Recognizing the Stranger: Recognition Scenes in the Gospel of John* (*Biblical Interpretation Series* 93). Leiden: Brill.

Lash, E. 1995. *St. Romanos the Melodist, Kontakia: On the Life of Christ (The Sacred Literature Series)*. New York: HarperCollins Publishers.

LXX. Rahlfs, A. (ed.) 1935. *Septuaginta*. Stuttgart: Würtemberg Bible Society.

McGuckin, J.A. 2008. "Poetry and Hymnography (2): The Greek World", in: Harvey, Hunter 2008, 641-56.

NRSV. *New Revised Standard Version Bible*. 1989. The Division of Christian Education of the National Council of the Churches of Christ in the United States of America. Used by permission. All rights reserved.

NTNA. *Novum Testamentum Graece*, Nestle-Aland 28th ed. Accessible online.

ODB. Kazhdan, A.P. (ed.) 1991. *Oxford Dictionary of Byzantium* I-III. Oxford: Oxford University Press.

Peel, M.L. 1979. "The 'Descensus ad Inferos' in 'The Teachings of Silvanus' (CG VII,4)". *Numen* 26 (1), 23-49.

PG. Migne, J.P. *Patrologia Graeca*.

PL. Migne, J.P. *Patrologia Latina*.

Puchner, W. 1979. "Zur liturgischen Frühstufe der Höllenfahrtsszene Christi". *Zeitschrift für Balkanologie* 15, 98-133.

Puchner, W. 2002. "Acting in the Byzantine Theatre: Evidence and Problems", in: Easterling, Hall 2009, 304-24.

SC. *Sources Chrétiennes*. Paris: Les éditions du cerf.

Stiefenhofer, D. 1909. *Die Geschichte der Kirchweihe vom 1 -7 Jahrhundert*. Munich: Verlag der J.J. Lentnerschen Buchhandlung.

Toit, M. du 2007. "The Origin of the Christian Doctrine on the 'Descensus Christi ad Inferos'". *Ekklesiastikos Pharos* 89 (18), 102-20.

Wellesz, E. 1961. *A History of Byzantine Music and Hymnography*, 2nd ed., revised and enlarged. Oxford: Clarendon Press.

Winling, R. 2003. "Le *Psaume 23* (24) et son utilisation dans la tradition patristique pour le theme de la résurrection." *Cahiers de Biblia Patristica* 7, 13-31.

Remembering or Concealing Mythical and Historical Events in the Cityscape of Early Roman Ephesus

Alcock, S.E. 2002. *Archaeologies of the Greek Past: Landscape, Monuments, and Memories.* Cambridge: Cambridge University Press.

Alzinger, W. 1974. *Augusteische Architektur in Ephesos* (*Sonderschriften* 16). Wien: Österreichischen Archäologischen Institut.

Alzinger, W. 1999. "Das Zentrum der Lysimachischen Stadt", in: Friesinger, Krinzinger 1999, 389-92.

Alzinger, W. & Bammer, A. 1971. *Das Monument des C. Memmius* (*Forschungen in Ephesos* 7). Wien: Österreichisches Archäologisches Institut.

Assmann, J. 1988. "Kollektives Gedächtnis und kulturelle Identität", in: Assmann, Hölscher 1988, 9-19.

Assmann J. & Hölscher T. (eds.) 1988: *Kultur und Gedächtnis* (*Suhrkamp Taschenbuch Wissenschaft* 724), Frankfurt am Main: Suhrkamp.

Bammer, A. 1972-5. "Die politische Symbolik des Memmiusbaues". *Jahreshefte des Österreichischen archäologischen Instituts in Wien* 50, 220-2.

Bammer, A. 2007. "Zum Monument des C. Memmius in Ephesos", in: Meyer 2007, 57-61.

Barrandon, N. & Kirbihler, F. (eds.) 2011. *Les gouverneurs et les provinciaux sous la République romaine.* Rennes: Presses universitaires de Rennes.

Beard, M. & North, J. (eds.) 1990. *Pagan Priests: Religion and Power in the Ancient World.* London: Duckworth.

Benndorf, O., Niemann, G. & Heberdey, R. 1906. *Forschungen in Ephesos* (*Forschungen in Ephesos* 1). Wien: Österreichische Archäologischen Institut.

Bier, L. 2011. *The Bouleuterion at Ephesos* (*Forschungen in Ephesos* 9.5). Wien: Verlag der Österreichischen Akademie der Wissenschaften.

Birk, S. & Poulsen, B. (eds.) 2012. *Patrons and Viewers in Late Antiquity* (*Aarhus Studies in Mediterranean Antiquity* 10). Aarhus: Aarhus University Press.

Bok, S. 1982. *Secrets: On the Ethics of Concealment and Revelation.* New York: Pantheon Books.

Brandt, B., Gassner, V. & Ladstätter, S. (eds.) 2005. *Synergia. Festschrift für Friedrich Krinzinger* I. Wien: Phoibos Verlag.

Broughton, T.R.S. 1952. *The Magistrates of the Roman Republic* II. *99 B.C. – 31 B.C.* Lancaster/Oxford: Lancaster Press/B.H. Blackwell.

Calinescu, M. 1994. "Secrecy in Fiction: Textual and Intertextual Secrets in Hawthorne and Updike". *Poetics Today* 15 (3), 443-65.

Chaniotis, A. 2013. "Mnemopoetik: die epigraphische Konstruktion von Erinnerung in den griechischen Poleis", in: Dahly et al. 2013, 132-69.

Connerton, P. 2004. *How Societies Remember*, 12th ed. Cambridge: Cambridge University Press.

Coşkun, A. (ed.) 2005. *Roms auswärtige Freunde in der späten Republik und im frühen Prinzipat.* Göttingen: Duehrkohp & Radicke.

Dahly, O. et al. (eds.) 2013. *Medien der Geschichte. Antikes Griechenland und Rom.* Berlin: De Gruyter.

D'Andria, F. & Romeo, I. (eds.) 2011. *Roman Sculpture in Asia Minor* (*Journal of Roman Archaeology Supplement* 80). Portsmouth: Journal of Roman Archaeology.

Dickenson, C.P. & Nijf, O.M. van (eds.) 2013. *Public Space in the Post-Classical Polis: Proceedings of a One Day Colloquium held at Fransum 23rd July 2007* (*Caeculus. Papers in Mediterranean Archaeology and Greek & Roman Studies*). Leuven/Paris/Walpole: Peeters.

Dignas, B. & Smith R.R.R. (eds). 2002. *Historical and Religious Memory in the Ancient World.* Oxford/New York: Oxford University Press.

Dreyer, B. 2005. "Rom und die griechischen Polisstaaten an der westkleinasiatischen Küste in der zweiten Hälfte des zweiten Jahrhunderts v.Chr. Hegemoniale Herrschaft und lokale Eliten im Zeitalter der Gracchen", in: Coşkun 2005, 56-74.

Elsner, J. 1995. *Art and the Roman Viewer: The Transformation of Art from the Pagan World to Christianity.* Cambridge: Cambridge University Press.

Engelmann, H. 1993a. "Celsusbibliothek und Auditorium in Ephesos". *Jahreshefte des Österreichischen archäologischen Instituts in Wien* 62, 105-11.

Engelmann, H. 1993b. "Zum Kaiserkult in Ephesos". *Zeitschrift für Papyrologie und Epigraphik* 97, 279-89.

Engelmann, H. 1996. "Das Grab des Androklos und ein Olympieion (Pausanias VII 2,9)". *Zeitschrift für Papyrologie und Epigraphik* 112, 131-3.

Fejfer, J., Moltesen, M. & Rathje, A. (eds.) 2015. *Tradition: Transmission of Culture in the Ancient World* (*Acta Hyperborea: Danish Studies in Classical Archaeology* 14). Copenhagen: Museum Tusculanum Press.

Fontani, E. 2002. "Le città della provincia d'Asia e la memoria delle loro origini". *Mediterraneo Antico. Economie società culture* 5 (1), 27-37.

Foxhall, L. 1995. "Monumental Ambitions: The Significance of Posterity in Greece", in: Spencer 1995, 132-49.

Friesinger, H. & Krinzinger, F. (eds.) 1999. *100 Jahre österreichische Forschungen in Ephesos. Akten des Symposions Wien 1995* (*Österreichische Akademie der Wissenschaft. Archäologische Forschungen* 1). Wien: Verlag der Österreichischen Akademie der Wissenschaften.

Gerrig, R.J. 2010. "Reader's Experiences of Narrative Gaps". *StoryWorlds. A Journal of Narrative Studies* 2, 19-37.

Gordon, R. 1990. "The Veil of Power: Emperors, Sacrificers and Benefactors", in: Beard, North 1990, 201-31.

Groh, S. 2001. "Die Topographie der Oberstadt von Ephesos". *Jahreshefte des Österreichischen archäologischen Instituts in Wien* 70, 21-33.

Groh, S. 2006. "Neue Forschungen zur Stadtplanung in Ephesos". *Jahreshefte des Österreichischen archäologischen Instituts in Wien* 75, 47-116.

Halfmann, H. 2001. *Städtebau und Bauherren im römischen Kleinasien. Ein Vergleich zwischen Pergamon und Ephesos* (*Istanbuler Mitteilungen Beiheft* 43). Tübingen: Ernst Wasmuth Verlag.

Hall, J.M. [1997] 1998. *Ethnic Identity in Greek Antiquity*, repr. Cambridge: Cambridge University Press.

Hofbauer, M. 2002. "Zum Theater von Ephesos. Eine kurze Darstellung der Grabungsgeschichte zwischen 1866 und 2001". *Jahreshefte des Österreichischen archäologischen Instituts in Wien* 71, 177-87.

I.Eph. Inschriften von Ephesos (*Inschriften Griechischer Städte aus Kleinasien* 11-17). Bonn: Rudolf Habelt.

Iser, W. 1978. *The Act of Reading: A Theory of Aesthetic Response*. London/Henley: Routledge & Kegan Paul Ltd.

Jones, C.P. 1999. *Kinship Diplomacy in the Ancient World* (*Revealing Antiquity* 12). Cambridge/London: Harvard University Press.

Kader, I. 1995. "Heroa und Memorialbauten", in: Wörrle, Zanker 1995, 199-229.

Keil, J. 1964. *Ephesos. Ein Führer durch die Ruinenstätte und ihre Geschichte*. Wien: Rudolf M. Rohrer.

Kermode, F. 1983. *The Art of Telling: Essays on Fiction*. Cambridge: Harvard University Press.

Kerschner, M., Kowalleck, I. & Steskal, M. 2008. *Archäologische Forschungen zur Siedlungsgeschichte von Ephesos in geometrischer, archaischer und klassischer Zeit. Grabungsbefunde und Keramikbefunde aus dem Bereich von Koressos* (*Ergänzungshefte zu den Jahresheften des Österreichischen Archäologischen Institutes* 9). Wien: Österreichisches Archäologisches Institut.

Kirbihler, F. 2007. "Die Italiker in Kleinasien, mit besonderer Berücksichtigung von Ephesos (133 v. Chr. – 1. Jh. n. Chr.)", in: Meyer 2007, 19-27.

Kirbihler, F. 2011. "Servilius Isauricus proconsul d'Asie: un gouverneur populaire", in: Barrandon, Kirbihler 2011, 249-72.

Knibbe, D. 1985. "Der Asiarch M. Fulvius Publicianus Nikephoros, die ephesischen Handwerkszünfte und die Stoa des Servilius". *Jahreshefte des Österreichischen archäologischen Instituts in Wien* 56, 71-7.

Knibbe, D. 1991. "Das "Parthermonument" von Ephesos: (Parthersieg)altar der Artemis (und Kenotaph des L. Verus) an der "Triodos"". *Berichte und Materialen des österreichischen archäologischen Institutes* 1, 5-18.

Knibbe, D. & Thür, H. 1995. *Via Sacra Ephesiaca* II. *Grabungen und Forschungen 1992 und 993* (*Österreichisches Archäologisches Institut Berichte und Materialien* 6). Wien: Druckhaus Grasl.

Koester, H. (ed.) 1995. *Ephesos: Metropolis of Asia. An Interdisciplinary Approach to its Archaeology, Religion, and Culture*. Valley Forge: Trinity Press International.

Kraft, J.C., Brückner, H. & Kayan, İ 2005. "The Sea under the City of Ancient Ephesos", in: Brandt, Gassner, Ladstätter 2005, 147-56.

Laale, H.W. 2011. *Ephesus (Ephesos): An Abbreviated History from Androclus to Constantine XI*. Bloomington: WestBow Press.

Ladstätter, S. (ed.) 2009. *Neue Forschungen zur Kuretenstraße von Ephesos. Akten des Symposiums für Hilke Thür vom 13. Dezember 2006 an der Österreichischen Akademie der Wissenschaften* (*Österreichische Akademie der Wissenschaften, Archäologische Forschungen* 15). Wien: Verlag der Österreichischen Akademie der Wissenschaften.

Langmann, G. & Knibbe, D. 1993. *Via Sacra Ephesiaca* I (*Österreichisches Archäologisches Institut. Berichte und Materialen* 3). Wien: Schindler.

Madsen, J. M. 2010. "Mithradates VI: Rome's Perfect Enemy". *Proceedings of the Danish Institute at Athens* 6, 223-36.

Magie, D. [1950] 1975. *Roman Rule in Asia Minor to the End of the Third Century after Christ*, repr. Princeton: Princeton University Press.

Meyer, M. (ed.) 2007. *Neue Zeiten – Neue Sitten. Zu Rezeption und Integration römischen und italischen Kulturguts in Kleinasien* (*Wiener Forschungen zur Archäologie* 12). Wien: Phoibos Verlag.

Mortensen, E. 2015. "Ktistes: Mythical Founder Hero and Honorary Title for New Heroes", in: Fejfer, Moltesen, Rathje 2015, 213-37.

Ng, D.Y. 2007. *Manipulation of Memory: Public Buildings and Decorative Programs in Roman Cities of Asia Minor*. PhD dissertation, University of Michigan.

Nijf, O.M. van 1997. *The Civic World of Professional Associations in the Roman East* (*Dutch Monographs on Ancient History and Archaeology* 17). Amsterdam: J.C. Gieben.

Outschar, U. 1990. "Zum Monument des C. Memmius". *Jahreshefte des Österreichischen archäologischen Instituts in Wien* 60, 57-85.

Parrish, D. (ed.) 2001. *Urbanism in Western Asia Minor. New Studies on Aphrodisias, Ephesos, Hierapolis, Pergamon, Perge, and Xanthos.* (*Journal of Roman Archaeology Supplement* 45). Portsmouth: Journal of Roman Archaeology.

Patterson, L.E. 2010. *Kinship Myth in Ancient Greece*. Austin: University of Texas Press.

Pesely, G.E. 1998. "The Date of Thrasyllos' Expedition to Ionia". *The Ancient History Bulletin* 12, 96-100.

Price, S.R.F. 2002. "Memory and Ancient Greece", in: Dignas, Smith 2002, 15-36.

Quatember, U. 2010. "The "Temple of Hadrian" on Curetes Street in Ephesus: New Research into Its Building History". *Journal of Roman Archaeology* 23 (1), 376-94.

Raja, R. 2012. *Urban Development and Regional Identity in the Eastern Roman Provinces, 50 BC-AD 250: Aphrodisias, Ephesos, Athens and Gerasa*. Copenhagen: Museum Tusculanum Press.

Rathmayr, E. 2010. "Die Präsenz des Ktistes Androklos in Ephesos". *Anzeiger der Philologisch-historische Klasse* 145, 19-60.

Rathmayr, E. 2011. "Die Skulpturenausstattung des C. Laecanius Bassus Nymphaeum in Ephesos", in: D'Andria, Romeo 2011, 130-49.

Robert, L. 1948. *Hellenica. Recueil d'épigraphie de numismatique et d'antiquités grecques* VI. *Inscriptions grecques de Lydie*. Paris: Adrien-Maisonneuve.

Rowlands, M. 1993. "The Role of Memory in the Transmission of Culture". *World Archaeology* 25 (2), 141-51.

Saxkjær, S.G. 2013. "A Figure-Decorated Plate from the Sanctuary on the Timpone della Motta", in: Thomasen, Rathje, Johannsen 2013, 179-96.

Scherrer, P. 1990. "Augustus, die Mission des Vedius Pollio und die Artemis Ephesia." *Jahreshefte des Österreichischen archäologischen Instituts in Wien* 60, 87-101.

Scherrer, P. (ed.) 2000. *Ephesus: The New Guide*, revised ed., trans. L. Bier & G. Luxon. Selçuk: Ege Yayınları.

Scherrer, P. 2001. "The Historical Topography of Ephesos", in: Parrish 2001, 57-93.

Scherrer, P. & Trinkl, E. 2006. *Die Tetragonos Agora in Ephesos. Grabungsergebnisse von archaischer bis in byzantinische Zeit – ein Überblick. Befunde und Funde klassischer Zeit* (*Forschungen in Ephesos* 13.2). Wien: Verlag der Österreichischen Akademie der Wissenschaften.

Schwandner, E.-L. & Rheidt, K. (ed.) 2004. *Macht der Architektur – Architektur der Macht. Bauforschungskolloquium in Berlin vom 30. Oktober bis 2. November 2002 veranstaltet vom Architektur-Referat des DAI.* Mainz am Rhein: Verlag Philipp von Zabern.

SEG. Supplementum Epigraphicum Graecum. Leiden: Brill.

Spencer, N. (ed.) 1995. *Time, Tradition and Society in Greek Archaeology. Bridging the 'Great Divide'.* London: Routledge.

Steskal, M. 2010. *Das Prytaneion in Ephesos* (*Forschungen in Ephesos* 9.4). Wien: Verlag der Österreichischen Akademie der Wissenschaften.

Thomasen, H., Rathje, A. & Johannsen K.B. (eds.) 2013. *Vessels and Variety: New Aspects of Ancient Pottery* (*Acta Hyperborea* 13). Copenhagen: Museum Tusculanum Press.

Thür, H. 1990. "Arsinoe IV, eine Schwester Kleopatras VII, Grabinhaberin des Oktogons von Ephesos? Ein Vorschlag." *Jahreshefte des Österreichischen archäologischen Instituts in Wien* 60, 43-56.

Thür, H. 1995a. "Der ephesische Ktistes Androklos und (s)ein Heroon am Embolos." *Jahreshefte des Österreichischen archäologischen Instituts in Wien* 64, 63-103.

Thür, H. 1995b. "The Processional Way in Ephesos as a Place of Cult and Burial", in: Koester 1995, 157-99.

Thür, H. 1995c. "Die Ergebnisse der Arbeiten an der innerstädtischen Via Sacra im Embolosbereich", in: Knibbe, Thür 1995, 84-96.
Thür, H. 1999. "Der Embolos: Tradition und Innovation anhand seines Erscheinungsbildes", in: Friesinger, Krinzinger 1999, 421-8.
Thür, H. 2004. "Ephesos – Bauprogramm für den Kaiser", in: Schwandner, Rheidt 2004, 221-30.
Thür, H. 2005. "Altarstudien aus Ephesos", in: Brandt, Gassner, Ladstätter 2005, 355-62.
Tilley, C. 1994. *A Phenomenology of Landscape: Places, Paths and Monuments*. Oxford/Providence: Berg.
Tilley, C. 2010. *Interpreting Landscapes: Geologies, Topographies, Identities* (*Explorations in Landscape Phenomenology* 3). Walnut Creek: Left Coast Press.
Torelli, M. 1988. "Il monumente efesino di Memmius. Un capolavoro dell'ideologia nobiliare della fine della repubblica". *Scienze dell'Antichita: Storia, archeologia, antropologia* 2, 403-26.
Tuchelt, K. 1979. *Frühe Denkmäler Roms in Kleinasien. Beiträge zur archäologischen Überlieferung aus der Zeit der Republik und des Augustus* I. *Roma und Promagistrate*. Tübingen: Verlag Ernst Wasmuth.
Van Dyke, R.M. & Alcock, S.E. 2003. *Archaeologies of Memory*. Malden/Oxford/Melbourne/Berlin: Blackwell.
Waldner, A. 2009. "Heroon und Oktogon. Zur Datierung zweier Ehrenbauten am unteren Embolos von Ephesos anhand des keramischen Fundmaterials aus den Grabungen von 1989 und 1999", in: Ladstätter 2009, 283-315.
Wiplinger, G. & Wlach, G. 1996. *Ephesus: 100 Years of Austrian Research*. Wien/Cologne/Weimar: Böhlau.
Wörrle, M. & Zanker, P. (eds.) 1995. *Stadtbild und Bürgerbild im Hellenismus. Kolloquium, München, 24. bis 26. Juni 1993*. München: Beck.
Zabehlicky, H. 1995. "Preliminary Views of the Ephesian Harbor", in: Koester 1995, 201-15.
Zuiderhoek, A. 2009. *The Politics of Munificence in the Roman Empire: Citizens, Elites and Benefactors in Asia Minor*. Cambridge: Cambridge University Press.
Zuiderhoek, A. 2013. "Cities, Buildings and Benefactors in the Roman East", in: Dickenson, Nijf 2013, 173-92.

A Secretive Muse: Hidden References in a Neo-Latin Eclogue

Bloom, H. 1973. *The Anxiety of Influence. A Theory of Poetry*. New York: Oxford University Press.
Brask, P. et al. (eds.) 1984. *Dansk litteraturhistorie* 2: *Lærdom og magi*. Copenhagen: Gyldendal.
Calinescu, M. 1993. *Rereading*. New Haven/London: Yale University Press.
Calinescu, M. 1994. "Secrecy in Fiction: Textual and Intertextual Secrets in Hawthorne and Updike". *Poetics Today* 15 (3), 443-65.
Friis-Jensen, K. 1987. "Syvårskrig og salmesang. En gendigtning af Johannes Pratensis' latinske hyrdedigt til Hans Thomesens bryllup 1563". *Museum Tusculanum. Dansk tidsskrift for græske og latinske studier* 57, 94-103.
Friis-Jensen, K. & Skafte Jensen, M. 1984. "Latindigtningens spejl", in: Brask et al. 1984, 368-438.
Hardin, J. & Reinhart, M. (eds.) 1997. *Dictionary of Literary Biography* 179: *German Writers of the Renaissance and Reformation, 1280-1580*. Detroit: Gale Research.
Hass, T.A. 2013. "Galathea, Amaryllis, and Fictive Chronology in Petrarch's Bucolicum Carmen". *Analecta Romana Instituti Danici* 38, 79-94.
Hessus, H.E. 1509. *Bucolicon*. Erfurt: J. Knappe.
Hessus, H.E. 1528. *Bucolicorum Idyllia*. Hagenau: J. Setzer.
Hessus, H.E. 1539. *Operum farragines duae*. Schwäbisch Hall: P. Braubach.
Kermode, F. 1983. *The Art of Telling: Essays on Fiction*. Cambridge: Harvard University Press.
Kirkham, V. & Maggi, A. (eds.) 2009. *Petrarch: A Critical Guide to the Complete Works*. Chicago: The University of Chicago Press.
Lætus, E. 1560. *Bucolica*. Wittenberg: Heirs of G. Rhaw.
Martinez, R.L. 2009. "*The Book without a Name*: Petrarch's Open Secret (*Liber sine nomine*)", in: Kirkham, Maggi 2009, 291-9.
Patterson, A. 1988. *Pastoral and Ideology: Virgil to Valéry*. Cambridge: Clarendon Press.
Pedersen, V.A. et al. (eds.) 2007. *Dansk litteraturs historie* 1: *1100-1800*. Copenhagen: Gyldendal.
Petrarca, F. 1974. *Sine nomine. Lettere polemiche e politiche*, ed. U. Dotti. Bari/Rome: Laterza.
Petrarca, F. 1985. *Letters on Famliar Matters. Rerum familiarium libri XVII-XXIV*, trans. A.S. Bernardo. Baltimore/London: The Johns Hopkins Press.

Petrarca, F. 1997. *Opera Omnia*, ed. P. Stoppelli. Rome: Lexis.

Pratensis. H.P. 1563. *Daphnis*. Copenhagen: L. Benedikt.

Scheppele, K.L. 1988. *Legal Secrets: Equality and Efficiency in the Common Law*. Chicago: Chicago University Press.

Schnur, R. et al. (eds.) 2010. *Acta Conventus Neo-Latini Budapestinensis: Proceedings of the Thirteenth International Congress of Neo-Latin Studies (Budapest 2006)*. Tempe: Arizona.

Servius Honoratus, M. 1887. *Servii Grammatici qui feruntur in Vergilii Carmina Commentarii*, ed. G. Thilo. Leipzig: Teubner 1887.

Skafte Jensen, M. 2004. *Friendship and Poetry: Studies in Danish Neo-Latin Literature*, ed. Pade, M., Skovgaard-Petersen, K. & Zeeberg, P. Copenhagen: Museum Tusculanum Press.

Skovgaard-Petersen, K. & Zeeberg, P. 2007. "En glemt litteratur", in Pedersen et al. 2007, 244-67.

Theocritus c. 1482. *Idyllia*, trans. M. Filetico. Rome: E. Silber.

Theocritus 1531. *Idyllia triginta sex, Latino carmine reddita*, trans. H.E. Hessus. Haguenau: J. Setzer.

VD 16. *Verzeichnis der im deutschen Sprachbereich erschienenen Drucke des 16. Jahrhunderts* (www.gateway-bayern.de/index_vd16.html, accessed November 2014).

Vredeveld, H. 2004. *The Poetic Works of Helius Eobanus Hessus* 1: *Student Years at Erfurt, 1504-1509*. Tempe: Medieval and Renaissance Texts and Studies.

Zeeberg, P. 2008. "Virgilian Imitation in Johannes Pratensis' Latin Pastoral *Daphnis* (Copenhagen 1563)." *Symbolae Osloenses* 83, 96-103.

Zeeberg, P. 2010 "The Bucolica (1560) of Erasmus Laetus", in: Schnur et al. 2010, 839-45.

Better to Reveal than to Conceal? Christian Attitudes to Secrecy in the Early Islamic Period

Bāšā, Q. 1905. *Un traité des œuvres Arabes de Théodore Abou-Kurra, évêque de Haran*. Tripoli de Syrie/Rome: L'auteur/Père Procureur des Basiliens de Saint-Sauveur.

Bulliet, R.W. 1979. *Conversion to Islam in the Medieval Period: An Essay in Quantitative History*. Cambridge: Harvard University Press.

Bulliet, R.W. 1990. "Conversion Stories in Early Islam", in: Gervers, Bikhazi 1990, 123-33.

Dammen McAuliffe, J. 2004. *Encyclopaedia of the Qur'ān* 4. Leiden: Brill.

Gervers, M. & Bikhazi, R.J. (eds.) 1990. *Conversion and Continuity: Indigenous Christian Communities in Islamic Lands. Eighth to Eighteenth Centuries*. Toronto: Pontifical Institute of Mediaeval Learning.

Ginkel, J.J. van, Murre-van den Berg, H.L. & Lint, T.M. van (eds.) 2005. *Redefining Christian Identity: Cultural Interaction in the Middle East since the Rice of Islam*. Leuven: Peeters Publishers.

Griffith, S.H. 2005. "Answering the Call of the Minaret: Christian Apologetics in the World of Islam", in: Ginkel, Murre-van den Berg, Lint 2005, 91-126.

Griffith, S.H. 2008. *The Church in the Shadow of the Mosque*. Princeton: Princeton University Press.

Griffith, S.H. 2013. *The Bible in Arabic: The Scriptures of the "People of the Book" in the Language of Islam*. Princeton: Princeton University Press.

Gutas, D. 1998. *Greek Thought, Arabic Culture: The Graeco-Arabic Translation Movement in Baghdad and Early ʿAbbāsid Society (2nd-4th/8th-10th centuries)*. New York: Routledge.

Haddad, W.Z. 1990. "Continuity and Change in Religious Adherence: Ninth-Century Baghdad", in: Gervers, Bikhazi 1990, 33-53.

Hoyland, R.G. 1997. *Seeing Islam as Others Saw It – A Survey and Evaluation of Christian, Jewish and Zoroastrian Writings on Early Islam*. Princeton: The Darwin Press.

Keating, S.T. 2006. *Defending the "People of Truth" in the Early Islamic Period; the Christian Apologies of Abū Rāʾiṭah*. Leiden: Brill.

Kugel, J.L. (ed.) 1990. *Poetry and Prophecy*. Ithaca/London: Cornell University Press.

Lamoreaux, J.C. 2005. *Theodore Abū Qurrah*. Provo: Brigham Young University.

Mingana, A. 1922. *The Book of Religion and Empire: A Semi-Official Defence and Exposition of Islām Written by Order at the Court and with the Assistance of Caliph Mutaakkil (A.D. 847-861) by ʿAli Ṭabari*. Manchester: The University Press Longmans, Green and Company.

Morony, M.G. 1990. "The Age of Conversions: A Reassessment", in: Gervers, Bikhazi 1990, 135-50.

Ricks, T.W. 2013. *Early Arabic Christian Contributions to Trinitarian Theology: The Development of the Doctrine of the Trinity in an Islamic Milieu.* Minneapolis: Fortress Press.

Rubin, U. 2004. "Prophets and Prophethood", in: Dammen McAuliffe 2004, 289-307.

Stroumsa, S. 1985. "The Signs of Prophecy: The Emergence and Early Development of a Theme in Arabic Theological Literature". *The Harvard Theological Review* 78 (1), 101-14.

Thomas, D. 1994. "The Miracles of Jesus in Early Islamic Polemic". *Journal of Semitic Studies* 39 (2), 221-43.

Thomas, D. (ed.) 2003a. *Christians at the Heart of Islamic Rule: Church Life and Scholarship in ʿAbbasid Iraq*. Leiden: Brill.

Thomas, D. 2003b. "Early Muslim Responses to Christianity", in: Thomas 2003a, 231-54.

Zwettler, M. 1990. "A Mantic Manifesto: The Sūra of "The Poets" and the Qurʾānic Foundations of Prophetic Authority", in: Kugel 1990, 75-119.

The Secrets of the Funerary Buildings in Palmyra during the Roman Period

Alcock, S.E. 1997. *The Early Roman Empire in the East.* Oxford: Oxbow Books.

Amy, R. & Seyrig, H. 1936. "Recherches dans la nécropole de Palmyre". *Syria* 17 (3), 229-66.

Attfield, J. 2000. *Wild Things: The Material Culture of Everyday Life.* Oxford/New York: Berg.

Baker, J.L. 2012. *The Funeral Kit: Mortuary Practices in the Archaeological Record.* Walnut Creek: Left Coast Press.

Balty, J.C. 1996. "Palmyre entre Orient et Occident: Acculturation et Résistances". *Annales Archéologiques Arabes Syriennes* 42, 437-41.

Bell, C. 1992. *Ritual Theory, Ritual Practice.* New York/Oxford: Oxford University Press.

Bellman, B.L. 1981. *The Language of Secrecy: Symbols & Metaphors in Poro Ritual.* New Brunswick: Rutgers University Press.

Bernhard, M.-L. (ed.) 1966. *Mélanges offerts à K. Michalowski.* Warszawa: Panstwowe Wydawnictwo Naukowe.

Bille, M., Hastrup, F. & Sørensen, T.F. (eds.) 2010. *An Anthropology of Absence: Materializations of Transcendence and Loss.* London/New York: Springer Science+Business Media B.V.

Birk, S. 2013. *Depicting the Dead: Self-Representation and Commemoration on Roman Sarcophagi with Portraits* (*Aarhus Studies in Mediterranean Antiquity* 11). Aarhus: Aarhus University Press.

Blakely, S. 2012. "Toward and Archaeology of Secrecy: Power, Paradox, and the Great Gods of Samothrace". *Archaeological Papers of the American Anthropological* 5 (1), 49-71.

Bok, S. 1982. *Secrets: On the Ethics of Concealment and Revelation.* New York: Pantheon Books.

Brück, J. 2005. "Experiencing the Past? The Development of a Phenomenological Archaeology in British Prehistory". *Archaeological Dialogues* 12 (1), 45-72.

Böhme, A. & Schottroff, W. 1979. *Palmyrenische Grabreliefs.* Frankfurt am Main: Herbert Beck.

Carroll, M. 2006. *Spirits of the Dead: Roman Funerary Commemoration in Western Europe.* Oxford: Oxford University Press.

Carroll, M. 2011. "*Memoria* and *Damnatio Memoriae*: Preserving and Erasing Identities in Roman Funerary Commemoration", in: Carroll, Rempel 2011, 65-90.

Carroll, M. & Rempel, J. (eds.) 2011. *Living through the Dead: Burial and Commemoration in the Classical World.* Oxford and Oakville: Oxbow Books.

Colledge, M.A.R. 1976. *The Art of Palmyra.* London: Thames & Hudson.

Cubitt, G. 2007. *History and Memory.* Manchester: Manchester University Press.

Cummings, V. 2003. "Building from Memory", in: Williams 2003, 25-44.

Cussini, E. 1995. "Transfer of Property at Palmyra". *Aram periodicals* 7 (1), 233-50.

Cussini, E. (ed.) 2005a. *A Journey to Palmyra: Collected Essays to Remember Delbert R. Hillers.* Leiden/Boston: Brill.

Cussini, E. 2005b. "Beyond the Spindle: Investigating the Role of Palmyrene Women", in: Cussini 2005a, 26-43.

Derderian, K. 2001. *Leaving Words to Remember: Greek Mourning and the Advent of Literacy.* Leiden: Brill.

Fejfer, J. 2008. *Roman Portraits in Context.* Berlin/New York: Walter de Gruyter.

Franz, H.G. 1987. "Die Kunst von Palmyra zwischen Okzident und Orient", in: Ruprechtsberger 1987, 163-78.

Gardin, J.-C. & Peebles, C.S. (eds.) 1992. *Representations in Archaeology*. Bloomington/Indianapolis: Indiana University Press.

Gawlikowski, M. 1970. *Monuments funéraires de Palmyre.* Warszawa: Ed. Nauk.

Gillespie, S.D. 2001. "Personhood, Agency, and Mortuary Ritual: A Case Study from the Ancient Maya". *Journal of Anthropological Archaeology* 20, 73-112.

Hastorf, C.A. 2007. "Archaeological Andean Rituals: Performance, Liturgy, and Meaning", in: Kyriakidis 2007, 77-108.

Hamilakis, Y., Pluciennik, M. & Tarlow, S. (eds.) 2002. *Thinking through the Body: Archaeologies of Corporeality.* New York/Boston/Dordrecht/London/Moscow: Kluwer Academic/Plenum Publishers.

Hekster, O. & Mols, S.T.A.M. (eds.) 2010. *Cultural Messages in the Graeco-Roman World: Acta of the Babesch 80th Anniversary Workshop. Radboud University Nijmegen, September 8th 2006.* Leuven: Peeters.

Henning, A. 2013. *Die Turmgräber von Palmyra. Eine lokale Bauform im kaiserzeitlichen Syrien als Ausdruck kultureller Identität.* Rahden: Verlag Marie Leidorf.

Heyn, M. 2010. "Gesture and Identity in the Funerary Art of Palmyra". *American Journal of Archaeology* 114 (4), 631-61.

Higuchi, T. & Saito, K. 2001. *Tomb F – Tomb of BWLH and BWRP: Southeast Necropolis in Palmyra.* Nara: Research Center for Silk Roadology 2.

Hillers, D.R. & Cussini, E. 1996. *Palmyrene Aramaic Texts.* Baltimore/London: The Johns Hopkins University Press.

Hodder, I. 1985. "Postprocessual Archaeology". *Advances in Archaeological Method and Theory* 8, 1-26.

Hope, V.M. 2003. "Remembering Rome", in: Williams 2003, 113-40.

Hope, V.M. 2007. *Death in Ancient Rome: A Sourcebook.* Oxon: Routledge.

Hvidberg-Hansen, F.O. & Ploug, G. 1993. *Palmyra Samlingen.* Copenhagen: Ny Carlsberg Glyptotek.

Ingholt, H. 1928. *Studier over Palmyrensk Skulptur.* Copenhagen: C. A. Reitzels Forlag.

Ingholt, H. 1934. "Palmyrene Sculptures in Beirut". *Berytus* 1, 32-43.

Ingholt, H. 1935. "Five Dated Tombs from Palmyra". *Berytus* 2, 58-120.

Ingholt, H. 1938. "Inscriptions and Sculptures from Palmyra, II". *Berytus* 5, 93-140.

Ingholt, H. 1954. *Palmyrene and Gandharan Sculpture.* Yale: Yale University Art Gallery.

Ingholt, H. 1966. "Some Sculptures from the Tomb of Malkû at Palmyra", in: Bernhard 1966, 457-76.

Ingholt, H. 1974. "Two Unpublished Tombs from the Southwest Necropolis of Palmyra, Syria", in: Kouymijan 1974, 37-54.

Kaizer, T. 2010. "Funerary Cults at Palmyra", in: Hekster, Mols 2010, 23-31.

Kouymijan, D.K. (ed.) 1974. *Near Eastern Numismatics, Iconography, Epigraphy and History: Studies in Honor of George C. Miles.* Beirut: American University of Beirut.

Kus, S. 1992. "Toward an Archaeology of Body and Soul", in: Gardin, Peebles 1992, 168-77.

Kyriakidis, E. 2007. *The Archaeology of Ritual.* Los Angeles: Cotsen Advanced Seminars.

Laurence, R. & Wallace-Hadrill, A. (eds.) 1997. *Domestic Space in the Roman World: Pompeii and Beyond.* Portsmouth: Thomson-Shore.

Laurence, R. & Newsome, D.J. (eds.) 2011. *Rome, Ostia, Pompeii: Movement and Space.* Oxford: Oxford University Press.

Lavan, L. (ed.) 2001. *Recent Research in Late-Antique Urbanism* (*Journal of Roman Archaeology, Supplement* 42). Porthsmouth: Journal of Roman Archaeology.

Lefebvre, H. [1974] 1991. *The Production of Space*, trans. D. Nicholson-Smith. Oxford: Blackwell Publishing.

Levy, T.E. 2006a. "Archaeology, Anthropology and Cult: Exploring Religion in Formative Middle Range Societies", in: Levy 2006b, 3-33.

Levy, T.E. (ed.) 2006b. *Archaeology, Anthropology and Cult: The Sanctuary at Gilat, Israel.* London: Equinox Publishing Ltd.

Nilsson Stutz, L. 2007. *Embodied Rituals & Ritualized Bodies: Tracing Ritual Practices in Late Mesolithic Burials.* Lund: Wallin & Dahlholm Boktryckeri AB.

Nooter, M.H. (ed.) 1993. *Secrecy: African Art that Conceals and Reveals.* Munich: Prestel Verlag.

Parker Pearson, M. 1999. *The Archaeology of Death and Burial.* Stroud: Sutton.

Parlasca, K. 1988. "Ikonographische Probleme palmyrenischer Grabreliefs". *Damaszener Mitteilungen* 3, 215-21.

Piersimoni, P. 1995. "Compiling a Palmyrene Prosopography: Methodological Problems". *ARAM periodicals* 7, 251-60.

Piot, C.D. 1993. "Secrecy, Ambiguity, and the Everyday in Kabre Culture". *American Anthropologist* 95, 353-70.

Pugalis, L. 2009. "A Conceptual and Analytical Framework for Interpreting the Spatiality of Social Life". *FORUM* 9, 77-98.

Rosaldo, R. 1993. *Culture and Truth: The Remaking of Social Analysis.* Boston: Beacon Press.

Ruprechtsberger, E.M. (ed.) 1987. *Palmyra. Geschichte, Kunst und Kultur der syrischen Oasenstadt. Einführende Beiträge und Katalog zur Ausstellung.* Linz: Druck- und Verlagsanstalt Gutenberg.
Sadurska, A. & Bounni, A. 1994. *Les Sculptures Funéraires de Palmyre.* Rome: Giorgio Bretschneider Editore.
Saito, K. 2005. "Palmyrene Burial Practices from Funerary Goods", in: Cussini 2005a, 150-65.
Schmidt-Colinet, A. 1997. "Aspects of "Romanization": The Tomb Architecture at Palmyra and its Decoration", in: Alcock 1997, 157-77.
Simmel, G. 1906. "The Sociology of Secrecy and of Secret Societies". *American Journal of Sociology* 11 (4), 441-98.
Simmel, G. 1950. *The sociology of Georg Simmel,* trans. and ed. K.H. Wolff. New York: Free Press.
Starcky, J. 1952. *Palmyre.* Paris: Adrien-Maisonneuve.
Sørensen, T.F. 2010. "A Saturated Void: Anticipating and Preparing Presence in Contemporary Danish Cemetery Culture", in: Bille, Hastrup, Sørensen 2010, 115-30.
Tanner, J. 2000. "Portraits, Power, and Patronage in the Late Roman Republic". *The Journal of Roman Studies* 90, 18-50.
Tarlow, S. 1999. *Bereavement and Commemoration: An Archaeology of Mortality.* Oxford: Blackwell Publishers Ltd.
Tarlow, S. 2012. "The Archaeology of Emotion and Affect". *The Annual Review of Anthropology* 41, 169-85.
Thomas, J. 1996. *Time, Culture and Identity: An Interpretive Archaeology.* London, New York: Routledge.
Thomas, J. 2002. "Archaeology's Humanism and the Materiality of the Body", in: Hamilakis, Pluciennik, Tarlow 2002, 29-46.
Tilley, C. 2010. *Interpreting Landscapes: Geologies, Topographies, Identities (Explorations in Landscape Phenomenology* 3). Walnut Creek: Left Coast Press.
Wallace-Hadrill, A. 1994. *Houses and Society in Pompeii and Herculanuem.* Princeton: Princeton University Press.
Will, E. 1951. "Le relief de la tour de Khitôt et le banquet funéraire à Palmyre". *Syria* 28 (1-2), 70-100.
Williams, H. (ed.) 2003. *Archaeologies of Remembrance: Death and Memory in Past Societies.* New York: Plenum Publishers.
Yon, J.-B. 2001. "Evergetism and Urbanism in Palmyra", in: Lavan 2001, 173-81.
Yon, J.-B. 2002. *Les Notables de Palmyre.* Beyrouth: Institut français d'archéologie du Proche-Orient.
Zanker, P. & Ewald, B.C. 2004. *Mit Mythen leben. Die Bilderwelt der römischen Sarkophage.* München: Hirmer Verlag.

Lucius Iulius Optatus: A Salacious Doctor Revealed?

Adams, J.N. 1982. *The Latin Sexual Vocabulary.* London: Duckworth.
Bargfeldt, N. 2015. "Newly Invented Tradition: The Individual and the Community at the Northern Frontier of the Roman Empire", in: Fejfer, Moltesen, Rathje 2015, 17-41.
Bargfeldt, N. (forthcoming). "Elite Societies on Display within Military Zones: The Meagre Beginnings of a Leading Municipal Class in Brigetio", in: Vagalinski (forthcoming).
Betz, A. 1963. "Epigraphischer Anhang. Das Grabmal des Optatus medicus". *Carnuntum Jahrbuch 1961/62. Römische Forschungen in Niederösterreich Beiheft* 7, 84-6.
Bibauw, J. (ed.) 1969. *Hommages à Marcel Renard* II. Bruxelles: Latomus.
Bille, M., Hastrup, F. & Sørensen, T.F. (eds.) 2010. *An Anthropology of Absence: Materializations of Transcendence and Loss.* London/New York: Springer Science+Business Media B.V.
Birk, S. 2013. *Depicting the Dead: Self-Representation and Commemoration on Roman Sarcophagi with Portraits (Aarhus Studies in Mediterranean Antiquity* 11). Aarhus: Aarhus University Press.
Birley, A. 1979. *The People of Roman Britain.* Letchworth: The Garden Press Limited.
Breitwieser, R. 1998. *Medizin im römischen Österreich (Linzer Archaeologische Forshungen* 26). Linz: Nordico-Museum der Stadt Linz.
Carroll, M. 2006. *Spirits of the Dead: Roman Funerary Commemoration in Western Europe.* Oxford: Oxford University Press.
CIG. Corpus Inscriptionum Graecarum.
CIL. Corpus Inscriptionum Latinarum.
Cooley, A.E. 2012. *The Cambridge Manual of Latin Epigraphy.* Cambridge: Cambridge University Press.
Croxford, B. 2008. "Humour in Roman Archaeology". *Theoretical Roman Archaeology Conference* 2007, 151-62.
Doneus, M., Gugl, C. & Doneus, N. (eds.) 2013. *Die Canabae von Carnuntum. Ein Modellstudie der Erforschung*

römischer Lagervorstädte (*Der römische Limes in Österreich* 47). Wien: Verlag der Österreichischen Akademie der Wissenschaften.
Dunbabin, K.M.D. 2003. *The Roman Banquet: Images of Conviviality.* Cambridge: Cambridge University Press.
Fejfer, J., Moltesen, M. & Rathje, A. (eds.) 2015. *Tradition: Transmission of Culture in the Ancient World* (*Acta Hyperborea: Danish Studies in Classical Archaeology* 14). Copenhagen: Museum Tusculanum Press.
Franzen, P. 2009. "The Nijmegen Canabae Legionis (71-102/105 AD): Military and Civilian Life on the Frontier", in: Morillo, Hanel, Martín 2009, 1271-83.
Funari, P.P. de A. 1995. "Apotropaic Symbolism at Pompeii: Reading of the Graffiti Evidence". *Revista de História* 132, 9-17.
Genser, K. 2005. *Römische Steindenkmäler aus Carnuntum* I. *Steindenkmäler in den beiden Loggien und im Garten des Museums Carnuntinum sowie im Kurpark Bad Deutsch-Altenburg.* Horn: Ferdinand Berger & Söhne Gesellschaft.
Genser, K. 2006. "Die Entwicklung des oberpannonischen Limes bis Kaiser Hadrian", in: Humer 2006, 73-84.
HD. *Epigraphische Datenbank Heidelberg*: edh-www.adw.uni-heidelberg.de.
Humer, F. (ed.) 2006. *Legionsadler und Druidenstab. Vom Legionslager zur Donaumetropole. Sonderausstellung aus Anlass des Jubiläums "2000 Jahre Carnuntum".* Horn: Ferdinand Berger & Söhne Gesellschaft.
Jackson, R. 1993. "Roman Medicine: Practitioners and their Practices", in: Temporini, Haase 1993, 79-100.
Kajanto, I. 1969. "Balnea vina Venus", in: Bibauw 1969, 357-67.
Kandler, M., Humer, F. & Zabehlicky, H. 2004. "Carnuntum", in: Kos, Scherrer 2004, 11-66.
Keppie, L. 1991. *Understanding Roman Inscriptions.* Baltimore: Johns Hopkins University Press.
Kos, M.S. & Scherrer, P. (eds.) 2004. *The Autonomous Towns of Noricum and Pannonia/Die autonomen Städte in Noricum und Pannonien.* Ljubljana: Narodni muzej Slovenije.
Lund, A.A. 2006. *I seng med romerne. Køn og sex i det antikke Rom.* København: Museum Tusculanum Forlag.
Lupa. *Ubi Erat Lupa*: www.ubi-erat-lupa.org.
McMullen, R. 1982. "The Epigraphic Habit in the Roman Empire". *The American Journal of Philology* 103 (3), 233-46.
Mócsy, A. 1974. *Pannonia and Upper Moesia: A History of the Middle Danube Provinces of the Roman Empire.* London/Boston: Routledge & Kegan Paul.
Morillo, A., Hanel, N. & Martín, E. (eds.) 2009. *XX International Limes Congress 2006 in León.* Madrid: Ediciones Polifemo.
PAS. Portable Antiquity Scheme: www.finds.org.uk.
Petrikovits, H. von 1976-91. *Beiträge zur römischen Geschichte und Archäologie* 2. Bonn: Rheinland-Verlag.
Petrikovits, H. von 1991. "Lixae", in: Petrikovits 1976-91, 75-9.
Scheppele, K.L. 1988. *Legal Secrets: Equality and Efficiency in the Common Law.* Chicago: Chicago University Press.
Selinger, R. 2006a. "Der fututor aus Carnuntum (AE 1969/70, 502). Moderne Altertumswissenschaften und römische Sexualität". *Klio. Beiträge zur alten Geschichte* 88 (2), 516-24.
Selinger, R. 2006b. "Sex in Carnuntum". *Historische Sozialkunde. Geschichte – Fachdidaktik – Politische Bildung* 1, 43.
Sørensen, T.F. 2010. "A Saturated Void: Anticipations and Preparing Presence in Contemporary Danish Cemetery Culture", in: Bille, Hastrup, Sørensen 2010, 115-30.
Temporini, H. & Haase, W. (eds.) 1993. *Aufstieg und Niedergang der römischen Welt* 2.37.1. Berlin: de Gruyter.
Vagalinski, L. (ed.) (forthcoming). *XXII International Limes Congress 2012 in Ruse.*
Vishnia, R.F. 2002. "The Shadow Army: The Lixae and the Roman Legions". *Zeitschrift für Papyrologie und Epigraphik* 139, 265-72.
Vorbeck, E. 1980. *Zivilinschriften aus Carnuntum.* Wien: Amt der NÖ Landesregierung Verlag.
Weiler, I. 1963. "Gräberstraße 1961". *Carnuntum Jahrbuch 1961/62. Römische Forschungen in Niederösterreich Beiheft* 7, 61-70.
Williams, C.A. 1999. *Roman Homosexuality: Ideologies of Masculinity in Classical Antiquity.* New York/Oxford: Oxford University Press.
Zanker, P. 2010. *Roman Art*, trans. H. Heitmann-Gordon. Los Angeles: Getty Publications.

"The Lord has Bidden Us to Pray in Secret": Reconciling Personal and Collective Identity through 'Secret Prayer' in 3rd-Century Christianity

Berchman, R.M. (ed.) 2005. *Porphyry: Against the Christians.* Leiden: Brill.

Bindley, T.H. 1914. *St. Cyprian on The Lord's Prayer (Early Church Classics)*. London: SPCK.
Bitton-Ashkelony, B. 2012. "'More Interior than the Lips and Tongue': John of Apamea and Silent Prayer in Late Antiquity". *Journal of Early Christian Studies* 20 (2), 303-31.
Brubaker, R. & Cooper, F. 2000. "Beyond 'Identity'". *Theory and Society* 29, 1-47.
Buchinger, H. 2003. "Gebet und Identität bei Origenes", in: Gerhards, Doeker, Ebenbauer 2003, 307-34.
Dover, K.J. 1974. *Greek Popular Morality in the Time of Plato and Aristotle*. Oxford: Blackwell.
Dunn, G.D. 2004. *Tertullian*. New York: Routledge.
Engberg, J. 2007. *Impulsore Chresto: Opposition to Christianity in the Roman Empire c. 50-250*. Frankfurt am Main: Peter Lang.
Gerhards, A., Doeker, A. & Ebenbauer, P. (eds.) 2003. *Identität durch Gebet. Zur gemeinschaftsbildenden Funktion institutionalisierten Betens in Judentum und Christentum*. Paderborn: Ferdinand Schöningh.
Heine, R.E. (ed.) 1993. *Commentary on the Gospel According to John, Books 13-32* (*The Fathers of The Church* 89). Washington: The Catholic University of America Press.
Horst, P.W. van der 1994. "Silent Prayer in Antiquity". *Numen* 41, 1-25.
Keener, C.S. 2009. *The Gospel of Matthew: A Socio-Rhetorical Commentary*. Michigan: William B. Eerdmans Publishing Company.
Koetschau, P. (ed.) 1899. *Origenes Werke* (*Die Griechischen Christlichen Schriftsteller* 3). Leipzig: J.C. Hinrichs.
Leary, M.R. 2003. *Handbook of Self and Identity*. New York: The Guilford Press.
Lewis, C.T. & Short, C. 1879. *A Latin Dictionary*. Oxford: Clarendon Press.
LSJ. Liddell, H.G., Scott, R. & Jones, H.S. et al. (eds.) 1950. *A Greek-English Lexicon*. Oxford: Clarendon Press.
Louth, A. 1981. *The Origins of the Christian Mystical Tradition*. Oxford: Oxford University Press.
McGuckin, J.A. 2004. *The Westminster Handbook to Origen*. Louisville: Westminster John Knox Press.
Mead, G.H. 1934. *Mind, Self & Society*. Chicago: The University of Chicago Press.
NASB. *The New American Standard Bible*. 1995. The Lockman Foundation. California: Foundation Publications.
Nestle-Aland. Kurt Aland et al. (eds). 2001. *Novum Testamentum Graece*. 27th ed. Stuttgart: Deutsche Bibelgesellschaft.
Perrone, L. 2003. "Prayer and the Construction of Religious Identity in Early Christianity". *Proche-Orient Chrétien* 53, 260-88.
Pickering, W.S.F. (ed.) 2003. *Marcel Mauss: La Prière, 1909*. New York/Oxford: Durkheim Press.
Reynolds, L.T. & Herman-Kinney, N.J. (eds.) 2003. *Handbook of Symbolic Interactionism*. Maryland: Rowman & Littlefield.
Réveillaud, M. (ed.) 1964. *L'orasion dominical par saint Cyprien*. Paris: Presses universitaires de France.
Rives, J.B. 1995. *Religion and Authority in Roman Carthage from Augustus to Constantine*. Oxford: Clarendon Press.
Schleyer, D. (ed.) 2006. *Tertullian: De baptismo, De oratione/Von der Taufe, vom Gebet*. Turnhout: Brepols.
Stachel, P. 2005. "Identität. Genese, Inflation und Probleme eines für die zeitgenössischen Sozial- und Kulturwissenschaften zentralen Begriffs". *Archiv für Kulturgeschichte* 87 (2), 395-425.
Stewart-Sykes, A. 2004. *On the Lord's Prayer: Tertullian, Cyprian, Origen*. New York: St Vladimir's Seminary Press.
Stritzky, M.-B. von 1989. *Studien zur Überlieferung und Interpretation des Vaterunsers in der frühchristlichen Literatur*. Münster: Aschendorff.
Stouck, M.-A. 2009. *A Short Reader of Medieval Saints*. Toronto: University of Toronto Press.
Stryker, S. 2008. "From Mead to a Structural Symbolic Interactionism and Beyond". *Annual Review of Sociology* 34, 15-31.
Versnel, H.S. (ed.) 1981. *Faith, Hope and Worship: Aspects of Religious Mentality in the Ancient World*. Leiden: Brill.

Trick or Treat? Secrecy and Performative Space in the Sanctuary of Glycon Neos Asclepius

Bergmann, M. 2010. "Sarapis im 3. Jh. v.Chr.", in: Weber 2010, 109-35.
Bonnet, C. & Motte, A. (eds.) 1999. *Les syncrétismes religieux dans le monde méditéranéen antique. Actes du colloque international en l'honneur de Franz Cumont*. Brussels: Brepols.
Bouvrie, S. des 2012. "Greek Festivals and the Ritual Process: An Inquiry into the Olympia-cum-Heraia and the Great Dionysia", in: Brandt, Iddeng 2012, 53-94.

Brandt, J.R. & Iddeng, J.W. (eds.) 2012. *Greek and Roman Festivals: Content, Meaning and Practice.* Oxford: Oxford University Press.

Branham, R.B. 1989. *Unruly Eloquence: Lucian and the Comedy of Traditions.* Cambridge/London: Harvard University Press.

Burkert, W. 1995. "Der geheime Reiz des Verborgenen: Antike Mysterienkulte", in: Kippenberg, Stroumsa 1995, 79-100.

Chaniotis, A. 2002. "Old Wine in a New Skin: Tradition and Innovation in the Cult Foundation of Alexander Abonuteichos", in: Dabrowa 2002, 67-85.

Chaniotis, A. 2012a. "Constructing the Fear of Gods: Epigraphic Evidence from Sanctuaries of Greece and Asia Minor", in: Chaniotis 2012b, 205-34.

Chaniotis, A. (ed.) 2012b. *Unveiling Emotions: Sources and Methods for the Study of Emotions in the Greek World.* Stuttgart: Steiner.

Clinton, K. 1994. "The Epidauria and the Arrival of Asklepios in Athens", in: Hägg 1994, 17-34.

Cole, S.G. 1988. "The Use of Water in Greek Sanctuaries", in: Hägg, Marinatos, Nordquist 1988, 161-5.

Dabrowa, E. (ed.) 2002. *Tradition and Innovation in the Ancient World* (*Electrum* 6). Krakow: Jagiellonian University Press.

De Miro, G., Sfameni Gasparro, G. & Cali, V. (eds.) 2009. *Il culto di Asclepio nell'area mediterranea. Atti del convegno internazionale, Agrigento 20 – 22 novembre 2005.* Rome: Gangemi.

Ehrenheim, H. von 2011. *Greek Incubation Rituals in Classical and Hellenistic Times.* Stockholm: University Press.

Eliade, M. 1959. *The Sacred and the Profane: The Nature of Religion.* New York: Harcourt.

Elm von der Osten, D. 2006. "Die Inszenierung des Betruges und seiner Entlarvung. Divination und ihre Kritiker in Lukians Schrift 'Alexander oder der Lügenprophet'", in: Elm von der Osten, Rüpke, Waldner 2006, 141-57.

Elm von der Osten, D., Rüpke, J. & Waldner, K. (eds.) 2006. *Texte als Medium und Reflexion von Religion im römischen Reich.* Stuttgart: Steiner.

Elsner, J. 2012. "Material Culture and Ritual: State of the Question", in: Westcoat, Ousterhout 2012, 1-26.

Fischer-Lichte, E. 2004. *Ästhetik des Performativen* (*Edition Suhrkamp* 2373). Frankfurt am Main: Suhrkamp.

Flinterman, J. 1997. "The Date of Lucian's Visit to Abonuteichos". *Zeitschrift für Papyrologie und Epigraphik* 119, 280-2.

Friese, W. 2010. *Den Göttern so nah. Architektur und Topographie griechischer Orakelheiligtümer.* Stuttgart: Steiner.

Friese, W. 2011. "Zwischen Kult und Kommerz. Architektur als erfahrbarer Raum in antiken Orakelheiligtümern". *Mosaikjournal* 1, 159-89.

Friese, W. 2013a. *Die Kunst vom Wahn- und Wahrsagen: Orakelheiligtümer in der antiken Welt.* Darmstadt: Verlag Philipp von Zabern.

Friese, W. 2013b. "Through the Double Gates of Sleep (Verg. Aen. 6.236.): Cave-Oracles in Graeco-Roman Antiquity", in: Mavridis, Jensen 2013, 228-38.

Gennep, A. van 1909. *Les rites de passage.* Paris: Picard.

Gerlach, J. 2005. "Die Figur des Scharlatans bei Lukian", in: Pilhofer et al. 2005, 151-97.

Hägg, R. (ed.) 1994. *Ancient Greek Cult Practice from the Epigraphical Evidence: Proceedings of the Second International Seminar on Ancient Greek Cult, Organized by the Swedish Institute at Athens, 22-24 November 1991.* Stockholm: Svenska Institutet i Athen.

Hägg, R., Marinatos, N. & Nordquist, G. (eds.) 1988. *Early Greek Cult Practice: Proceedings of the Fifth International Symposium at the Swedish Institute at Athens, 26-29, June, 1986.* Stockholm: Svenska Institutet i Athen.

IG. Inscriptiones Graecae.

Jones, C.P. 1986. *Culture and Society in Lucian.* Cambridge: Harvard University Press.

Kippenberg, H.G. & Stroumsa, G.G. (eds.) 1995. *Secrecy and Concealment: Studies in the History of Mediterranean & Near Eastern Religions* (*Studies in the History of Religions* 65). Leiden/New York/Köln: Brill.

Kunnert, U. 2011. "Archäologische Funde und Befunde in den Territorien von Pompeiopolis und Abonuteichos-Ionopolis", in: Summerer 2011, 207-14.

Kyriakidis, E. 2007. *The Archaeology of Ritual.* Los Angeles: Cotsen Institute of Archaeology.

Lane Fox, R. 1988. *Pagans and Christians.* San Francisco: Harper.

Leschhorn, W. & Miron, A.V.B. & Miron, A. (eds.) 1996. *Hellas und der griechische Osten. Studien zur Geschichte und Numismatik der griechischen Welt. Festschrift für Peter Robert Franke zum 70. Geburtstag.* Saarbrücken: SDV.

Maran, J. 2006. "Mycenaean Citadels as Performative Space", in: Maran et al. 2006, 93-116.

Maran, J. et al. (eds.) 2006. *Constructing Power: Architecture, Ideology and Social Practice.* Hamburg: Lit-Verlag.

Marek, C. 2003. *Pontus et Bithynia. Die römischen Provinzen im Norden Kleinasiens.* Mainz: Zabern.
Mastrocinque, A. 2009. "Alessandro di Abonouteichos e il culto di Asclepio", in: De Miro, Sfameni Gasparro, Cali 2009, 195-200.
Mavridis, F. & Jensen, J.T. (eds.) 2013. *Stable Places and Changing Perceptions: Cave Archaeology in Greece.* Oxford: Archeopress.
Miron, A.V.B. 1996. "Alexander von Abonuteichos. Zur Geschichte des Orakels des Neos Asklepios Glykon", in: Leschhorn, Miron, Miron 1996, 153-88.
Mitchell-Boyask, R. 2008. *Plaque and the Athenian Imagination: Drama, History and the Cult of Asclepius.* Cambridge: Cambridge University Press.
Mylonopoulos, J. 2006. "Greek Sanctuaries as Places of Communication through Ritual: An Archaeological Perspective", in: Stavrianopoulou 2006, 69-110.
Mylonopoulos, J. 2008. "The Dynamic of Ritual Space in the Hellenistic and Roman East". *Kernos* 21, 49-79.
Nielsen, I. 2001. *Cultic Theatres and Ritual Drama* (*Aarhus Studies in Mediterranean Antiquity* 4). Aarhus: Aarhus University Press.
Nielsen, I. 2014. *Housing the Chosen: The Architectural Context of Mystery Groups and Religious Associations in the Ancient World.* Turnhout: Brepols.
North, J.A. & Price, S.R.F. 2012. *The Religious History of the Roman Empire: Pagans, Jews and Christians* (*Oxford Readings in Classical Studies*). Oxford: Oxford University Press.
Petsalis-Diomidis, A. 2010. *Truly Beyond Wonders: Aelius Aristides and the Cult of Asklepios.* Oxford: Oxford University Press.
Pilhofer, P. et al. (eds.) 2005. *Lukian: Der Tod des Peregrinos: Ein Scharlatan auf dem Scheiterhaufen.* Darmstadt: WBG.
Renfrew, C. & Zubrow, E. (eds.) 1994. *The Ancient Mind: Elements of Cognitive Archaeology*, Cambridge: Cambridge University Press.
Riethmüller, J. 2005. *Asklepios. Heiligtümer und Kulte.* Heidelberg: Verlag Archäologie und Geschichte.
Rostad, A. 2011. "The Magician in the Temple: Historicity and Parody in Lucian's Alexander". *Classica et Mediaevalia* 62, 207-30.
SEG. Supplementum Epigraphicum Graecum. Leiden: Brill.
Sfameni Gasparro, G. 1999. "Alessandro di Abonutico, lo 'pseudo-profeta' ovvero come contruirsi un'identità religiosa. II. L'oracolo e i misteri", in: Bonnet, Motte 1999, 275-305.
Sfameni Gasparro, G. 2012. "Mysteries and Oriental Cults: A Problem in the History of Religions", in: North, Price 2012, 276-324.
Stavrionapoulou, E. (ed.) 2006. *Ritual and Communication in the Graeco-Roman World* (*Kernos Supplement* 16). Liège: Centre International d'Ètude de la Religion Greque Antique.
Summerer, L. (ed.) 2011. *Pompeiopolis* I. *Eine Zwischenbilanz aus der Metropole Paphlagoniens nach fünf Kampagnen (2006 – 2010).* Langenweissbach: Beier und Beran.
Turner, V.W. 1969. *The Ritual Process: Structure and Antistructure.* Ithaca: Cornell University Press.
Victor, U. 1997. *Lukian von Samosata. Alexander oder der Lügenprophet. Eingeleitet, herausgegeben, übersetzt und erklärt.* Leiden/New York/Köln: Brill.
Weber, G. (ed.) 2010. *Alexandreia und das ptolemäische Ägypten. Kulturbegegnungen in hellenistischer Zeit.* Berlin: Verlag Antike.
Westcoat, B. & Ousterhout, R. (eds.) 2012. *Architecture of the Sacred: Space, Ritual and Experience from Classical Greece to Byzantium.* New York: Cambridge University Press.
Wickkiser, B.L. 2008. *Asklepios, Medicine and the Politics of Healing in Fifth-Century Greece: Between Craft and Cult.* Baltimore: Johns Hopkins University Press.

The Locrian *Pinakes*: Revealing Secrets of Cult Practice?

Barra Bagnasco, M. (ed.) 1977. *Locri Epizefiri.* Florence: Sansoni.
Bernabé, A. 2009. "Imago Inferum Orphica", in: Casadio, Johnston 2009, 95-130.
Boardman, J. 1971. "Helmut Prückner: Die lokrischen Tonreliefs. Beitrag zur Kultgeschichte von Lokroi Epizephyrioi". *The Classical Review* 1971, 144-5.
Borelli, L.V. 1995. "Premessa". *Atti e Memorie della Società Magna Grecia* 1994-1995, 145-9.

Bosher, K. 2012. *Drama in Greek Sicily and South Italy*. Cambridge: Cambridge University Press.
Bottini, A. (ed.) 2005. *Il rito segreto: misteri in Grecia e a Roma*. Milano: Electra.
Cardosa, M, Grillo, E. & Schenal Pileggi, R. 1999. "Caratteristiche tecniche", in: Caronna, Sabbione, Borelli 1999, 25-45.
Caronna, E.L., Sabbione, C. & Borelli, L.V. (eds.) 1999. *I pinakes di Locri Epizefiri, Museo di Reggio Calabria e di Locri*. (*Atti e Memorie della Società Magna Grecia, Quarta Serie I (1996-1999)*, 1-4). Roma: Società Magna Grecia.
Caronna, E.L., Sabbione, C. & Borelli, L.V. (eds.) 2003. *I pinakes di Locri Epizefiri, Museo di Reggio Calabria e di Locri*. (*Atti e Memorie della Società Magna Grecia, Quarta Serie II (2000-2003)*, 1-5). Roma: Società Magna Grecia.
Casadio, G. & Johnston, A. (eds.) 2009. *Mystic Cults in Magna Graecia*. Austin: University of Texas Press.
Gennep, A. van. [1908] 1960. *The Rites of Passage*. Chicago: University of Chicago Press.
Giannelli, G. 1924. *Culti e miti della Magna Grecia. Contributo alla storia più antica delle colonie greche in Occidente*. Firenze: R. Bemporad & figlio.
Gleba, M. & Horsnæs, H. (eds.) 2011. *Communicating Identity in Italic Iron Age Communities*. Oxford: Oxbow Books.
Gluckman, M. 1962. "Les Rites de Passage", in: Gluckman, Forde 1962, 1-52.
Gluckman, M. & Forde, C.D. (eds.) 1962. *Essays on the Ritual of Social Relations*. Manchester: Manchester University Press.
Graf, F. 2013. "Dionysiac Mystery Cults and the Gold Tablets", in: Graf, Johnston 2013a, 137-66.
Graf, F. & Johnston, S.I. (eds.) 2013a. *Ritual Texts for the Afterlife: Orpheus and the Bacchic Gold Tablets*. London: Routledge.
Graf, F. & Johnston, S.I. 2013b. "The Tablets: An Edition and Translation", in: Graf, Johnston 2013a, 1-47.
Grillo, E. 1996. "Le testimonianze architettoniche del santuario di Persefone alla Mannella", in: Lattanzi 1996, 43-5.
Johnston, S.I. 2013. "The Myth of Dionysus", in: Graf, Johnston 2013a, 66-93.
Junker, K. 2012. *Interpreting the Images of Greek Myths: An Introduction*. New York: Cambridge University Press.
Kimbali, S.T. 1960. "Introduction", in: Gennep [1908] 1960, v-xix.
La Fontaine, J. 1985. *Initiation: Ritual Drama and Secret Knowledge across the World*. Manchester: Manchester University Press.
Lattanzi, E. (ed.) 1996. *Santuari della Magna Grecia in Calabria*. Napoli: Electra.
Lincoln, B. 1979. "The Rape of Persephone: A Greek Scenario of Woman's Initiation". *The Harvard Theological Review* 72, 223-35.
MacLachlan, B. 2012. "The Grave's Fine and Funny Place: Chthonic Rituals and Comic Theatre in the Greek West", in: Bosher 2012, 343-64.
Mertens Horn, M. 2005. "I pinakes di Locri: immagini di feste e culti misterici dionisiaci nel santuario di Persephone", in: Bottini 2005, 48-57.
Mertens Horn, M. 2006. "Initiation und Mädchenraub am Fest der lokrischen Persephone". *Mitteilungen des Deutschen Archäologischen Instituts, Römische Abteilung* 112, 7-77.
Müller, C.O., Welcker, F.G. & Leitch, J. 1852. *Ancient Art and Its Remains; Manual of the Archaeology of Art*. London: Henry G. Bohn.
Niutta, F. 1977. "Le fonti letterarie ed epigrafiche", in: Barra Bagnasco 1977, 253-355.
Osanna, M. 1992. *Chorai coloniali da Taranto a Locri: documentazione archeologica e ricostruzione storica*. Roma: Instituto poligrafico e zecca dello stato.
Parca, M. & Tzantou, A. (eds.) 2007. *Finding Persephone: Women's Rituals in the Ancient Mediterranean*. Indianapolis: Indiana University Press.
Petersen, J.H. 2011. "Constructing Identities in Multicultural Milieux: The Formation of Orphism in the Black Sea Region and Southern Italy in the Late 6th and Early 5th Centuries BC", in: Gleba, Horsnæs 2011, 167-76.
Pi.LE I. Caronna, Sabbione, Borelli 1999.
Pi.LE II. Caronna, Sabbione, Borelli 2003.
Price, T.H. 1978. *Kourotrophos: Cults and Representations of the Greek Nursing Deities*. Leiden: E. J. Brill.
Prückner, H. 1968. *Die lokrischen Tonreliefs*. Mainz am Rhein: Verlag Philipp von Zabern.
Quagliati, Q. 1908. "Rilievi votivi arcaici in terracotta di Lokroi Epizephyrioi". *Ausonia* 3, 136-234.
Redfield, J.M. 2003. *The Locrian Maidens: Love and Death in Greek Italy*. Princeton: Princeton University Press.
Rubinich, M. 1999. "Storia e metodologia dell'attuale edizione", in: Caronna, Sabbione, Borelli 1999, 3-21.
Rubinich, M. 2003. "Gruppo 5 – Introduzione", in: Caronna, Sabbione, Borelli 2003, 229-61.
Sabbione, C. 1996. "Il santuario di Persefone in contrada Mannella", in: Lattanzi 1996, 32-9.

Saxkjær, S.G. 2013. "A Figure-Decorated Plate from the Sanctuary on the Timpone della Motta", in: Thomasen, Rathje, Johannsen 2013, 179-96.

Schenal Pileggi, R. 1999. "Gruppo 2 – Tipo 2/24", in: Caronna, Sabbione, Borelli 1999, 814-25.

Schenal Pileggi, R. 2003. "Gruppo 7 – Introduzione", in: Caronna, Sabbione, Borelli 2003, 729-38.

Stehle, E. 2007. "Thesmophoria and Eleusinian Mysteries: The Fascination of Women's Secret Rituals", in: Parca, Tzanetou 2007, 165-88.

Sourvinou-Inwood, C. 1973. "The Young Abductor of the Locrian Pinakes". *Bulletin of the Institute of Classical Studies* 20, 12-21.

Sourvinou-Inwood, C. 1974. "The Votum of 477/6 B. C. and the Foundation Legend of Locri Epizephyrii". *The Classical Quarterly* 24, 186-98.

Sourvinou-Inwood, C. 1978. "Persephone and Aphrodite at Locri: A Model for Personality Definitions in Greek Religion". *The Journal of Hellenic Studies* 98, 101-21.

Thomasen, H., Rathje, A. & Johannsen K.B. (eds.) 2013. *Vessels and Variety: New Aspects of Ancient Pottery* (*Acta Hyperborea* 13). Copenhagen: Museum Tusculanum Press.

Webster, H. 1908. *Primitive Secret Societies: A Study in Early Politics and Religion*. New York: The Macmillian Company.

Zancani Montuoro, P. [1935] 1995. "Il giudizio di Persephone in un *pinakion* locrese". *Atti e Memorie della Società Magna Grecia* 1994-1995, 159-75.

Zancani Montuoro, P. [1940] 1995. "Tabella fittile locrese con scena del culto". *Atti e Memorie della Società Magna Grecia* 1994-1995, 177-94.

Zancani Montuoro, P. [1954] 1995. "Il rapitore di *Kore* nel mito locrese". *Atti e Memorie della Società Magna Grecia* 1994-1995, 195-202.

Zancani Montuoro, P. [1961] 1995. "I pinakes di Locri". *Atti e Memorie della Società Magna Grecia* 1994-1995, 153-6.

Index